COMPARATIVE POETICS

EARL MINER

❏

Comparative Poetics

An Intercultural Essay on Theories of Literature

Princeton University Press, Princeton, New Jersey

Library of Congress Cataloging-in-Publication Data

Miner, Earl Roy.
Comparative poetics : an intercultural essay on theories
of literature / Earl Miner.
p. cm.
Includes bibliographical references.
ISBN 0-691-06860-7 (alk. paper)
ISBN 0-691-01490-6 (pbk. : alk. paper)
1. Literature—History and criticism—Theory, etc.
2. Poetics. I. Title.
PN81.M535 1990   90-33553   801—dc20

Publication of this book has been aided by the
Whitney Darrow Fund of Princeton University Press

IN MEMORIAM

James J. Y. Liu

CONTENTS

MY FIRST little book dealt with the reception of Japan by British and American writers and in a remote way has been the progenitor of this essay. Much has happened in comparative study (and to my thoughts) since then. Out of so much that is difficult to place, the immediate inspiration of this study was a sudden invitation to give three lectures at Tamkang University. At the time, I was teaching on a Fulbright lectureship at the Chinese University of Hong Kong both an undergraduate course on American literature and a graduate seminar on comparative poetics. As in so many other matters during that stay in Hong Kong, I consulted with my host, John J. Deeney, who had spent time in Taiwan and who had participated in that graduate seminar. He suggested that I lecture on the subject of that course. I thank him for his suggestion, as well as for a good deal else during that visit. And for their hospitality at Tamkang University I thank Chi Ch'iu-lang and Lin Yun-shan. (I follow their ways of representing their names, elsewhere using the pinyin system of romanizing Chinese.) Those lectures are long since thrown away, but the order of the three middle chapters follows theirs. Some of the examples are the same, although the proportion taken from Chinese literature has shrunk.

I have tried to be scrupulous in acknowledging material taken from others. The method of citation used is the "scientific" one: the bibliography contains works actually cited in the text and notes. No method can account for some kinds of indebtedness. My general debts for literary understanding are given over as a lost cause. Too much is owed to too many. Students in various versions of my courses on comparative poetics have furnished me with many engaging examples from literatures east and west, north and south, times old and times contemporary. Numerous faculty colleagues have endured my interrogations, assisting with their responses and their suggestions for where to turn. The account will blend the tradition of the epic hero's shield with the annals of the Japanese *Record of Ancient Matters*.

Among senior colleagues, René Etiemble has been a source of inspiration, as René Wellek has been a source of knowledge and support. Horst Frenz—to whom we owe the institutionalizing of intercultural study of comparative literature—deserves special gratitude for inviting me to a conference that seemed to open the world to me, since it was there I first met Peter H. Lee, James Liu, and A. K. Ramanujan. There have been numerous others who have been model colleagues: Qian Zhongshu, Makoto Ueda, and, particularly for this study, Janet A. Walker.

Richard Martin and Barbara Miller have advised me on Indian matters, Charles Segal on Greek matters, and David Quint on an Italian matter. Although responsibility for translations is my own, unless otherwise credited, I wish to acknowledge the assistance or vetting by Anne-Sophie Cremers (French), Hu Ying (some Chinese), Rafael Newman (some Latin), and Steven Wlodek (some German). I wish that I knew more languages and that I commanded much better those I use, particularly English.

This is the first book for which I have used a word processor. Older stagers with the machine than I will recall what adventures one has. For cheerful assistance, occasionally at moments of dire need, I wish to thank Alice Augenti, John Ferguson, Gary Weston Fuchs, Annette Lewis, Andrea Smart, and above all, David Kramer—*il pastor fido* to an errant lamb.

I wish particularly to thank the readers of this study for the Princeton University Press—J. T. Rimer and Mario Valdés—for encouragement, amendments and challenges. I owe a good deal to the consideration and unflappable good cheer of Robert Brown, literature editor of Princeton University Press.

I am grateful for a grant for photocopying from the Mary Cross Fund of the Department of Comparative Literature at Princeton.

It gives me pleasure to acknowledge permission by the Gest Oriental Library and East Asian Collections at Princeton University to print the picture and text of the first page of Santō Kyōden's *Edo Umare Uwaki no Kabayaki* in Chapter 4. I am also pleased to acknowledge permission of the International Comparative Literature Association and Iudicum Verlag, Munich, to reuse in Chapter 4 "Common, Proper, and Improper Place," published in 1990 as part of the Proceedings of the Twelfth Congress of the International Comparative Literature Association. Likewise, I am pleased to acknowledge permission from Professor Maria-Alzira Seixo, president of the Portuguese Comparative Literature Association, again for Chapter 4, "Narrative Point of View Reviewed," published in the proceedings of the inaugural meeting of the Portuguese Comparative Literature Association, Lisbon, 1990. The previous publications amount to excerpts from an already completed manuscript, with various changes to make them understandable on their own.

Some related matters follow in the "Introduction." And yet others will be found in the notes and citations of the succeeding chapters of this essay.

Final additions are necessary. I am most grateful to Janet A. Walker for going through the whole manuscript at a late hour for corrections and encouragement. And once again I have enjoyed the privilege of having work edited by Cathie Brettschneider. Since she has handled much more complex manuscript text for me with ease, I was equally assured and delighted to have her expert, collegial assistance. Under great pressure of time, Judith Olson cheerfully assisted in reading proof. I have enjoyed what assistance others could give and am deeply grateful.

Princeton 1987–1989

COMPARATIVE POETICS

INTRODUCTION

THERE is no dearth of avenues of approach to comparative poetics. In practice, however, there have been obstacles more determined by collective will and conception than by difficulties in the topic. Many of those obstacles are formidable and some possibly irremediable (Etiemble, 1963 or 1966). Collective will has restricted the scope of evidence for reasons that no longer make sense. Comparative Romanticisms constitute an important subject, but its historical and cultural bounds are severely limited—if, that is, we wish to study something other than what are, all things considered, the short and simple annals of one cultural parish at one historic moment. In other words, it is an assumption of this study that the phrase "comparative poetics" is meaningful only if the evidence is intercultural and taken from a reasonably full historical range.

Another impediment has been lack of attention to the meaning of "comparative" in "comparative literature." In the almost complete absence of attention to what may justly be assumed to constitute comparison, one must lamely say that "comparative literature" refers to the practice of "comparatists" and socially sanctioned entities like departments of comparative literature in our institutions of higher learning and in certain academies. In the first chapter readers will find an attempt to offer at least a practical account of what literary comparison may entail.

Comparative poetics is, then, by its nature an extensive, complex subject. Any effort to address the subject makes grand claims. One part at least of the title of this book is modest, "An . . . Essay," an attempt: the necessary description for a first book-length comparative exploration of poetics conceived interculturally. In practice only a small range of possible issues is dealt with in this essay. The range reflects my teaching over several years and a number of previous publications that have developed concepts brought together and developed here. Because of the novelty of the essay, and because I hope to reach students as well as their teachers, I have tried to smooth and clarify not only my own work but also that of others. I do not expect readers to become my followers, but I do wish all who read to follow my argument. The works cited, my own and others, will afford context, complexities, and further readings. As for my own, it is not only the case with that of others, that the studies on which this rests have much more in the way of dotted "i's" and crossed "t's." I have also found it necessary here to uncross some earlier "i's" and undot some earlier "t's."

Attentive readers will observe what is emphasized and what subordinated or ignored. Such understanders will also come to appreciate that many commonly used terms—"fictionality," "representation," and "the novel"—are far from coextensive with literature or narrative. They are idols of the marketplace and of the tribe.

Along with more grandly carved theoretical chess pieces, the pawns of usual talk in western languages derive from but one game, whose rules are so far from being universal that if we played by the rules used elsewhere we would soon suffer checkmate, if indeed we knew how to move at all. Intercultural comparative study does not imply addition of alien "new" ideas to a familiar stock but rather large sets of alternative stocks. As we shall see, the western shop is the one whose wares are most idiosyncratic and unusual.

"Poetics" may be defined as conceptions or theories or systems of literature. James J. Y. Liu entered a distinction. Theories of literature are, he wrote, concerned "with the basic nature and functions of literature," whereas literary theories deal "with aspects of literature, such as form, genre, style, and technique" (Liu, 1975:1). Some may know of needs for which that distinction is too fine. Others may be beckoned by the prospect of a yet larger, more philosophical, more contextualized, or even more abstract theory of literature.

Comparatists (whoever we are), but not only comparatists, have been drawn by visions of the full largess of literary theory. Many find greatest appeal in a theory presumed to be immune to qualification by historical and other relative factors. To others that appeal is spurious, and what cannot be grounded historically is not to be taken seriously. Yet others invite plague on the claims of both the theoretical Capulets and the historical Montagues. In fact, none of us is totally immune to the desire for literary conceptions safe from time and change, and few of us are able to write as if we had doubts about possessing such a theory. As we strive to render immutable our constantly changing medley of thought, we join— if only as canceled footnotes—the history of the mutation of literary ideas. The seconds tick and the calendar turns as we earnestly, and not without a certain engaging charm, devise our transtemporal theories.

Let it be said that our problem is not the indeterminacy of language. Language is irresistibly predicative, given to claim and determination— even in conditional and subjunctive moods. The constraints of language allow me no more freedom than they do the next person. My best hope lies in designating this study to be an essay, an attempt. Otherwise the title is circular: "Intercultural . . . Theories of Literature" is simply another way of saying "Comparative Poetics."[1]

[1] It is also a way so strongly urged by one of the readers of this study, Mario Valdés, that

One may easily tick off representative poetics. More or less comprehensive *western* versions run from Aristotle and Horace to Minturno, Vida, and Julius Caesar Scaliger, then on to Sidney and Hobbes. Thereafter—from Corneille, Le Bossu, and Dryden—it becomes more and more the case that a given poetics is avowedly partial: an *examen* of a single play, an essay of *dramatic* poesy. The narrowing derives in part from sophistication (which is not necessarily identical with insight) and from an altered social institutionalizing of literature in which the general critic yields to the more specialized man, and occasionally woman, of letters.

We have yet to awaken, and perhaps never will, from the dream of a pantascopic poetics, even while our theories have come to be based on ever smaller selections of the increasingly available evidence. Because effort is required to be recognized as an authority on Ovid or Virginia Woolf, we have good reasons to batten our sheep on narrowly defined pastures and to pipe with a few pastoral friends. It is equally human, on discovery of some versions of pastoral, to inquire about remoter places. The discovery—instead of sheep, of camels and fish and dragons—sends all of us some of the time back to our local pastures. It also leads some of us much of the time to consider how the camels, fish, and dragons fit with the sheep and what their counterparts must be to the Euroamerican pastures. Necessity in the guise of curiosity is one parent of comparative poetics.

In existing practice, comparison is dominantly *intra*cultural, even *intra*national. Goethe and Schiller have often been compared, whereas Takamura Kōtarō and Neruda never have been, as far as I know. *Comparative* literature clearly involves something more than comparing two great German poets, and something different from a Chinese studying French literature or a Russian studying Italian literature.

Among the extraordinarily few discussions we have had of the larger matter, there is one thought-provoking statement by James J. Y. Liu.

> I believe that comparative studies of historically unrelated critical traditions, such as the Chinese and the Western, will be more fruitful if conducted on the theoretical rather than practical level, since criticism of particular writers and works will have little meaning to those who cannot read them in the original language, and critical standards derived from one literature may not be applicable to another, whereas comparisons of what writers and critics belonging to different cultural traditions have thought about literature may reveal what critical concepts are universal, what concepts are confined to certain cultural traditions, and what concepts are unique to a particular tradition. This

---

I have readily acceded to his advice. He seemed to feel that there might be a narrower comparative poetics of western Europe for which all else was *terra incognita australis*.

in turn may help us discover (since critical concepts are often based on actual literary works) what features are common to all languages, what features are confined to literature written in certain languages or produced in certain cultures, and what features are unique to a particular literature. Thus a comparative study of theories of literature may lead to a better understanding of all literature. (Liu, 1975:2)

This is counsel from a man of the highest standards. Higher, in fact, than he seems to have realized, since there was no divorce in his work between understanding of practice and knowledge of theories.

René Etiemble would have us learn many languages. Besides his familiar cavalry charges of wit, there are his fusillades of names and bombardments of titles in numerous languages. Yet he remains a staunch defender of translations, and of the study of them. He is as sympathetic as Liu with rigorous standards and as desirous that comparative study be intercultural. Yet he also recognizes the benefits of reading work in translation.[2] I would speak rather of the inevitability and desirability of reading works translated from languages one does not know, since otherwise one is *entirely* cut off from important, revealing varieties of human experience. Of course all of that is premised on one's knowing *some* literary works in the originals of some variety of languages.

Liu's aim for "a better understanding of all literature" comprehends in "literature" the literary corpus, its history or histories, and theories about it. Not everyone thinks alike today as to the priorities of those three entities. Rather than argue with this or that imagined enemy, I shall simply declare my hand. The literary corpus cannot be understood without historical and theoretical knowledge, whether that be tacit or explicit—as anyone knows after first discovering with mystification a poem from some tradition very different from those theretofore familiar. And yet, historical and theoretical knowledge *about* literature logically presumes the priority of the poem and the poet. There is always the poet's and the poem's implicit poetics, and they are of paramount importance. It has been the business of about four centuries of thought to seek to understand what it was that Shakespeare knew about his art. That process of study makes up, along with performance and translations, the history of the plays. That process of study has certainly uncovered theoretical and historical implications of those plays and of drama more generally, even while revealing what the searchers needed to discover.

If we find interest in a single major author, tradition, or set of theories, there can be only greater attraction in considering other varieties. In this essay, the emphasis will fall chiefly on theories of literature, with some

[2] This is a reductive, but not inaccurate, summary of Etiemble, 1966.

stress on literary history. But I hope that rays of appreciation of individual poems will also be seen to shine. In any event, as with given poems and poets, so with poetics: to consider those of but one cultural tradition is to investigate only a single conceptual cosmos, however intricate, subtle, or rich that may be. To consider the other varieties of poetics is by definition to inquire into the full heterocosmic range, the full argument from design, of literature. And to do so comparatively is to establish the principles and the relations of those many poetic worlds.

That is the necessary hope. My present study is ineluctably an essay. Enlargement of our view involves risks or, more positively, a set of criteria that may be sustained by logically as well as historically validated principles and evidence. That will be essayed in the first chapter.

Since this is an introduction, a brief sketch seems in place. It is argued in what follows that there are two kinds of general poetics. One is implicit in practice, and such a poetics belongs to every culture that distinguishes literature as a distinct human activity, a distinct kind of knowledge and social practice. The other is an explicit "originative" or "foundational" poetics, and this kind of poetics is to be found in some cultures but not in others.

The thesis of this essay is that an originative poetics develops when a critic or critics of insight defines the nature and conditions of literature in terms of the then most esteemed genre. By "genre" is meant drama, lyric, and narrative. These "foundation genres" may be termed by other names—kinds, modes, radicals of presentation, whatever. But I hold that that is how, historically, explicit poetics have been devised. For example, and to reveal no great secret, western poetics was established by Aristotle's defining literature on the basis of drama. His poetics would be a very different thing if founded on Homeric narrative or Greek lyric.

Because my term "genre" is vexed, I shall detour for a moment to give a brief account of it. To Goethe's concept of "die Bauformen der Poesie" (drama, lyric, narrative) and my own concept, Paul Hernadi has offered a useful if friendly challenge in *Beyond Genre: New Directions in Literary Classification* (1972). The best account of western genre theory, that by Irene Behrens, *Die Lehre von der Einleitung der Dichtkunst* (1940) shows that the triadic conception begins to emerge with Antonio Sebastiano Minturno's influential book, *L'Arte Poetica* (1564).[3]

Milton and Dryden were the first in England to adopt the triadic conception of genres (treating, as has often been the case since, narrative by its subclass, epic). Perhaps because of Goethe's influence, that conception

---

[3] Full citations of Behrens and others following, except Minturno, will be found in the bibliography.

has often been explored by writers in German. Emil Staiger's beautifully titled book, *Die Zeit als Einbildungskraft des Dichters* (1939), should be mentioned along with his (to me) more useful *Grundbegriffe der Poetik* (1939). A more recent study, Wolfgang Kayser's *Das sprachliche Kunstwerk* (1962) has much to teach, and it is a pity that it has not been translated into English as well as Spanish, among whose readers it has had considerable impact. Since I have gradually moved "beyond genre," I add two more works. I particularly sympathize with the blend of realism and skepticism in Mario Valdés's *Shadows in the Cave* (1982), whose last chapter (10) has particular relevance to my fourth. And to end with genre, there is Alastair Fowler's valuable *Kinds of Literature* (A. Fowler, 1982), which ranges extensively, at least through wide fields of western literature.

Even those who approach talk of genres with suspicion must admit the utility, in fact the necessity, of concepts grouping portions of a literary corpus larger than a single example and smaller than that entity, "literature" (Miner, 1986A). Because our ideas of those middle ranges differ and because vocabulary is not fixed, we all need to define our terms. My chief one is of course "genre," and definition of the three kinds is partly what this study is about.

Aristotle's founding his *Poetics* on drama illustrates the validity of the very concept of genre—at least if it can be shown that other cultural poetics are also founded on my putative genres. Examination of the issue reveals something very curious: all other examples of poetics are founded not on drama, but on lyric.[4] Western literature with its many familiar suppositions is a minority of one, the odd one out. It has no claim to be normative.

A triadic conception of genre is necessary, then, for the inception of a poetic system, whether that beginning be implicit (as lyric is for near Eastern cultures) or explicit (as drama is for Eurowestern). The conception is also necessary for later stages of the development of theories of literature along with attendant practice in literary criticism and history. That is shown with particular clarity by Japanese conceptions of literature, which begin with lyric and then are successively modified (and enlarged) to accommodate the explicit and implicit poetics of first narrative and then drama. There are further stages for which the assumptions of generic relevance are crucial. At those later stages, features of the funda-

---

[4] Indian poetics presents a very complex conception with names, titles, and terms quite unfamiliar to most of us. In an earlier draft of this study, I failed in the effort to present a brief, readable account of Indian poetics, as the two readers for Princeton pointed out. Although I shall publish a revised version elsewhere, I offer here my conclusion: Indian poetics closely resembles the lyric-based poetics of all but western theory.

mental poetics remain, even if people who talk about literature are un-aware of it or would deny it. Also at those later stages, features of the poetics of a given genre may be assumed tacitly, unawares, or even re-jected. English criticism the past two centuries gives a particularly telling example. The English Romantic critics drew on lyricism for language and affect as fundamental criteria. Since then, affect has been rejected and language has been made more and more central, explicit. That lyric po-etics was used to discuss chiefly narrative until the last stage of the nou-velle critique. Drama was utterly ignored, and yet both concern with is-sues like fictionality and representation and antimimetic claims have testified to a continuing mimetic presence, something there although ig-nored or denied.

It will be evident, then, that given the historical vicissitudes, terms like "western" or "mimetic" are very roughshod. For lyric-based poetics, I have devised the term "affective-expressive." I do not term that "non-western" for two good reasons. One is that comparison is infeasible be-tween what is (western) and what is not (nonwestern)—not to mention the imperialistic legacy and hegemonic presence of the notion. The other is to have a reasonably accurate nickname to set against "mimetic."

It is passing strange that there is no originative poetics founded on nar-rative. The nearest thing to it is the incorporation of narrative into Japa-nese lyric-based poetics so very early: within a century of definition of poetry by lyric, the greatest work in the literature, *The Tale of Genji*, had appeared. It is also true that in China, Korea, and Japan, certain kinds of narrative history were included with lyric, so that to some extent narra-tive was present from the beginning, even if lyric was the dominant element.

Western poetics has of course also been dynamic. Horace's *Ars Poetica* is of crucial importance, since it introduced a strongly affective (and to a considerable extent expressive) poetics into western currency. For many stretches of western literary history, "mimetic-affective" is a more accu-rate description than simple "mimetic." As we shall see, however, it is quite surprising how strong the residual western mimetic assumptions are at the present time. That fact is scarcely creditable, as I am well aware—until one enters the world of *comparative* poetics. Then the scene changes.

Readers will have ample reason to hold reservations about what has been posited. Let me assure them that this introduction is the entry rather than the house, whatever the necessary connection. In the ensuing chap-ters complications and exceptions will be noted. There was the loss of Aristotle's *Poetics* and bafflement among its principal recoverers. There are forms of didactic poetry. There is Romantic expressionism. There is the absurdity of Ionesco and the nihilism of Beckett. These matters will be discussed in their places. Seen from the western parish, western ideas about literature appear to be very numerous. So do Chinese theories seen from the Chinese parish. In that wider, intercultural context in which alone fundamental comparison is feasible, the local and temporary are less significant than the prominent and enduring.

The genres (as defined here) are certainly not the only bases of comparative poetics. There is a fallacy of the single explanation (to which attention will be paid in Chapter 5). The generic explanation is, I believe, true but incomplete and even mistaken if assumed to be the only explanation. Yet the genres are used here with reason: they enable and require us to consider theoretical origins along with historical development. There are numerous other limits to this study, some of which its author is aware. Once again: the account is an *essay*, because it is a first book-length attempt to address the issues in the breadth assumed necessary here.

Of course any "first" attempt is so in only a most qualified extent. Horst Frenz and the leadership of his colleagues at Indiana University were the first in the United States to bring the engagement of American comparatists with Indian, Chinese, Japanese, and Korean literature. (Princeton and Stanford followed suit: the first Ph.D. in comparative literature at Princeton was granted Wai-lim Yip for intercultural study of Pound and Chinese poetry.) René Etiemble has been tireless in proclaiming the need to know the literatures of all cultures, including African and little-studied Asian literatures. René Wellek has repeatedly urged the study of literature in the most comprehensive, international sense.

We have seen progress, or this study would have been infeasible. Our professional associations more and more feature literatures less familiar to many of us (including the hidden literatures within our own culture) as real parts of their programs, not merely as largely unattended sideshows.

There is, however, a curious imbalance. Our social, including university, organization assists those of us who study western literatures in ignoring the intellectual obligation to read widely.[5] On the other hand, people in the departments we have marginalized are more or less forced to keep abreast of what goes on in study of western literature. They know what we do, but we do not know what they know otherwise. Obviously none of us knows as much as is desirable, or even in principle necessary, for adequate understanding of the literatures, of comparative poetics.

---

[5] I obviously support "changing the canon": among other salutary advances, reading things written before 1800.

True study of comparative literature and of poetics requires a larger reach of our imaginations than we have been accustomed to require of ourselves.

The intellectual canons of comparative study also have clear, strong ethical corollaries. Just as the feminist argument rests on the unshakable rock that justice be done to that half of the race that bears us, so consideration of the other three-quarters or four-fifths of the race must enter into any literary study denominating itself comparative.

I wish I could claim to sing of the literatures of the race, invoking most of the Muses at once. But in terms used in East Asia, what follows will no doubt lack the grandeur of peaks and waters. It will not be fine enough to concern flowers and birds. It will deal instead with fields and gardens, above the pastures and below the georgics. *Paulo maiora*, just a little higher in this first essay.

❏

CHAPTER 1

Comparative Poetics

. . . comparative literature would then be
irresistibly drawn to comparative poetics.

—René Etiemble

COMPARATIVE POETICS. The phrase is familiar enough not to seem outlandish. It is not so frequently heard, however, as to have a range of definite meanings, or perhaps definite meaning at all. In fact, the familiarity may be only apparent, coming from our acquaintance with the words separately. Those independent meanings do derive, however, more from the practice of comparatists and students of literary theory than from theoretical inquiry into the nature of conceptions about literature construed comparatively.

Insofar as it refers to anything, "comparative" refers to the kinds of study engaged in by people who do "comparative literature." "Poetics" naturally recalls Aristotle's perhaps briefest work; it recalls for some people Julius Caesar Scaliger (whose *Poetices Libri Septem* still awaits adequate translation and commentary); and it finds echo in such modern adaptations as "a poetics of dance." Adequate, strict definitions do not exist and may be infeasible. It is therefore all the more necessary to specify what the phrase is taken to mean, and imply, in this essay.

POETICS

Aristotle's example enables us to define the word as an account of the nature and practice of (in his case dramatic) literature considered as an autonomous subject. The autonomy of literature has been severely questioned in recent years. We know many reasons to emphasize what literature shares with other kinds of human expression. We know how readily we transform literary to nonliterary knowledge, and vice versa. We also know how fuzzy matters may be at their intellectual margins. But it is altogether evident from the works of Aristotle that his *Poetics* was conceived of as a subject distinct from his works on ethics, metaphysics, politics, rhetoric, zoology, and the other matters designated by his titles.

Moreover, this separation of human knowledge into distinct categories is an essential prior step to the formation of a poetics in any culture.

Aristotle's is the purest example we have of an explicit originative study of the nature of literature as a distinct, separate branch of human knowledge. Brief it may be, but the *Poetics* is the most sustained of what has just been termed the originative poetics that have appeared in various cultures (Miner, 1979B). In principle, his poetics is separate enough to be presumed free of contamination by other concerns, although (as we reflect on it) we can lay bare what was invisible to him, his deep involvement in social and other ideological matters. We also observe that mingling of descriptive and normative considerations that seems to characterize all attempts to explain literature. But in presumption at least, Aristotle sets about to describe what literature is, to define its constituents, and to show what are its means and ends.[1]

Aristotle was not a poet. Yet there were, as he necessarily recognized, not only the dramatists who were his main concern, but also a number of other writers, and chiefly Homer. This is not surprising: there cannot be a poetics without literature to describe. But the corollaries are less obvious and less palatable to some critics. The subject of poetics begins, if but by implication, with a practice on which the Aristotles must draw. This is to say that the subject of poetics deals with what is hitherto implicit in the writings by the poets.

We can go back a step farther to a time before which there was not even an implicit poetics, since poetry and poets were not distinguished as things autonomous. This holds true for those cultures today in which "la pensée sauvage" contains—in undifferentiated, nonautonomous status—the elements or kinds of thought we are used to presuming as distinct entities.[2] The clear sign of differentiation is the naming of the poets, of authors of works. Because writers are designated as proprietary creators before painters and musicians, implicit theories such as those of the Homeric poems long antedate implicit theories of painting and music. This is not the place to argue whether Homer existed, or whether he was a transitional figure between an oral and a literate culture. The fact is that not only did the Greeks assume his real existence, but that most of them (although not Aristotle) regarded him as their greatest poet. Hesiod certainly existed, as did the dramatists Aristotle mentions. His naming of them in a work titled *Poetics* implies the effort to differentiate literature as

---

[1] In what follows there will be numerous contrasts between mimetic and expressive-affective poetics. I shall be emphasizing that neither is monolithic or immune to change. But without some general characterization, one gets lost in details. For recognition of differing kinds of mimesis, see Doležel, 1988:475–96, especially n. 1.

[2] See Konishi, 1984: index, under "primitives, modern."

an autonomous activity whose principles had earlier formed the implicit poetics of what they wrote. Aristotle sets about to make them explicit.

It is noteworthy that he proceeds a logical step farther. He differentiates as his main subject a single kind of literature, tragedy, whose autonomy he demonstrates by his distinguishing, all too briefly, another kind of drama, comedy, and another kind of literature generally—although not by him—preferred to tragedy, the Homeric epic. (He also glances at satire.)

Aristotle's *Poetics* has a few important counterparts in other literary traditions, although they are not as abstract or sustained as his work. The conditions of the Athenian Academy were special if not ideal in every way, and he had the work of Plato to challenge him. The originating poetics in other cultures are as explicit but not as treatise-like: for example, the "Great Preface" to *The Classic of Poetry* (*Shijing*; probably dating from the early portion of the Han Dynasty, which ran from 206 B.C. to A.D. 220) and Ki no Tsurayuki's Japanese preface to the *Kokinshū* (ca. 910).[3] In their own cultures, these writings were as originative as was Aristotle's in his, and only the long domination of our thought by Aristotle's assumptions makes them seem less originative, less like a poetics than they are. From what has been said earlier, there is obvious significance in Tsurayuki's naming actual authors from earlier times and his own. It is also significant that the Confucian commentary on *The Classic of Poetry* should assign authorship by allegoresis to this body of anonymous poems.[4]

Names designate authors of works that are identifiable, separable from those by other named authors, from anonymous writing, and from other writings not deemed autonomously literary. Until such distinctions of authorship and kinds of knowledge are reached, a poetics is infeasible. That is also to say that a poetics presumes the existence of other distinct, autonomous kinds of knowledge. Once a culture is advanced in writing, and certainly once it has means to duplicate what has been composed, the products can and, so people believe, must be ordered and stored. The old libraries of Alexandria and China, like the modern ones of our universities, reflect in their intellectual ordering autonomies of kinds of knowledge. It is clearly significant that the major classification used (when the information is available) from late oral to advanced print cultures is the

---

[3] See Liu, 1975; Rickett, 1978; Miner, 1979B.

[4] There is serious question about the ways in which allegory and allegoresis are to be understood in Chinese practice. The issue will be discussed in Chapter 3. Given Chinese assumptions about the factuality of literature, and given zoological fact, there is great justice in Dore J. Levy's correction. The day after I acquainted her with Mrs. Malaprop's "allegory on the banks of the Nile," she told me, "There are no allegories in Egypt—only chronicles on the banks of the Nile."

author's name, since the presumption of authorship is the continuing basis of assumptions about poetics.

Of course the autonomy of poetics, economics, religion, and other kinds of knowledge is not complete. Various kinds of knowledge can be transferred, for given purposes, from one category to another. Even so, once we begin to think in terms of autonomous kinds of knowledge, we order our social institutions to reflect them: the Chinese literatus, the renaissance patron and poet, school curricula, departments of universities, even publishers' catalogues.

Moreover, the transferability of knowledge from one category to another has some important and variable constraints (Miner, 1979A). Mathematics shows this. Probably no other kind of knowledge is so widely used by other kinds of thought, and probably no other finds other kinds so useless. Only logic, which is almost a twin, is radically useful to mathematics. History offers a suggestive counterpart. Since everything that exists has undergone some inception and development, everything has a history. Even mathematics. But the utility of those histories to other kinds of knowledge is not as great as is that of mathematics. The utility of literature to other classes of knowledge is even less (although still far from negligible), whereas it is a kind of knowledge that seems able to incorporate—in one version or to one degree or another—every other kind of knowledge. There is one of us who has derived his no doubt shaky knowledge of Czarist Russia almost entirely from reading translations of the poems, novels, and criticism written at that time. To the extent that we can derive our knowledge from literature, that literature has already been absorbent of many other kinds of knowledge. (We cannot similarly derive knowledge of nineteenth-century Russian society from nineteenth-century mathematics.) It is as if literary transformation of other kinds of knowledge is not a complete thing; certainly much at least of what has been absorbed may be subsequently resorted out. A corollary is that to be understandable literature cannot be wholly fictional.

The positing of the literary autonomy necessary for a poetics to exist does not, then, involve a black hole but a constellation of kinds of knowledge. For literature itself to exist, other kinds of distinguishable knowledge must also. It is a necessary corollary that certain factors specific to the literary and perhaps to the aesthetic more generally must give it the means to exist, and that a major purpose of poetics is to identify them. In the ensuing discussion important factors of literature will be identified, beginning with the most elementary. Fuller discussion of many must await discussion in ensuing chapters. And, like Milton, I must invoke "the meaning not the name," for it will be evident that there are numerous alternatives in various languages (and even English) and that some terms are used differently in this account from meanings given or implied in other usages.

LITERARY FACTORS

For a poem to exist, there must be a poet, so giving the first two elementary factors. Reason tells us, along with historical evidence from known titles of nonexisting books, that many poems have been made and are now lost. Without a text, we have no evidence of the writer's work, no possibility to make our readers' poems. Or again, without readers commanding the language in the text, the poem ceases to exist except potentially, against the day when someone decodes Linear A. The reader can have access to the authorial creation only by means of a text, by which is meant here some physical coding, whether in our familiar black marks on paper, in the sound waves of a recitation and theater, or in the recollective memory of the poet or anyone else who can summon memory of the creation. The more often the physical text is multiplied, the more variations will be introduced. The differences are physical in terms of coding but cognitive in respect to the person doing the knowing. It is also evident that the multiplication of readers leads to varying reception of what there is to know. Although everyone may be clear that they are reading Faulkner's rather than Shakespeare's *Hamlet*, we can predict differences in what is known, even if not what those differences will be.

It is therefore useful to make elementary distinctions between that work which is wrought by a poet and that poem which is made by a reader. In brief, we have a simple, invariable pattern.

Poet
Work
Text
Poem
Reader

At either end are the human agents. We next have what is known and, at the textual center, the means of knowing.

Contrary to usual practice in writing about literature, I feel it necessary to risk labor of the obvious so that at least my meanings are in fact obvious. Everybody will understand that the Poet is the author figure, whether in prose or verse, and the Reader the receiving, re-creating figure, whether hearing or reading. Similarly, it should be clear that it is not always necessary to distinguish between the Work and the Poem. Also, different meanings may be attached to Text without ascending or descending to textuality à la mode. In addition to the physical coding, a text may be taken as the main body of writing as opposed to interlinears, notes, or indexes and other appendages. In an edition, the text is opposed to the commentary. Or it may be a selection specified from a whole, as in the sense of the preacher's text being 2 Corinthians 3:13. None of these meanings is far from a physical sense, and none permits me the luxuries of, say, "intertextualities," phenomena I therefore need not define but which I could explain, if I could ascertain that a meaning really is meant, by other means.

The five factors are obviously necessary but not sufficient ones. The poet (literary writer in any kind), the reader (or audience, receiver), and the text exist in what all of us presume to be a "world," however poorly understood or illusory that may be. The world involves times and places—all that we mean by culture—that will differ for the poet and the reader. The difference may be relatively small, as when Pound read the work of T. S. Eliot, or it may be great, as when one of us in an English-speaking country today reads the Sanskrit epics. The world also involves cultural features such as language, the distinguishing medium of literature among the various kinds of aesthetic knowledge. For poet and reader alike—although commonly on different bases—both the diachronic and synchronic features of language are involved.

A digression or pause for emphasis seems necessary here. Talk of language in the terms given resembles the earlier limited sense offered for "text," so raising as it were the other eyebrow of some readers. People of many persuasions might well agree with the sense of Hans-Georg Gadamer's sentence: "Language is not just one of man's possessions in the world, but on it depends the fact that man has a world at all."[5] I would go farther than that sentence alone suggests and claim that language is inescapably referential and predicative, predicative in the sense of constantly entering truth claims. (Special signs or conventions are necessary for us to know that a fiction is implied, a very different, less definitive predication.) Whether the references or predications work is another matter. There is fundamentally no reply to the skeptic's claim that the existence of the world cannot be proved. There is fundamentally an eloquent testimony to the world in the skeptic's acting, in the daily conduct of life, as if that world does exist. In any event we can know the world only as we are equipped to know it and as we are able in language to learn of it by

---

[5] Gadamer, 1982:401. My sympathy with the third part of his work will be as evident as is the foundation it provides for many of my own views. Cf. also Timothy J. Reiss on the "episteme" that would emerge, by his reckoning, ca. 1600: "literary discourse will be equated rigorously with the material (and ethical) order insofar as its status regarding veracity, actuality, and reality is concerned" (Reiss, 1982:34; the rest of the first chapter provides the context and argument in favor of the assertion). We may question the utility of that model for many purposes, but it does allow for certain simple, grand distinctions.

reading or by talking with others. Whether or not the world exists is therefore in a manner of speaking a moot point. Our behavior and our use of language constantly presume that it is more efficient to assume that it does than that it does not.[6]

What has been termed the world here clearly entails such other cultural features as social organization. We may call this large body of knowledge (including language) the cultural sphere inhabited and explored by poets and their readers. To represent that sphere, one could draw a circle around the five elementary terms set forth. It hardly seems necessary, since the matter is so obvious (if not entirely fashionable) as not to admit rational opposition. Also, "sphere" is metaphorical, whereas the terms set forth are of the literal kind we do well to pursue so that they may be more readily judged for their truth or falsehood, or at least for their utility or inutility.

A full poetics would also account for the means of production. This seems a small or incidental topic, one unimportant except to Marxists. And in fact most English-speaking critics ignore it most of the time—at least in its Marxist terms. Those concerned with drama do devote themselves to the immediate means of production: players, directors, stages, and costumes. Of all the many other features of this matter, the social means of production are too important to be left to Marxists alone.

For our example, let us take a restricted topic, the identity of the poet as producer. Quite different implications about the nature of literature may be found in five brief identifications of persons who produce literature. In chronological order, they are the Greek view that tragedy is written by male Athenian citizens in a state competition; the Chinese view that the select male, Han literati and royalty do, with a few others; the early Japanese view that everybody (male or female) does, including illiterates; the western renaissance view that the male nobility might and that patronized male writers do; the prevailing modern view that anybody (women as well as men) may try, but that the successful ones are professionals (however subsidized they may be in their society).

APART from the poet as producer, there are as yet not wholly adequately recognized implications of a feature of modern literary production: the teaching and writing about it by a guild of teachers and professors. To apply one of these concepts out of place—or not to apply one in place— is to make a category error. Acknowledging the existence of the differ-

---

[6] Nor is language necessary either to assume that the world exists or to refer to it. As I perform one of my favorite relaxations, gardening, perhaps I am thinking wordlessly as I act some two-thirds of the time. That rest from thought in language is, with the physical exercise, a major therapeutic benefit.

ences in conception of the identity of the poet is part of the duty of *comparative* poetics.

We have begun this discussion of what a poetics entails by identifying five factors (poet . . . reader), the world (in its cultural conditions), and production (in some of its forms). Let them stand for all the terms and assumptions that literature entails (which is by no means the case), and we have something that no single poetics can encompass. The deviser would have to know all the terms and assumptions of the literary cultures of the world—then, now, and in the future. And since there are actual contradictions between various available poetics, a *summa* is possible only to the divine poet. Inevitably, every poetics is only partial because of the restricted evidence drawn on. To go no farther, the choice of one of the five factors listed, or of some feature of the world, or some feature of production is a choice that rules out most while allowing dominance to one—or more likely, a small number—of crucial matters. Once again, there is a fallacy of the single explanation.

Another way of saying this (the examples will be merely illustrative) is to observe that, whether from the implicitness of literary practice or the explicitness of theorizing, we can distinguish between the elements stressed in certain dominant poetics during the nineteenth and twentieth centuries. The Romantic poets emphasized above all the poet, so stressing an expressive poetics. That hypostatized entity, "the classical realistic Victorian novel," stressed almost equally the work-poem and the world, so giving rise to assumptions of literary realism. To skip ahead to a contrary poetics, for about two decades (the mid-1960s to the mid-1980s) critics either conferred unusual powers on literature or abstracted, from the world, language as the center of a skeptical poetics.

As an example of the one, we may take Peter Szondi, who declared, "Drama is primary. It is not the (secondary) representation of something else (primary); instead, it represents itself, is itself" (1965:16). As an example of the other, we may take the distinguished and distinguishable author whom it is appropriate not to name even anon, the author who proclaimed the death of the author (in a work to which he attached his name as author). Language was said to rule its users, the poets (although somehow it did not rule, apparently, the critics who proffered their "readings"). Literary language was found to be untrustworthy, contradictory, given to aporia, abysmal. During those same two decades, other poetics were actively promulgated. Socialist realism has been the official poetics set for well over half the human race. It was said that in Latin America "magical realism" prevailed: a special combination of poet, world, and language.

In all this, what we choose to emphasize implies the omission of other things. The nature of our gain determines the nature of our losses for, as in the rest of life, so in poetics, we are willing to sustain certain disadvantages in order to possess what we value more highly.

"THE COMPARATIVE"

It is now time to give the adjective its due (Miner, 1987). One useful approach in these matters is to inquire what people of the given kind—our people are the "comparatists"—actually do. They engage in influence study, in literary parallels (e.g., Romanticism, realism, or Symbolism in France, Germany, and England), in literary theory of one or more kinds, in literary history of one or more kinds, and in study of translation. Yet even Macaulay's prodigious schoolboy would find it difficult to discover actual *comparison* in the work of the comparatists. His labor would be lengthier than Psyche's and more trying than Hercules' if he sought to find out what made a comparison just, how one should set about to compare.

It seems to be assumed that a comparatist knows one or more foreign languages and writes about their literatures. One is particularly recognizable as a comparatist if one writes about the nineteenth- or twentieth-century novel in two or three European countries, and superlatively so if the languages are English, French, and German. It has been said, and the idea is still often honored in practice, that the field of comparative literature should be restricted to national literatures related to each other within a single culture, which somehow seems to mean European and North American. Not only that, but the emphasis of practice has fallen on modern European literature—taking "modern" in the sense of ancient, medieval, and modern—and in the later stretches of modernity at that. It is left to students of the Renaissance, the Middle Ages, and antiquity to do pretty much what the comparatists are thought to do, only under other names. Although students of modernity may not feel the need to know classical tongues, classicists need to know modern languages. That is because, as the matter was once explained to me by a Hellenist friend, a classicist need not know Greek but must command German.

Why, however, should our "comparative literature" lack an eastern and a southern hemisphere?

Even years of acquaintance with our human waywardness fail to prepare one adequately for understanding that comparatists do not talk about comparison. A basic reason is no doubt that so much of what is called comparative study is not comparative at all. But given the name, and given the need to introduce students to the subject, it might be

COMPARATIVE POETICS · 21

thought that there would be concern with comparison.[7] What *is* literary comparison? What *are* the principles of adequacy in comparison?

One may as well satirize oneself to make the point. It must be true that, both in teaching and writing, I have more often compared writers *within a single literature and period* (whether English, other European, or Japanese) than I have writers from more than one literature. There is a certain feeling of security, if little pride of originality, in comparing Jonson with Donne or Dryden with Milton. In such acts we feel secure, because we sense that we honor, somehow, canons of comparability. There should not be category error in comparing writers contemporary with each other and writing in the same language. Unfortunately, even that safety may be illusory, and at best it gives only modest help to consideration of the nature of comparative literature, of principles of comparison, or of comparative poetics. Its modest contribution is this: we must establish a basis for comparison between things possessing elements in common to degrees of likeness higher than resemblance or analogy. Otherwise there can be no certainty that we have avoided category error.

It is clear that the major problem is assurance of sufficient resemblance between or among the things compared. Nobody is likely to make the opposite error of comparing the identical, although in practical terms the act should be borne in mind, as we shall see.

The nub of this problem is what elements constitute, or what procedure guarantees, *sufficient* comparability. It is also clear that scale determines the nature, and certainly the results, of comparison. Donne and Jonson may make a sound comparison, because they were contemporaries, indeed friends, who often wrote in the same literary kinds and subkinds. Even that comparison could go wrong, however, by comparing the dramatic elements in Donne's lyrics with Jonson's plays. The differences are too great. Counterparts of the Donne–Jonson comparison exist in other literatures. Chinese are fond of comparing Li Bo (or Li Bai; d. 762) with Du Fu (712–70), and Japanese Matsuo Bashō (1644–94) with Yosa Buson (1716–83). On the Chinese scale, the two Tang poets are enough alike to compare, but they seem very different. The same holds for the Japanese poets.

When, however, we undertake comparison of the Chinese with the Japanese poets, the Chinese now seem very similar but different from the Japanese, who now seem quite like. If we then enlarge the scale further, introducing Donne and Jonson (or Hugo and Baudelaire, etc.), we are

---

[7] These considerations were borne in on me as I readied myself to teach a graduate course, "Introduction to Comparative Literature." I could find nothing on literary comparison, whether by my own searches or in questions to colleagues. To my surprise, philosophers were equally dumb. The results of that search are recounted in Miner, 1987.

struck by the resemblances of the Chinese and Japanese poets to the one side and those of the west to the other. Various other factors affect comparison. A few are orality vs. literacy, religious vs. secular, and drama vs. lyric vs. narrative.

These considerations are rudimentary. But the art (not to mention the *Wissenschaft*) of comparison has a long way to go before clear canons are provided us. A similar situation has existed in the social sciences, many practitioners of which professedly execute comparative studies. In the sole reliable study of comparison known to me, from any field, Morris Zelditch exposes flimsy pretenses to comparison with an unerring hand for the jugular (Zelditch, 1971). It is a brilliant exercise, developing a portion of the logic of John Stuart Mill. Unfortunately, his clear logic seems to be unavailable to the practice of literary and social comparison alike, since it allows for no more than two variables, whereas we are not yet certain how to identify or deal with literary variables.

Because both European and east Asian literatures interest me, and because this book concerns comparative poetics, it has been necessary for me—in the absence of a valid theory—to fashion conditions of practice that seem to work. I shall describe the practical principle and seek to clarify it by three examples, one not undertaken as far as I know, the other two previously undertaken by me. The practical principle holds that comparison is feasible when presumptively or formally identical topics, conditions, or elements are identified. Of course what is presumptively but not actually identical soon betrays difference. With tact and luck, however, we may find the difference just great enough to provide interest, and the presumed identity strong enough to keep the comparison just.

For a book on comparative poetics, the examples must be intercultural rather than intracultural. One that holds interest to me, although I have never investigated it, is the nontitling of lyric poems. One would soon find, I believe, that certain things needed sorting out. There might be no numbers of any kind, as with most editions of Donne's lyrics (which do have titles) and the compilations of *haikai* (Japanese linked poetry of lower decorum). Or there could be division of a collection into a number of books, as with Japanese royal and certain other collections. And there can be division into books with numbering of poems, as is now the case with Horace, although it was not the case at the outset. There may also be headnotes in lieu of titles, as is the case once again with the Japanese royal collections. The cultural assumptions that allowed Japanese to anthologize lyric poems without titles or numbers differed from assumptions about the integrity and scope of the lyric unit as found in the titled poems of Wordsworth and Coleridge's *Lyrical Ballads*. Such things are involved as reading for the whole collection vs. reading only one or more chosen poems. Hence when the individual poems in the Japanese royal collections and in Horace's first three books of *Odes* came to be numbered, reading shifted from the collection as the integral object of attention to individual poems as the integers. Only centuries later, in each case, was the original concept of the collection recovered. Numbering may also be used in the absence of titles, as with Donne's satires and holy sonnets. Or it may be introduced to suggest editorial rigor and exactitude, as with some recent editions of Donne. Like what is done, what is not done (for there is more) to identify lyrics would provide, I am convinced, a fruitful subject for comparative study.

The subject of literary collections is one I have undertaken (Miner, 1985B). Although the range of study included the Jewish and Christian scriptures along with Buddhist, and although secular prose evidence was also drawn on, the presumed identity was that of the poetic collection: Greek, Roman, modern European, Chinese, and Japanese. The last named was the central object of study, because Japanese are more given to prizing collections than are other peoples. Intercultural evidence was employed to isolate features of Japanese poetic collections and their units that might explain Japanese conceptions about the relation of the individual to the collective, not only in poetic but also in social terms.

The other study actually undertaken involved the origin and development of systematic poetics in various cultures.[8] Because that study provides one theoretical basis for this book, its thesis must be set forth at somewhat greater length. The presumptively identical topic was what I have designated here the creation of an originative poetics. To enlarge on what was earlier mentioned briefly, an originative poetics appears in a given culture, not at its outset but at a subsequent period, after poets have moved from anonymity to stated authorship and poetry has been granted autonomous status. Two striking features of Aristotle's *Poetics* require attention. One is that although the greatest name in Greek literature, Homer, was associated with narrative poetry, epic, Aristotle defines his poetics out of drama. The other is that his act required a mind of great powers within the terms of its tradition; to effect his poetics he had to use Plato's concept of mimesis to ends contrary to those of his teacher. From those two important facts it was possible to develop a thesis that a system-

---

[8] Miner, 1979B. Given the importance of this study to the conception and organization of this book, it may not be amiss to point out that it also exists in different versions. Leaving aside one in Japanese, there is "Toward a New Conception of Classical Japanese Poetics," *Studies on Japanese Culture*, 2 vols. (Tokyo: The P. E. N. Club of Japan, 1973), 1:99–113. A briefer and adapted version appears in Miner-Odagiri-Morrell, 1985:3–17.

atic, explicit, originative poetics emerges in a culture when a gifted critic defines a conception of literature from the genre thought most prestigious.

The next step was to verify the thesis. It held for China on the basis of the "Great Preface" to *The Classic of Poetry*. (The preface is "great" only in normative terms, since it is actually far briefer than the "Little Preface.") The thesis also held for Japan, on the basis of Ki no Tsurayuki's Japanese preface to the *Kokinshū*. The Chinese—Korean and Japanese, too—category of the literary is expressed by a written character pronounced *wen* (K. *mun*; J. *bun, fumi*). The category includes certain kinds of history more or less foundational and legendary along with the central item, lyric poetry. The presence of history is highly important, as is the mention Aristotle makes of Homer, but the originative poetics occurred in the immediate contexts of lyrics.

Since the thesis held for east Asian as well as the earliest European poetics, it seemed worthwhile to inquire into other traditions. That meant asking questions of people who knew some literatures I did not, and it yielded a surprise. It transpired that with one exception (the complex Indian one) they all emerged, usually implicitly, by definition out of lyric.[9] That is another way of saying two things: there appears to be no originative poetics defined out of narrative; and the western is the sole one derived initially from drama alone. There are various complexities (Miner, 1979B), but these two central facts have rich implications.[10]

It is no wonder that Aristotle's poetics should be a mimetic one: it is founded on drama, the representing kind. Only Eurocentrism allows one to term the other poetics—those of the world besides—nonmimetic; if any, western poetics is the true *non*entity. Another designation is therefore necessary. I have termed the various lyric-based poetics *affective-expressive* because they presume that a poet is moved by experience or observation to give expression in words, and that that expression is the cause

[9] Although the error in Miner, 1979B, is not apparent, it is too serious not to castigate it here. It was assumed there that the world has produced a large number of *explicit* and *originative* poetics, whereas in fact the number of poetics is large but, outside the classical west and Asia, the various poetics are implicit. The exact nature of a given poetics therefore depends, by definition, not upon critics but poets, upon the genre most esteemed, on whether a genre exists and is esteemed, on whether verse or prose is considered normative, and on other factors. In short, the situation is at once more complex and more interesting than I had implied (and assumed). Hereafter, even when the distinction is not made, it should be borne in mind that a generative poetics need not be explicit.

[10] On his penultimate page—Ricoeur, 1984–85:vol. 3:273—the author recalls that he had said that "Lyric poetry . . . borders on dramatic poetry" ("La poésie lyrique côtoie ainsi la poésie dramatique"). No explanation is offered for what seems to me untenable: it is lyric and narrative (as I hope to show) that are closer together. The added condition of poetry (poésie) seems immaterial to me. But if Ricoeur is correct, an alignment of lyric and drama might explain why they are the world's sole foundation genres.

of moving the listener or reader. Although we must consider the subsequent developments of the poetics devised in any literature, it is striking that the affective-expressive and the mimetic poetics do share what may be termed a prior presumption. Both have traditionally held to the philosophically realist ground that the world is real and knowable. It was only on that assumption that a poet could be moved and find words, only on that presumption that a poet could imitate features of humanity in its world. The comfort given by that unstated prior presumption perhaps explains the enduring powers of these generative poetics. A great deal of contemporary western literature has broken with the prior presumption and therefore with mimetic principles as well. That antimimesis must be distinguished from affective-expressive unmimesis. By a beneficent irony, however, western readers' familiarity with (western) antimimetic writing has made it easier to teach things written in the affective-expressive traditions, whether of Asia or of Islamic literatures in various parts of the world. It should also be added that in Japan there is writing today that also denies the prior realist assumption, but—and this is of great import—doing so does not bring into being an antimimetic theory but an antiexpressivist poetics.

Certain features of the development of European and east Asian poetics will assist our understanding of their differences. Aristotle emphasizes the fear and pity evoked by tragedy and once, to our remaining uncertainty, he mentions *katharsis*. This clearly implies an affective view of literature and inclusion of the reader in his poetic scheme. The situation in the Academy, however, prevented Aristotle from positing the affective as a differentia for poetics. The philosophers, notably Aristotle's teacher, held that philosophy was more moving (and more justly so) than was literature: hence Plato's remark on "the ancient war between philosophy and poetry" (*Republic*:10, 607). There was, moreover, a third group of contenders, the Sophists, as Plato shows with consummate skill in the *Phaedrus*. Aristotle therefore fails to account adequately for two of the five factors distinguished above: the reader and the reader's poem.

The omission was repaired by Horace in his *Ars Poetica* (*Ad Pisones, De Arte Poetica*). Although the matter is uncertain enough to require fuller consideration (in Chapter 5), it appears that Horace had knowledge of Aristotle's *Poetics* through Alexandrian sources.[11] But we cannot claim

---

[11] On this complex issue, see Brink, 1963–82:vol. 2:77–83 and index "Varia," under "Aristotle." The issue appears to be how and how much Horace knew of the *Poetics* through which Alexandrian intermediaries. The issue involves interpretation of the *Ars Poetics* itself, since about a third of the poem is devoted to drama. That requires explanation, since Romans held the theater in low repute (e.g., see Plutarch's life of Mark Antony, ch. 9), and although plays were composed by many wellborn men, including of course Seneca, it is the consensus of classicists that those plays were declaimed rather than performed. Perhaps one

either that he draws on Aristotle very much or that he has his predecessor's power as an originator of poetics. It was too late to originate in the strict sense, but he could adjust the basic poetics. This he did by writing from his own practice as a poet of lyrics, satires, and epistles (about a third of which are satiric). He based his theory, then, on essentially affective kinds (although he does deal frequently with drama, too, and painting). It is striking how the result resembles affective-expressive poetics. His most famous conception is that poetry moves us, and in western centuries to come it would be said that the ends of poetry are the Horatian ones of teaching and delight and its means the Aristotelian one of imitation. With Horace, the reader became fully part of western poetics. So has the reader's poem, because although the fact is seldom remarked on, Horace devotes himself to *words* as strikingly as do the Chinese and Japanese. To do so, he draws on seemingly every possible Latin expression for "words" from his well-stocked thesaurus, including that quintessentially Horatian expression, *norma loquendi* (1. 72; the rule, model, pattern of speaking).

It cannot be emphasized strongly enough that concern with language is as symptomatic of lyric presumptions about literature as concern with representation is of dramatic presumptions.

It is worth a review of the central issue of comparative poetics: the striking contrast between the rest of the world's poetics and that of the west. Historically speaking, after Horace the western system may be thought mimetic and affective, or even mimetic, affective, and expressive. And we shall have reason later to consider various complexities occurring at different times. Granting as much, a logical and indeed comparative principle contravenes. The important feature of an idea is its identity, of course—that is, what distinguishes it from other things in its class. And the distinguishing feature of western poetics is precisely its congeries of mimetic assumptions.

Today most theoretically minded westerners would deny that they are heirs to mimesis, that their views are shaped by mimetic assumptions. There are, however, telltale signs that may be arbitrary as semioticians say. They are not neutral. One need only read or listen like a sentinel alert to the passwords. On hearing "representation," "fiction," "origin" or "originality," "literariness," "unity," "plot," or "character," one knows the talk is mimetic. ("Representation," *representation*, and *Darstellung* are particularly revealing.) Someone might object that these terms are not particularly mimetic but are simply terms everybody uses. Nothing

or more of the Pisos was known to Horace to have such ambitions; perhaps the attention to drama shows knowledge of Aristotle.

could be more Eurocentric. Those are precisely terms that everybody does not use, but only users whose assumptions continue to be mimetic. Another objection may be raised: Writer W or Critic C is clearly, openly antimimetic. But it does not matter if the crucial terms are preferred or quarreled with as long as they are presumed. Antimimesis is simply a variant that feeds on what it attacks.

Historical interests alone would lead us on. We might consider the debates, decided now this way, now that, whether moral teaching or delight was paramount. We might follow the vicissitudes of the central mimetic principle to the Romantics, considering for example Coleridge's acceptance of mimesis but depreciation of imitation. We might concern ourselves with the heyday of the novel, with its emphasis both on mimesis and its prior assumption. But let the *occupatio* be gone.

A better topic involves some fine distinctions between affectivisms. By comparison with east Asian poetics, Horace's affectivism is much more concerned with the reader and less with the poet.[12] This seems to be part of the mimetic legacy from Aristotle, whose affective concerns (which, as we have seen, could not have been a logical differentia for literature) account solely for the reader or the theatrical audience. As a representor of the world, the mimetic poet is accorded imitative powers rather than a motivating affect. Further distinctions are possible. As far as the reader is concerned, Chinese affectivism resembles Horace's in including teaching of moral kind along with delight. What one may term the official Chinese preference was clear: Confucianism held to a strict preference for teaching over delight. (Of course there was what might be termed soft Daoism to foster engaging dreams in the red chamber.) In Japan, which shares with China a premise of the affected poet, moral affectivism is difficult to discover. Apart from a few (but important) earlier exceptions, it was not until about 1600 that Confucianism, or rather Neoconfucianism, gained strength as a result of its being adopted as the official policy of the Tokugawa military aristocracy. Even then writers resisted it for the most part. We may say, therefore, that the Chinese conception of affectivism holds to a position between the Japanese and the Horatian versions.

In Sanskrit practice, teaching and delight exist together, being almost indistinguishable in the Indian merger of the sacred with the erotic; much the same is true of some Islamic mystical poetry. These matters are worthy of mention to show how the subsidiary as well as the governing pre-

---

[12] This point was made to me in conversation by a Japanese graduate student, whose name I did not catch, at a University of Tokyo symposium on comparative literature in June 1987. I argued with him, mentioning passages I remembered that implied the author. But his point is the major one, as reflection has shown me.

sumed identities yield to a differentiation making comparison at once feasible and controlled.

The excursion with Horace (the phrase seems in his spirit) has a counterpart in east Asian literature. In the absence of any originative poetics in the world based solely on narrative, Japanese poetics provides the best evidence we have as to what a narrative poetics might be like.[13] About three and a half centuries separate Aristotle and Horace, a period required for the Horatian adjustment of western poetics. Important changes occurred more quickly in Japan. It has been mentioned that Ki no Tsurayuki's Japanese preface to the *Kokinshū* (or more properly and in full, *Kokinwakashū*) is the originative poetics of Japan. In both the title (meaning *An Anthology of Older and Recent Japanese Poetry*) and in Tsurayuki's preface there are historical touches, or distinctions, that differentiate it from other originative poetics. When Tsurayuki writes about invisible gods and spirits, he shows signs of having read the early histories (or myth *cum* history), particularly no doubt the *Nihon Shoki* (or *Nihongi*, *Chronicles of Japan*; in Chinese and ca. 720). This is to suggest that Japanese affective-expressive poetics had from the outset a certain congeniality with the principle of narrative.

There is no other satisfactory way to explain the extraordinary, unparalleled fact that within just over a century after the founding of the generative poetics out of lyricism (and a kind of history) there should appear (with royal and noble support) the greatest work of Japanese literature, Murasaki Shikibu's *Tale of Genji*. This is a very lengthy narrative, albeit one with nearly four thousand lines of lyric poetry in the five-line *tanka* form, along with numerous allusions to Japanese and Chinese verse. Composition was necessarily protracted, and given the high price of paper, patrons were necessary. Murasaki Shikibu was fortunate in having a royal consort as her patron (and therefore the consort's male backers for support), not simply for the economic assistance but also for the prestige. Earlier *monogatari* had been written by men for women and children, although men also read them on the sly. Now a woman was writing a newly serious *monogatari* that would repay reading by the foremost men at court. It is significant that one of her readers should have been the reigning monarch, Ichijō (r. 986–1011) and that he should have commented that the author of the work had read the *Nihongi*, which has just

---

[13] As has been mentioned, east Asian poetics included history with lyric, so making factual literature a congenial conception and making easy the acceptance of narrative in Japan. Representative histories included as literature in the three nations include (in order of composition) the Chinese *Records of the Historian* (*Shiji*), the Japanese *Records of Ancient Matters* (*Kojiki*), and the Korean *Recollections of the Three Kingdoms* (*Samguk Sagi*). The affective differences among these three parallel those among the lyric poetics of the three peoples.

been mentioned: "She must have read the Chronicles of Japan. . . . She seems very learned" (Bowring, 1982:137).

It is striking that the greatest work in the language was written so soon after the definition of a systematic poetics out of lyric, and yet that that work should be a very lengthy prose narrative (inclusive of lyrics, to be sure). Of course, histories of certain kinds were also deemed literary, and there are works that combine lyric with what was deemed historical. Those include *The Tales of Ise* (*Ise Monogatari*), which offers "tales of poems," the real or supposed circumstances that produced the poems. There is also *The Tosa Diary* (*Tosa Nikki*), Tsurayuki's poetic diary, which records, in the guise of a woman, the return of his party to the capital from his governorship of Tosa. These writings and the *Nihongi* itself combine prose with poems, making it more natural than we might assume for prose narrative to combine with lyric to define the nature of literature.

Such matters are reflected in the famous passage in "The Fireflies" chapter (ch. 25) of *The Tale of Genji*, where the hero discusses the art of *monogatari*, the author's own art, the art of the story we are reading. Within the affective-expressive poetics, Genji posits a role for *monogatari* as a kind of supplementary history. His complex discussion (which will be examined in Chapter 4) involves religious matters as well, but for our present purpose the remarkable thing beyond the sheer greatness of *The Tale of Genji* is its appearance so soon after the devising of a lyric poetics. It is no less a wonder that the author should also be so explicit about her own and other arts, giving us the closest thing we possess to a narrative-based originative poetics.

No doubt Murasaki Shikibu's task was eased by the assimilative, syncretic nature of Japanese thought. A very major allowance for narrative was possible within the essentially lyric-based poetics. This might be thought due solely to the presence of history along with lyric in literature (*bun*). If so, explanation is required for the nonemergence for so much longer of comparable writing in China and Korea. The example of *nō* and *kyōgen* also shows otherwise. Not only the serious *nō* but also the comic *kyōgen* were allowed status as premier arts long before drama was accorded serious purpose in China. In brief, the general postulate of the genesis of an explicit originative poetics does require an engagement with the then most esteemed literary kind. But it does not preclude our ability to make further, finer or smaller distinctions, whether of Horatianism, of early prestige for prose narrative and for drama in Japan, or of other historical developments reflecting changes in a culture's poetics.

Comparative evidence also bears on the fact/fiction issue. I confessed earlier that my knowledge of Czarist Russia derives from reading its literature in translation. There is no question but that that literature is, as we say, fictional, whether in a poem like Pushkin's *Evgeni Onegin*, in the major Russian novels, or in Gogol's play, *The Inspector General*. But of course a fictional work is not *entirely* fictional. If it were, we could not comprehend it. There is no cause for surprise that we can derive something approaching a picture of historical actuality from fictional literature, providing of course we as readers know how to sort out what the author takes to be fact and what fiction.

Perhaps it is the romance heritage of the novel, surviving in popular romance to this day, that leads booksellers and so many of us in common usage to classify novels as "fiction." But that is misleading on many grounds. We may consider *The Tale of Genji* again. It is there on the "fiction" shelf, too. It is treated as if it were a novel, which it is not. (It is a *monogatari*.) It certainly is fictional in many respects, and what one learns historically is that to which a female author had access in the late tenth and early eleventh centuries. Even the opening of the legend-like first chapter points in a factual direction: "In which reign was it?" or "In an earlier reign. . . ." We are given features of real monarchs to go with fictional heroes and heroines, and the fictional characters wear factual clothes, have factual concerns, and believe factual things of that time (e.g., spirit possession).

The strong (and sound) east Asian thesis is that fact has priority, not because it is imagined that literature imitates or represents the world. Rather, in the absence of evidence to the contrary, that which moves us in literature is considered factual. If a lyric is fictional, Chinese critics will seek ways to obtain fact nonetheless, commonly by presuming another meaning. As a corollary, in the absence of countervailing evidence, it is presumed that poets speak *in propria persona*. Not only that. Passages in *monogatari* of what seem like narratorial comment or intrusion to the Western eye are termed, in a centuries-old distinction, "the author's words" (*sakusha no kotoba*). Of course, in one sense all the words constituting a work are inescapably "the author's words." The author is the one who has chosen them in their order. But the east Asian idea holds that the author is speaking out to the reader, commonly as if there were no lyric speaker, no narrator of a story. This conviction runs at such odds to modern western ideas that it will seem downright wrong to many people.

During the next three chapters, we shall have reason to discover the merit of the factual presumption. And in the last chapter the reader will find some consideration of issues of comparative literature that are often ignored. They may be termed the issues of ethics and relativism: if all is relative to a given culture, we face the issue—and in a double sense the responsibility—of choosing between claims of rival poetic systems.

Most of this chapter has been devoted to defining comparative poetics and to propounding a thesis on the genesis, to some extent also the development, of a systematic poetics—whether explicit or implicit—within cultures. The thesis depends for its value on any explanatory power it possesses. Knowing no other account, I can point only to a few features of this one. The explanation is historical in depending on successions of events. It is theoretical in that the pattern is abstracted from the historical, with elements of the pattern defined. For example, the triad of drama, lyric, and narrative (to follow the order of the ensuing chapters) is shown to be necessary to an explanation of views of literature. We may agree that "Lyric, epic [narrative], and drama grow from systematic to historical categories" (Szondi, 1965:10), providing we may first presume the reverse.

Although these matters will be more adequately discussed in the next three chapters, enough evidence should have been given by this point to show that, far from being inevitable, the view of literature dominant in the west is in a minority of one. The mainstream is instead a version defined out of lyric, with or without other kinds of writing. In the general survey offered in this chapter, such matters have been discussed in terms of what may be meant more strictly than usual by "poetics" and "comparative."

To this point I have been as sparing as possible in special terminology, sparing in the sense of not wishing to impose meanings on familiar words. In what follows, I wish to be able to assume certain conceptions involving distinctions. To do so requires meanings, and meanings require terms. There is no necessity whatsoever for others to adopt my terminology, but there is a necessity that the reader know what I mean by certain words. For example, given their roles in the genesis of originative poetics, lyric and drama, along with narrative, will be called *genres*. The name is not important, but it is important that, when the term is used here, it be recognized that what is meant are the "foundation genres" (Lewalski, 1986:4). There is a certain awkwardness in schematic presentation, but it has the virtue of putting the definitions in one place and of allowing for a sense of the relations among them. The account is not complete, but it is probably long enough for the patience and memories of most readers.

Literary Distinctions

Rhythm: verse, prose
Mode: the relation taken by the poet between self and world (and others) on a spectrum from public to private

Attitude: conception by the poet (and the reader) of the degree of awe in the world and characters (whether higher, like, or lower)

Presentation: recited-oral; written-visual; theatrical; quasi-theatrical (radio, film, television)

Genre: lyric, dramatic, narrative

Other kinds (mostly poetic)

Affective kinds: tragedy, comedy, satire, panegyric

Occasional kinds: aubades, epithalamia, epicedes, banquet poems, parting poems

Topical kinds: poems on set topics (a season, love), compound topics (snow at a mountain village), prosodic topics (the same rhymes as in the poem responded to)

Formal kinds: elegy (in distichs), sonnet, sestina, shi, fu, chōka, hyangga, sijo, ru'bai

Genres and affective kinds can be taken attributively
  As: a *dramatic* lyric; the poem is lyric, with attributive dramatic features
  As: a *tragic, comic, satiric, praising* narrative

Genres and affective kinds may be mingled
  As: comic intervals in tragedies, lyric passages in a narrative

Drama and narrative may be doubled
  As: plays within a play, narratives within a narrative

This is incomplete, as promised, and it tends to emphasize poetry over prose writing. But it will be enough for a start as we now pursue the subject of comparative poetics more or less genre by genre.

COMPARATIVE POETICS IN BRIEF

Nothing in the preceding, nothing in what follows, is meant to argue for a single conception of comparative poetics. All that is argued, and it is quite enough, is that comparative poetics requires two things: a satisfactory conception and practice of comparison along with an attention to poetics (conceptions of literature) that rest on historically sound evidence. The route followed here is based on what can be inferred from the three genres conceptually and historically.

Not all roads lead to comparative poetics. That point also needs making. But others do besides that followed here. René Etiemble clearly envisioned another double route that others have tried to set asunder. "By combining the two methods that consider themselves enemies but that, in reality, must complement each other—[the putatively French] historical inquiry and [the putatively American] critical or aesthetic reflection— comparative literature would then be irresistibly drawn to comparative poetics."[14] The attitude is visionary in part, lofty, and set in a possible future. This essay is, in a sense, an attempt to act on that vision in the present. Others in the same enterprise may wish to follow different routes: ideology, interpretation, translation, the individual, society—the routes involve the manifold and familiar ones of literary study. It is, as Etiemble envisions, the purpose and the goal that determine whether a given route leads to comparative poetics. There is, finally, no reason to believe that there can be but one traveler per route. There are "defects of loneliness," as Donne observed in another connection. Similarly, as Bashō observed, there is comfort in being able to write, "I travel with a friend." My companions are variously identified in other pages of this essay, most explicitly in the forematter and bibliography.

And so to drama as our beginning.

[14] Etiemble, 1963:101; using and correcting 1966:54 by 1963.

❏

CHAPTER 2

Drama

Within recognizable likeness there will
be points of deviance.

— Chikamatsu

. . . the fear or strangeness or *terribilità*
which enters into the actor's power
over the audience.

— Michael Goldman

DRAMA OFFERS the natural beginning, the first of three chapters on the
poetics of the foundation genres. It is the genre by which Aristotle originated the traditional western mimetic poetics. The greatest English writer
is great because of his plays, rather than for those mannered narratives
that appealed so much to some of his contemporaries. In fact, as we shall
see, the distinguishing properties of drama are those normally associated
with literature by us in the west today. For that reason, to begin with
drama is to enter a consideration of comparative poetics by the familiar
western door. It is not entirely an accident that "drama" and "dramatic"
seem to "represent" the excitement of life: dialogue, role-playing, antagonism, reversals, climaxes, and even the final scene when we are carried
off dead from this theater of the world.

For all the truth that may be found in such reasons, however, creative
drama—the actual writing and performing of an important theatrical literature—is historically the rarest of the three foundation genres. There
are major cultures like the Hebraic and the several Islamic ones that lack
drama. After its flowering in Athens, drama ceases in Greece until modern revival. After another brief period in Rome, the west itself is without
drama until the late Middle Ages. When medieval critics wrote about
drama, they had the Ciceronian dialogue in mind. Tragedy was of the
narrative *de casibus* kind told by Chaucer's Monk. As the title of Dante's
masterpiece shows, comedy was that which ended happily.[1]

---

[1] For an excellent account, see Behrens, 1940; for a summary based on her work, see
Preminger, 1974:under "genre."

Although there are many kinds of performance loosely termed "Chinese Opera," none held esteem until relatively recently: they were not to be set beside *shi* in its wide sense of largely lyric poetry, or those histories that also entered with lyric to make up literature, premier writing (*wen*). In Japan, drama of certain kinds—*nō* and *kyōgen*—achieved prominence and obtained credit. But other forms were not credited, and the creative period for *nō* and *kyōgen* did not last long. Even in England, although there is that giant race before the flood, as Dryden said nostalgically, there is no Shakespeare in Restoration drama, in drama from Shaw to Beckett, or in medieval drama.

It is not difficult to identify reasons why drama should be so fragile. Living theater—the creation and production of enduringly esteemed new plays—requires elements that are paradoxical, hard to balance, combustible. Drama commonly originates when one kind of the sacred is crossed by another of profaning. Social approval by patronage exists alongside anger over the profanity of the stage and the loose living of the players. All's well that ends well, but until that belated and sometimes perfunctory assurance, we are treated to challenges to authority and violations of the assumptions of right-minded people. Most great plays are problem plays. Pompey's question figs authority: "Does your worship mean to geld and spay all the youth of the city?" (*Measure for Measure*, 2, 1). But the moral imaginations of Iago, Hamlet, King Lear, and others reach into viler ditches, and no water will cleanse them of their thoughts. In the Restoration, as was often remarked, the price of admission to the theater was the price of admission to a whore.

AMPHITRYON AND DON JUAN

Given the tinseled and sweaty nature of that fine glitter, it is quite appropriate that two of the most often treated western stories for the theater have been those of Amphitryon and Don Juan, both of which offer accounts of violations. Plautus's *Amphitruo* is the oldest surviving version of that story, although predecessors are known to have existed. The story should be set forth briefly, both because it is not as familiar as the Don Juan legend and because later we shall be using the conclusions of some of the Amphitryon plays for their exemplary character.

The plot involves Jupiter's assuming the guise of Alcmena's husband, Amphitryon, in order to bed her through a divinely lengthened night. Mercury appears as well, taking on the guise of Amphitryon's servant, Sosia, in wonderful comic scenes that—like those involving his master— center on questions of human identity and the brutality of the gods. It is variously appropriate for the prologue to this play (l. 59) to be the *locus classicus* of "tragicomedy." One major Plautine reason for the designation was the treatment of both divine and human characters in the same play, a mixture that would pose other problems and opportunities for Christian dramatists.

Molière's version is highly attractive, not least for the great beauty of its verse. Against that is set, with increasingly bleak clarity, the necessity of suffering and loss—because we are human—in those things that matter most to us. We human creatures must yield to the iron whim, the domineering power of the *grand seigneur*. In Dryden's version, the gods are of unspeakable scurrility and unbridled appetite. He adds to Molière's characters to redouble his point. And as Amphitryon, Alcmena, and Sosia seek to make some sense of their experience, to find some decency in lives violated by irresponsible gods, Dryden does not allow us even the luxury of supposing that, although weak, our kind is ideal. Sosia himself is no saint, and the best that can be said of one of the added characters, Phaedra ("queen of the gypsies"), is that only if a human character is a sufficient cheat to manipulate divine appetites is there a chance to work on equal terms. If it were not so very funny, this would be a tragedy.

Whether it is better to laugh or to cry is an issue picked up by Kleist. With his unusual gifts for depicting female psychology, Kleist develops the character of his Alkmena even more. The play closes with her divided in soul. There has been that experience of divine sexuality, after which she has been restored to a husband of her own kind and choice. What is a woman to say? Kleist's Alkmena, present at an unbearable conversation between Jupiter and her husband, has two one-word exclamations: "Amphitryon!" and "Ach!" There has been endless dispute over what she means, which direction her heart leads her, or even whether she herself knows—or knows herself.

The Don Juan story is better known. How can it fail, when it explores the gap between the rules over the erotic that we wish upon others and from which we wish to be free? Although the story may be said to originate from dark reaches of human (or at least male) desire, it achieved presentable greatness in *El Burlador de Sevilla* (1635) by Tirso de Molina (Gabriel Tellez). Thirty years later there appeared Molière's version, *Dom Juan ou le festin de Pierre*. Both were given English versions: it would be too much to say that they were translated. The Spanish play appeared, after a fashion, in the English of John Ozell (*The Libertine*, 1665). The version of Molière's play is so bad as to cause reflection.

People sometimes say, without adequate explanation, that the Anglo-Saxon mind is unable to deal with the Don Juan story. Given Byron's and Shaw's versions, it seems more likely that the story is intrinsically as difficult to deal with as it is irresistible when done well—and that few of any nation can handle the story well.[2] It is a perfect vehicle for the theater's capacity to violate norms. Yet the necessary aesthetic violation of drama may itself be violated, spoiled. At least we may consider what to one person seems the worst along with the best version.

Thomas Shadwell's *Don John* is based on Molière's play, and a more exemplary instance of degradation would be hard to discover. Shadwell seems to wish us to understand that Don John is a bad man. The hero and a fellow rakehell set fire to a convent in order to rape fleeing nuns. That is as nothing to incestuous rape. But the climax, the worst deed in an ascending series is, of course, Don John's killing of his father. By these apprisals we are meant to understand that such evil should be punished, and so morality closes the play. All's well that ends well, as previously observed.

Nothing, one feels, could be farther from Shadwell's moral dungheap than the grandeur and beauty of *Don Giovanni*. Who does not recall the loveliness of Don Ottavio's arias to Donna Anna, "Dalla sua pace" and "Il mio tesoro intanto"? But are they lovelier than Don Giovanni's seductive song with Zerlina, "Là ci darem la mano"? There are complexities here that Shadwell never could wake to. We recognize the evil in Don Giovanni's exploitation of others, but like the women of the opera we respond to his attractiveness—or is it his command? We all recognize the vitality of Leporello's catalogue ("Madamina") detailing to Donna Elvira his master's conquests throughout Europe: "And of the Spanish a thousand and three." Pitted against this indecent energy is the relentless rigidity of the moral statue, that statute of mortality.

There is no problem with the play's morality, except how to take it: which is to say how we really feel about the issues. At the end a sestet sings three lines, "the most ancient refrain," on how wrongdoers are punished. Those lines seem rather routine set beside three others sung earlier:

> Vivan la femmine,
> Viva il buon vino!
> Sostegno e gloria d'umanità!
>
> (Here's to kind women,
> Here's to good drinking!
> Sustainers and glory of our humankind!)

[2] Perhaps the most used account is Rank, 1975 (reprint), but his Freudianism is heavy-handed. Gendarme de Bérotte, 1911, is particularly useful: e.g., volume 2 contains a list of well over a hundred versions of the story.

The triumphant music here credits these three lines rather than the final three. The music tells us in a very complex way what the subtitle of Lorenza Da Ponte's libretto declares: *Don Giovanni* is a "Dramma Giocoso."

ESTRANGEMENT

Whether tragicomedy or jocose "dramma," these staged pieces illustrate the violation of law, the incursion of boundaries, that the energies of drama propel it to. But there are also limits necessary, partly for testing and partly for containing. For the moment they will be dealt with briefly by example. In both the Amphitryon and the Don Juan pieces, one unspoken limit is what we can suffer while laughter is yet possible, what we can laugh at while yet knowing it to be pain.

Japanese theatrical history provides another kind of limit. The comic interludes that go with *nō* are appropriately called by a name, *kyōgen*, that means "wild words." That is the spirit of drama. There were three principal schools for these interludes, patronized for centuries, along with *nō*, by samurai families. About 1900, the head of the Sagi school taught *kyōgen* principles to a *kabuki* actor. The enraged ex-samurai sponsors at once withdrew support, and the school vanished. As players have always known, the limits are often far greater than the possibilities to violate, although drama cannot exist without violation.

It is difficult to know whether to take heart or flight over the state of dramatic criticism and theory. We do have Aristotle and shall review him. In China, drama was all but ignored as an art worthy of critical speculation. In Japan, there has been great dramatic criticism: by Zeami (ca. 1364–ca. 1443), by Komparu Zenchiku (1405–?), and by Chikamatsu Monzaemon (1653–1724). It was, however, absorbed into a lyric-based poetics. We do have Corneille, whose *examens* initiate analytical criticism in Europe; we do have Dryden and Johnson; and we do have the academic Shakespeare industry. But it has been a hard season for dramatic theory since the Romantics insisted that Shakespeare's plays were too great for performance.

Because the three foundation genres imply distinct concepts of literature, and because critical practice varies as based on one or the other, it is as necessary to consider the implications of all three as it is to draw on intercultural evidence. Having never been achieved on the scale desired, the aim will not be achieved here, either. But the principles may be established, and examples may be brought forward. There is hope at least in this: attention to the implications of a single genre brings out sets of conceptions about literature that would otherwise be overlooked or understressed.

The essence of drama is presentation, in words and action, by players on a stage.[3] There are numerous mutations in mystery plays, *commedia dell'arte*, puppet theater (e.g., that so highly developed in Japan, *jōruri* or *bunraku*), along with opera, ballet, and other kinds of stage works. The common element is presentation by players in a spatially defined arena. The scripts of the greatest plays make engrossing reading, because the verbal medium as well as the theatrical medium has been so well realized. Many things that read strangely, however, perform very well. Yet more to the point, much that is strange is necessary to the dramatic temper of violation. What is true to some degree of all literature is truest and elemental for drama: estrangement.

A play begins with the discovery of one or more players *doing* (the meaning of *shite*, the principal character or role in *nō*). The doing is what we understand from the language we hear and the "language" we see in the total performance. The motions of thought and passion cannot be adequately understood without the visibilia of stage, costuming, and the players' "body language." They may be masked or barefaced, their faces painted or plain. They may be dressed up in the finery of a distant time and place. These days they may be dressed down into humble garb or bare forked nakedness. We know that we have paid our money or at least set aside our time to watch people *acting* persons they are not. To the extent that dramatic mimesis is, in Erich Auerbach's phrase, "The Representation of Reality in Western Literature," we are required to take an estranging illusion as a hypothetical but insisted upon truth. (His German is actually more exact, "dargestellte Wirklichkeit," represented reality.) We are estranged by being caught between what is *represented* as real and what we otherwise presume to be real. We feel a shock in the pressing need to set aside our assumptions about human identity, with the presentation of a strange world given the claim to be normal and yet violating our norms.

This shock, and‚the kind of people it usually requires to make it, are what have so often made drama the target of moralists. To them, the estrangement is real in the wrong terms: what is not true but dissembled is insisted on by a group of people of lewd and unfamilial natures.

This exaggerated and misplaced response testifies to the felt reality of shock, revealing more than one thing. It reveals first of all some explanation and implication of the old allegation that literature is a lie. Of course the boy playing Shakespeare's Cleopatra or the woman playing Dryden's are not the Egyptian queen, and perhaps their sexual morality is not all that it might be. But a lie is told with the intention to deceive,

[3] That means "the entire occasion of acted drama"—Goldman, 1975:vii.

and when it is exploded, the liar is dismissed, cognitively as the violator of truth and morally as a violator of trust. The players know that we know we know we have entered the theater expecting them to act roles of those they are not, and no lie is involved. But offering as real, being given as real, what is known not to be real is a powerful estrangement. It is a cognitive, potentially pleasurable violation of the real by the fictional.

The aesthetic blow forces us to realize that we are brought up against full-scale fiction. As is well known, *fictio* begins as a term in Roman law. The parables told in the *Lotus Sutra* are among many expedients or accommodations (Skt. *upāya*) that the merciful and wise Buddha employs to make enlightenment accessible to all sentient creatures. Both *fictio* and *upāya* have been more often employed to characterize nondramatic than dramatic literature.

That is a paradox. For, as we have seen in the first chapter, drama is the only one of the three genres that is necessarily fictional. The very fictionality of Chinese drama was the cause preventing its becoming respectable in a culture prizing literary fact above fiction. Those shelves labeled "fiction" in the bookshops of English-speaking countries offer novels, all but a few of which are indeed fictional to the degree and with the reservations expressed in the preceding chapter. But the signs in our bookshops are misplaced. Prose narrative literature need not be fictional. The unavoidable shock of the fictional is found in the theater, and inevitably in drama alone of the three genres.

Theatrical violation reveals the centrality of conventions to drama. Of course all literature rests on conventions, as does nonliterary writing, language itself, and our other social behavior. There is a wide range indeed of coding that we employ to do things efficiently, in fact to do them at all. Dramatic conventions are, by nature, just such coding, just such sign systems that we use. With usage, we lose our sense of their arbitrariness, as if they naturally signified what we take them to do.

MAKE-UP

Nonetheless there are two features of dramatic conventions that distinguish them from other sign codes. One is their blatancy. The soliloquy, the stage whisper, the aside are perpetually in danger of sounding false. The closer we are to the front row of seats, the more the paint and wig and saliva are obvious. This blatancy may be termed the make-up of drama, from one of its cosmetic practices. Of course we can learn the codes, and the paint may be only part of the glitter or a special sign: in one theatrical tradition, a red face designates a heroic figure and in another a debauched one. The blatancy of dramatic make-up will be evident to anyone recalling the first experience of seeing a completely different kind of theater, the "Chinese opera," for example. There is plenty of making up, whether on the face or in what at first seems an artificial straining of the voice, in the costumes, and in the singing by just one character—with the words of the song being flashed on the wall next to the stage opening.

Nō is better known, but a westerner in its theater well after the first time will still be disconcerted by the initial thumping and howling. The sounds we hear seem so contrary to what we *see* in that spare sumptuousness, the elegant abbreviation of nō. In time, but only in time, those thumps and howls will also come to seem necessary to the atmosphere of nō. Examples could be multiplied, but the first point is the *relative* extremity of the coding, the clear arbitrariness of the signs, the presence of make-up.

The second feature is the basic one and has been suggested already on different grounds. This is the founding convention of drama itself, the necessary estranging fiction: those people on the boards are acting as if they fall in love or argue, commit adultery, or betray a country. The fearsome because unconcealed strength of the make-up in the founding convention can be exemplified by a one-word stage direction that requires only body language, a player, and a stage: "*Dies.*" Only a player can fully assess the double risks of melodrama and comedy in dying while yet alive and ready to perform again at tomorrow's matinee. For ourselves, we consent (if all goes well on stage) to the fictional death in order that in our estranged world of the scene we may consider some of the implications of that final human moment.

The founding convention and the cultural conventions work together to produce dramatic representation, no more and no less. But if no more, the make-up of dramatic fiction is nonetheless the basis for entertaining, in a double sense, truth and falsehood. The playwright and the players have means at their disposal to represent situations in which we and certain deceivers know that the majority of persons being played are in cognitive error. The power of the make-up in such instances may be enormous, as with a slightly different example, that in *Oedipus the King*. Many matters of allied or different kinds can be so represented as to offer us a sense of the false or the unreal within the fictional make-up.

A play within a play and other forms of "metadrama" usually will require a higher degree of make-up—a different verse form, or a special stage area—but they also have the curious effect of giving by comparison a kind of credence, a certain licitness to the basic fiction of the play. The more extreme fiction of the metadramatic usually testifies to the relative reliability of the basic dramatic fiction, for although too heightened or too frequent a move to higher fictionalities may deprive us of ease with the basic fiction, within bounds we return from the metadramatic moment to what we take to be the "real" fictional norm.

The sense of a conditional real is not all we may discover. The real may be accompanied or displaced by the unreal or the surreal. Each may be means, each end. Each is based on the founding and cultural conventions of drama. Each is an estrangement for us, and in some sense making the fictional seem real may be thought the greatest—or highest—artifice of all.

There are many examples of a doubled sense of stage fiction. Besides dumbshows and plays within plays, there is that trick of having a player emerge from a seat in the audience, forsaking an identity like our own for that of a fictional character on stage. What is rarer by far and very exquisite is the opposite: a player's giving up a role within the fiction of the play and becoming, as an example will show, a version of her real self. In Dryden's *Tyrannick Love*, the comic actress and mistress of Charles II, Eleanor (Nell, Nelly) Gwynn, played Valeria, the daughter of the Tyrant Maximin, who martyrs St. Catherine. Distraught with love, Valeria takes her life. At the end of the play two stage hands come on stage to bear her "dead" body off. This is what we read, what the original audience heard and saw.

> *Spoken by* Mrs. Ellen, *when she was to*
> *be carried off dead by the bearers.*
>
> *To the Bearer*
> Hold; are you mad? you damn'd confounded dog!
> I am to rise and speak the Epilogue.
>
> *To the Audience*
> I come, kind gentlemen, strange news to tell ye:
> I am the ghost of poor departed Nelly.
> Sweet ladies, be not frighted; I'll be civil;
> I'm what I was, a little harmless devil. . . .

No longer Valeria, she reassumes her nonfictional identity as Mrs. Eleanor Gwynn. Since, however, she is still in costume and on the stage apron, her reassumption of her real identity is deliciously confusing in its handling of reality and fiction. Having died as Valeria, she becomes a fictionally dead Nell Gwynn. We see this in yet other terms when she curses the playwright—in words that, of course, he had written for her.

O poet, damn'd dull poet, who could prove
So senseless! to make Nelly die for love;
Nay, what's yet worse, to kill me in the prime
Of Easter-Term, in tart and cheesecake time!
I'll fit the fop, for I'll not one word say
T'excuse his godly out-of-fashion play,
A play which if you dare but twice sit out,
You'll all be slander'd and be thought devout.
But farewell, gentlemen, make haste to me;
I'm sure ere long to have your company.
As for my Epitaph when I am gone,
I'll trust no poet but will write my own.
Here Nelly *lies, who, though she liv'd a slattern,*
Yet di'd a princess acting in St. Cathar'ne.

The fictional situation is reduced to the delightful minimum, with our *awareness* of the fiction (e.g., "I'll trust no poet"—speaking lines by Dryden) heightened to the degree that the fiction lessens.

Other examples of manipulated dramatic fiction abound. There is the fine depiction of a character whose very name, "Le Menteur," invites us to see through him. Or there is another, Othello, who acts increasingly at variance from what we know is the nature of things. As these numerous examples show, depiction of a feigned reality requires another feigning. By the same token, depiction of the unreal or surreal requires a fictional reality to enable us to judge them unreal or surreal. If we may use the linguists' concept of markedness as an analogy, drama is the "marked" (although by no means necessarily mimetic) version of the "normal" world of our lives outside the theater: "*Dies.*"

The unreal and the surreal are versions of the foundation convention of drama that are marked still farther than the fictional reality of a stage. In some cases—as old as Aristophanes, as recent as Beckett—the unreal and the surreal may be used to question the very existence of reality. This also happens in narratives. But the situation is exquisite in drama. For, on the one hand, the reality put in question on stage can only have been a fiction to begin with. And, on the other, there must be a fictional reality to displace in order to establish that the unreal or the surreal has been substituted for it. No wonder, then, that in the absurdist plays of a dramatist as skilled as Eugène Ionesco, the stage may open upon a bourgeois sitting room in which the husband reads the newspaper and the wife darns socks. The humdrum and quotidian establish a fictional basis for admitting the absurd.

In its foundational nature, then, drama offers us what has been well called "the fear or strangeness or *terribilità* which enters into the actor's power over the audience" (Goldman, 1975:7). Yet to speak of estrangement or fear alone does not explain the appeal of drama, or of literature more generally. Clearly, there must be some other quality or qualities setting limits, modifying, redirecting our estrangement. Some would explain this dual repulsion and attraction by associating art with play: *homo ludens* is the human creature at play, finding amusement.[4] A *ludius* was a pantomimic actor. In a Juvenalian usage, he was a gladiator in an amphitheater of the real, a blood sport in which "*Dies*" brought a different, perverse pleasure to an audience. To those who appeared in that arena with the greeting, "We who are about to die salute you," the fictional foundation convention of drama did not exist.

Another explanation might be that what has been termed estrangement here frees us from many of the implications that a given matter would have if not presented but actual, and that that freedom permits us to contemplate the significance of other implications. This explanation does seem to have some force for drama, and indeed for all art. But in my judgment it does not get to the center. It does not account for the fact that our interests lie in the very things estranged. Aristotle touched on the matter: "it is also natural for all to delight in works of imitation. The truth of this . . . point is shown by experience: though the objects themselves may be painful to see, we delight to view the most realistic representations of them in art, the forms for example of the lowest animals and of dead bodies."[5] Aristotle seems to have in mind Greek vase painting, so called, and he assumes that we take pleasure in artistic copying, "the most realistic representations," of what would be too painful or disgusting to us if we saw the real thing. (Let us recall that the "realistic representations" by the Greeks included that of *painting* their statues.) There is something in what Aristotle says, but it does not account for the sense of estrangement we get in encountering art. I think another approach suits the nature of literature better, and of drama in particular.

One of the possible truth statuses of the aesthetic may be termed the "virtual," what is neither true nor false, neither not true nor not false. The *locus classicus* for this view is a pronouncement recorded, let it be stressed, from a playwright. The passage from Chikamatsu Monzaemon is rather lengthy to quote (haiku have overemphasized Japanese love of

---

[4] See Huizinga, 1949, for a general discussion. For a discussion far more germane to my interests, see Gadamer, 1982:91–119, on "The ontology of the work and its hermeneutical significance," specifically with "Play as the clue to ontological explanation."

[5] R. McKeon, 1947:627 (ch. 4). A somewhat more literal version of the ending words: "replicas of the most unprepossessing animals, and of cadavers" (Else, 1967:124).

brevity). But it offers a decisive insight into the nature of drama, as also of *art* so construed as to include all aesthetic varieties.

> Art is that which occupies the narrow margin between the true and the false. . . . It participates in the false and yet is not false; it participates in the true and yet is not true; our pleasure is located between the two. In this connection, there was a certain lady serving at the palace who developed a passionate relation with a certain lord. The lady's chamber was in the depths of a splendid apartment, and since he was unable to enter there [probably because it belonged to the higher-born lady whom she attended], she had only a look at him from time to time through a gap in the blinds. So great was her yearning for him that she had a wooden image of him carved. The countenance and other features differed from those of usual images in representing the lord to a cat's whisker. The coloring of the complexion was indescribably exact, each hair was in place, the ears and nose and the teeth in their very number were faultlessly made. Such was the work that if you placed the man and the image side by side the only distinction was which had a soul. But when she regarded it closely, the sight of a living person exactly represented so chilled the lady's ardor that she felt distaste at once. In spite of herself, she found that her love was gone, and so unpleasant was it to have the model by her side that before long she got rid of it. As this shows, if we represent a living thing exactly as it is, for example even [the legendary Chinese beauty] Yang Gueifei herself, there would be something arousing disgust. For this reason, in any artistic representation, whether the image be drawn or carved in wood, along with exact resemblance of the shape there will be some deviance, and after all that is why people like it. It is the same for the design of a play—within recognizable likeness there will be points of deviance . . . and since this is after all the nature of art, it is what constitutes the pleasure people take in it.[6]

What is represented must be recognizable (according to learnable conventions), or we would not have estrangement but the unknowable. For the rest, we expect and enjoy "deviance," a stylizing as attractive as it is estranging. Chikamatsu seems to have seen farther than Aristotle into the nature of dramatic and other art. He also offers what is, in every major respect, a reversal of the male-favoring, mimetic Pygmalion story.

Chikamatsu clearly posits a concept of the virtual for both the visual arts and painting. It is most appropriate that he includes his analogy from

---

[6] Chikamatsu's remarks were recorded by Hozumi Ikan (1692–1769) in *Naniwa Miyage*, pt. 1.

a kind of sculpture. Appropriate, because it reviews Aristotle's own re-peated concern; and appropriate also because, in contradicting that Pyg-malion story, it reveals how parochially western the concept of mimesis—represented reality—is. Last and above the others, the concept offers us a way of seeing that the virtual is a category larger than the fictional.

This issue is important enough for us to benefit from contemplating a series of examples involving a common element. Let us imagine seeing, as we walk along a path, a man's left shoe. We might wonder who lost it, and why he was not aware or troubled to lose it. We might place it on a stump or a fencepost to attract the loser's eye, should he come back searching for it. It is an actual, factual shoe. We might also see a beggar with his left shoe and hat off, placed side by side. In the shoe are pencils, and in the overturned hat banknotes suggesting a generous payment for a pencil. The shoe remains a factual shoe. We can also imagine going to an art gallery and finding, attached to the wall, a man's left shoe. Now there is a frame around it, on the bottom board of which there is a sign on a brass plate, "A Man's Left Shoe." It is in fact a left shoe. There is no fiction. But the shoe becomes something more than a fact, something other. It is now a virtual object, one to be viewed aesthetically rather than be worn, lost, or used for begging. For emphasis: it *is* a virtual object, aesthetic but not fictional.

In the gallery, as on the stage, conventions are used to shift the status of the real (the shoe as shoe, the players as real individuals) to what is presented as something else (an aestheticized shoe, represented people). In other words, the concept of the virtual explains the nature of estrange-ment in all the arts. It is strongest in drama of all literature. And in drama—unlike the other arts, unlike lyric and narrative—the version of the virtual is *necessarily* fictional. A painting or vase is not taken as some-thing true or false, but neither does it make sense to say it is fictional. What is not verbal cannot be fictional. With lyric and narrative, we may have the fictional, but we may have the factual instead. If the narrative is factual and aesthetic it is virtual, not fictional. There is estrangement in a factual lyric. As we shall see, all literature is inclusive of factuality. But such is the make-up of drama that it alone is necessarily fictional, and it is therefore the most given to estrangement.

We can characterize aesthetic estrangement by attention to a series of authorities whom we have consulted or shall consult.

Aristotle.
> Our pleasure derives from comparison of a representation with what is represented (ch. 4).

Chinese Historiography.
>These wonders are true and reveal how disorder in the state follows ignoring of right principles.

Ki no Tsurayuki.
>When the strange is moving, it reveals how someone has been led to give it expression (Preface to the *Kokinshū*).

Murasaki Shikibu.
>Although it seems strange, it is a device enabling us to understand how people really act ("Fireflies," *The Tale of Genji*).

William Shakespeare.
>O, what a rogue and peasant slave am I!
>Is it not monstrous that this player here,
>But in a fiction, in a dream of passion,
>Could force his soul to his own conceit
>That from her working all his visage wanned,
>Tears in his eyes, distraction in his aspect,
>A broken voice, and his whole function suiting
>With forms to his conceit? and all for nothing!
>For Hecuba!
>What's Hecuba to him or he to Hecuba
>That he should weep for her?   (*Hamlet*, 2, 2)

A Yuan Play (A Briefer "Chinese Opera").
>That is what the whole thing is about.

Chikamatsu Monzaemon.
>Art is that which occupies the narrow margin. . . .

Samuel Beckett.
>I don't know why I don't know (*Waiting for Godot*, et ubique).

That range of pronouncements is a tacit reminder that radio, film, and television can be considered dramatic. Many would hold that recently drama has simply forsaken the stage and taken to electricity—in the cinema or a rectangular box. Our favorite "programs" and films share the radical make-up of drama: people are playing the roles of persons they are not. The film may be a historical retelling of the death of Lincoln, and we accept as fact that Booth shot Lincoln (in a theater!). The players of the two roles are also actual, historical individuals. But since they are not the same actual individuals as those they play, the situation is necessarily fictional, as it is in live theater. On the other hand, news broadcasts and documentary films may have people playing their own roles, being themselves. There is no fiction, and no drama, because there are no players, no founding convention. It is unjust to exclude from drama many radio and television programs, and many films have even higher claims to being thought dramatic.

The claim is not complete, however, as many have recognized. Seeing a filmed performance of *Macbeth* is not the same as seeing it on stage. Film renders the theater photographic, so that the three-dimensional "presence of the representation" in the theater is reduced to two (Pfister, 1977:47). The production and reception of film approach (but only approach) those of narrative, departing from (but not entirely) those of drama.[7]

There is something yet more important. With radio, television, and film we simply are not in the players' immediate presence, participating with them in the estranged shock of present awareness that "they" are not who *they* are but "we" are who *we* are. With drama in the full sense, each performance differs according to the relationship established among the various players and between them and us in the audience at a specific performance. True drama, full theatricality is higher risk business, allowing for no extra "takes," never a replay. There is always possibility of innovation, of new success, of new failure. Interestingly enough, the risk of theater is approximated most closely by television in broadcasting sporting events, whose gladiatorial participants are also called "players." Yet we are aware the more keenly that we are an audience at a remove from the cheering crowds who see things in three dimensions rather than on a television screen. Nontheatrical performance cannot be dismissed from the category of drama, but it is not full drama.

Full drama is artisan theater rather than mass-produced theater. Let us allow that the mass-produced varieties belong to the same category as does live theater-drama, but to keep a comparative discussion under control, it seems desirable to restrict discussion to that purer kind, artisan theater.

The artisan variety shows estrangement in purer form than does film— or for that matter than do lyric and narrative. But estrangement alone is not enough for drama any more than for the other genres. To advance beyond concern with Goldman's "fearful energies," we may conclude discussion where we might have begun, with two conceptions similar to estrangement that have been advanced in the modern west.

One is the position held by the Russian Formalists, that literariness requires a use of language that is defamiliarized. This was called "making strange," *ostranenie* by Viktor Shklovsky and others.[8] The utility of the conception is that it posits as a property of all literature what is being discussed here as a characteristic of drama. The Formalists were clearly

---

[7] Pfister, 1977:47. We may recall the subtitle of Chatman, 1983: *Narrative Structure in Fiction and Film*, even if the pages allotted to film are few: 96–101, 158–61.

[8] For a convenient discussion, see T. Hawkes, 1977:59-73.

onto something that we all recognize at once, and onto something that is troublesome to reflection. The Formalists' account sets the problem at one remove without solving it. The fact is that all writing is, in linguistic terms, a marking of natural language. There is *ostranenie* in Cicero's orations if it exists anywhere, and in lawyer's language, and even down to the language of a weather or sports report in the morning newspaper. Neither the Formalists' account nor my own thus far explains literariness, since for that to be the case we require an account of a distinctive *literary* estrangement.

The other western example is of course Bertolt Brecht's "alienation effect" (*Verfremdungseffekt*). With his ideological and literary program clear in his mind to a degree rare among major artists, Brecht realized that the conventional estranging of the theater he inherited might continue to distance audiences from what they beheld and heard. But he was unhappy with the self-satisfying familiarity that the existing conventions had acquired. He therefore took strenuous efforts, in Pound's phrase, to "Make it new." His means was the foundation of an epic theater that used "narration on the stage" (*Erzählen auf der Bühne*). This had been done before in different but successful ways by Aeschylus, as later by Corneille and Racine. It was done, whether successfully or not, in the Restoration heroic play. Of course Brecht, with more than a glance at *nō*, was concerned with a socialist agenda rather than with Greek fatal metaphysics or *la gloire*. With his necessarily novel and therefore stronger alienation, he sought to jolt his audiences out of conventional, passive reception. By raising through novel estrangement the awareness of his attenders, he could get them to see issues afresh, properly, as he thought.

He could engage them.

Brecht's alienation is close to our idea of estrangement, but it is an issue whether the principle originates in a vision of art or of politics. We shall be seeing that, in his preface to the *Kokinshū* (ca. 910), Ki no Tsurayuki held that the moved human spirit is the generative factor of poetry and that the words one is moved to utter constitute the expressive factor. This explanation does not apply so neatly to drama, and in that respect Aristotle's mimesis is the superior account. Tsurayuki does, however, add a third term, *sama*, which in ordinary usage means something like "manner." That is, he posits style as well, not merely style as estranging language but as that which estranges in a particular, conventional set.

This additional concept seems essential to conceive justly of the literariness or nonliterariness of an example of writing. Conventions of estrangement tell us that what happens in the theater does so in a way that puts us off—so that we understand that what we recognize as a fiction offers us something we can sit back to appreciate. Next to the hand that would hold us off is another that beckons.

ENGAGEMENT

Like estrangement, engagement is crucial to all literature, but most necessary to drama, in which the estrangement is strongest, and most characteristic, by virtue of its founding convention.[9] To be literary, the engagement must also involve codifying certain human situations or ideas with conventions accepted as literary in a culture. Engagement follows immediately after estrangement, galling its kibe, holding us in our seats even while we jump with the shock of theatrical make-up. Involving skill as it does, *art* is necessarily something that can be done well or poorly. Among those of us fortunate enough to have seen a now legendary performance, like the Scofield-Brook *King Lear*, I know that it is possible to be so engaged by the theater as to forget where I was for long periods, until a momentary lull led me to notice that the Englishwoman sitting to my right was eating a chocolate from a box.

Theatrical magic does not always work. A passage of pastiche in Dryden's *Essay of Dramatic Poesy* declares that there may be a mishandling that

instead of making a play delightful, renders it ridiculous:

Quodcumque ostendis mihi sic, incredulus odi.

[It is so incredible that I hate whatever of this kind you show me.]

For the spirit of man cannot be satisfied but with truth, or at least verisimility; and a poem is to contain, if not *ta hetuma* [the truth], yet *hetumoioin omoia* [the likeness of truth], as one of the Greek poets expressed it. (Miner, 1985A:63)

Dryden raises the stakes of the game. Before his ante, engagement (like estrangement earlier) was being considered without attention to the whatness with which the play engages us. Issues of "truth," or at least verisimility," may be reserved; only this much need be said here. Engagement on the basis of encoded conventions (the only possible way) is fundamentally inseparable from the matter being encoded. Sometimes—as with farce or musicals or other popular art—the seriousness that engages us lies largely in the handling or manipulation of the codes. Yet even in

---

[9] Cohen, 1987, treats engagement as a deliberate aim of poets and painters ca. 1680 to 1880. I posit it as an essential feature of all literature and of other art, one presumable however only with the prior presumption of estrangement.

the greatest drama, "truth, or verisimility" is no more at stake for engagement than is the artistry that embodies it, the skill with the conventions that allow presentation.

We may decrease the distance between Dryden and ourselves by seeking answers to the question why the make-up of drama should engage us. Different answers are available. Because the originative western poetics begins with drama as its model, we may first examine the mimetic account of the nature of engagement. Mimesis provides us with an imitation of the world, or more particularly with enduring features, sometimes called universals, of human experience (Aristotle as in R. McKeon, 1947:636 [ch. 9]). In normative terms, this will be true by virtue of the criteria of probability or necessity (ibid., 635, 661 [chs. 9, 25]). In descriptive terms, we understand and take pleasure in the imitation by comparing it with those features of the world or experience imitated (627–28 [ch. 4]).

The descriptive version has a long history with numerous vicissitudes. For some time now it seems to have been rejected by sophisticated western critics as an account implausible or naive—until the stakes become too high. It has been my experience that when mimetic presumptions are challenged not by antimimetic opposition but in full by affective-expressive poetics, Aristotle will be recalled, his point made, fictionality will be insisted on, or the *representational* art/reality nexus will be invoked.[10] Some time ago, Robert Scholes and Robert Kellogg bravely faced an issue that is usually let lie: how do we derive meaning in narrative? The answer: from the world and its depiction compared.[11]

Aristotle of course emphasizes *mythos* as the first and most important part of tragedy, with character, thought, diction, sight, and sound in descending order (R. McKeon, 1947:632 [ch. 6]). Unfortunately there is not agreement as to what *mythos* means. "Plot" is held to be inadequate, but is "action" much better? The chief figure, the tragic hero (surely not identifiable with "character") is also important. Like Oedipus, he should be an able, gifted, and in many ways a good man in order to engage our sympathy. But since to Aristotle suffering is the most desirable tragic experience, an Oedipus must also have some fault, have made some mistake, or suffer from some pollution (ways of explaining *hamartia*) so that

---

[10] One example, taken from a well-known antimimetic critic may serve: "The critic suffers a breakdown of distinctions, for example . . . between the text and that extratextual reality which the text mirrors" (J. H. Miller, 1976:73). Here no challenge is being resisted, so the mimetic talk in an antimimetic passage must reflect long-ingrained habits of mind.

[11] Scholes-Kellogg, 1966:83. We must seek "the nature of the relationship between the author's fictional world and his real world." They mark this as a "complicated problem," not presuming any facile mimetic literalism. But the fictional/real distinction is so very western.

we do not think his suffering unjust or uncaused (639–40 [ch. 13]). In these comments, we have a Greek moral version of engagement and estrangement. Surely to posit so much is also to posit thought and its expression, diction.

It is particularly striking that Aristotle's poetics is *not* based on a conception of language. For that presumption, well based, we shall need to await discussion of lyric.

None of us knows how long it would take us to get used to the conventions of the Aeschylean or Sophoclean stage, not to mention the Euripidean. We really know too little about them to judge. Aristotle seems to think little of conventions himself, as is betokened by the lower status he assigns to words, sight, and sound (or music).[12] He writes almost as if the theater—as we know it to be from other traditions—did not exist, except as some place where mimesis goes on.[13] To that process he attributes a high degree of philosophical realism. That prior assumption of mimesis was no doubt necessary for an Academic philosopher to be willing to entertain a theory of drama. The result is a concept of mimesis well fraught with realism, as also with an almost grand neglect of the conventions, the total make-up of the theater. Freed from convention, the mimesis presents universals of human experience more convincingly than history, in which universals are lost in detail.[14]

Although Sidney follows Aristotle in this, he goes farther, elevating poesy above philosophy (as of course Aristotle never does), because poesy is a kind of golden world between historical detail lacking in general truth and philosophical generalization deficient in human detail.[15] Sidney seems to think mimesis a flawless medium, a perfect mirror in a golden frame. He therefore introduces and stresses the role of the poet who, "lifted up with the vigor of his owne invention, doth growe in effect an-

---

[12] Aristotle does not mention the audience, and I believe it true that the only time he clearly mentions actors is in chapter 9 (R. McKeon, 1947:637), where he says they are at fault for poets writing bad (i.e., episodic) plays.

[13] The conditions of Greek drama are not well known. The Periclean theater seated about 14,000 citizens. Unless the Academy had front-row seats reserved, it may be imagined that action did indeed strike the spectator more than words. Also, the plays themselves present "the most treacherous evidence" of staging. That is because "although Greek plays were written to be acted, the Greek playwright could not be certain of more than a single production, and therefore he always wrote for a reading public as well as his audience" (Webster, 1956:4, xi). Euripides left Athens in 508 B.C. Aristotle lived 384–22, nearly two centuries later. He must have seen revivals of plays by Aeschylus, Sophocles, and Euripides; he would certainly have read them. It really is remarkable that he should have defined literature out of drama.

[14] R. McKeon, 1947:636 (ch. 9). For a fine discussion of this passage, see Else, 1967:301–14.

[15] G. G. Smith, 1904:1, 164; see also 152–56. Features of those pages are written large by Sir William Davenant in his preface to *Gondibert*.

other nature" while "ranging onely within the Zodiack of his owne wit" (G. G. Smith, 1904:1, 156). Like the argument of his master Aristotle (and, as we shall see in the next chapter, his other master, Horace), Sidney's argument has very great power for all who have believed it these centuries. And like other strong claims, it derives its power not only from its propositions but also from what it leaves out.

AFFECTIVE-EXPRESSIVE POETICS OF DRAMA

The genuine alternative to a mimetic theory of drama is not antimimesis but that of the affective-expressive poetics. The absence of drama, until recently, in Hebrew and Islamic cultures is both a loss and a revelation of other literary priorities. Certainly the lyricizing of Aristotle's *Poetics* by the Arab translators speaks eloquently for affective-expressive poetics. But the fullest and most understandable dramatic versions, and their exposition, are the Japanese. *Nō* and *kyōgen* were held to constitute a premier art by 1400, an allowance remarkable to an affective-expressive poetics.

The central figure is Zeami (ca. 1364–ca. 1443), although in a full discussion we would also need to consider his son-in-law, Komparu Zenchiku. Zeami's father, Kan'ami, was as responsible as anyone for putting together the elements of dance, song, verse, prose, and selection of plots that characterize *nō*. Zeami himself is surely unique in world literature for excelling in four respects: as actor, director, playwright, and critic. It is therefore of very great importance that in his first principal work, *Teachings on Style and the Flower (Fūshikaden)*, the emphasis should fall on "imitation" *(monomane)*. The example of Aristotle shows how natural that emphasis should be to a person defining the nature of drama. But in the portions of that work in which imitation is meant, he is merely transmitting his father's teaching, not establishing his own.

When he spoke in his own voice, Zeami accommodated *nō* to the affective-expressive poetics developed by Tsurayuki. That poetics had already been extended to account for prose narratives like *The Tale of Genji* and had recently been made to govern the principles of *renga* (serious linked poetry). The establishment of *renga* as a premier art had been effected by Nijō Yoshimoto (1320–88), with whom Zeami composed linked poetry and from whom he learned the principles of one school of court poetry *(waka)* as well.

Zeami's terminology is the despair of translators. Clearly, he set the art of moving an audience as his theoretical goal. The moving of spectators obviously involves engagement, just as it is obviously indebted to Tsurayuki's poetics. (His concern with estrangement is obvious to anyone who has ever attended a *nō* performance and need not be traced.) The moving does not involve mimesis, and it is not a transparent medium.[16] An actor playing an old man is not to limp or drag the body but to arrest or otherwise qualify his usual grace slightly (Rimer-Yamazaki, 1984:55–56, 84 [*Fūshikaden, Kakyō*]). The art is made to seem complex by the stress laid on a number of styles characterized by Zeami in highly poetic imagery. These are ranked hierarchically, and an actor is told not to begin at the lowest but higher up, using elements of the lower styles only when supreme mastery has been achieved (ibid., 120–25 [*Kyūi*]). Expressivism has become an immensely complex art to describe. Affectivism of course involves success with audiences. It is also associated with the actor-playwright in terms of the religious contemplation or dedication such as characterized twelfth- and thirteenth-century *waka* poets like Fujiwara Teika.[17]

Zeami's treatises are marked in their discussions and in their titles by his central image, "the flower" (*hana* in the discussions, the Sinified *ka* in the titles).[18] No single English word can encompass what "the flower" means in Zeami's writings. We can understand that the flower is an artistic ideal related to performance. Aristotle has surprisingly little to say about performance, and nothing good about performers. As a man of the theater in every sense, Zeami is concerned with what goes on, what the actors says and sings, how he moves and dances. In other words, the flower is the ideal of a theorist and playwright concerned above all with performance. Zeami goes so far as to stipulate what actors of given ages should strive for (Rimer-Yamazaki, 1984:106–10 [*Kakyō*]). We should also observe the normative character of Zeami's poetics. It is true that he writes descriptively much of the time. But the concern to which he drives is always the ends to be sought, and the good or ill means of achieving the ends.

The normative character develops out of linked-poetry treatises. To take the conspicuous example, a *renga* sequence was required to be divided into three distinct parts. The first was a stately introduction or *jo*

[16] Like his father, Zeami also uses the word, *monomane*, on occasion in a central treatise, *Kakyō*. In his modern Japanese rendering, Konishi Jin'ichi renders Zeami's usage in different ways but normally as "performance" or "dramatic performance"; occasionally he uses other renderings to convey Zeami's meaning clearly: e.g., "gesture" or "acting the stage entrance of an altered character." See Konishi, 1974:215, 216, 220. The term is rendered "artifice" by Rimer-Yamazaki, 1984:97 (*Kakyō*). *Monomane* clearly does not mean "mimesis" to Zeami.

[17] See Chapter 3, pp. 115–17.

[18] Perhaps this is one of his debts to linked poetry (*renga*), since in it the most important stanzas are the four "flower stanzas" (*hana no ku*) required in the usual one-hundred-stanza *renga* sequence.

and the last a fast close or *kyū*. The two are relatively brief and of the same length. In between went the longest section, the *ha*, that of development (more literally, breakage). Zeami required that the *jo-ha-kyū* rhythm, as it is called, be embodied in the opening, long middle, and close of a play (Rimer-Yamazaki, 1984:83–87 [*Kakyō*]; 149–50 [*Sandō*]. The rhythm should extend from the five *nō* plays of a day's performance down to the last detail, as an actor's raising an open hand before a downcast face or mask to indicate weeping.[19]

It is clear that in Zeami's flower the ideal and the technical merge to a degree unknown in other traditional dramatic theories. So that if this flower, at once practically aesthetic and hypostatized, is to be translated by any single English term, that would have to be "art." As opposed to Zeami's "flower" (*hana*), "art" lacks the normative insistence and the suggestions for practice to attain an ideal. But no other word fits so well, and it is significant that in Zeami's day there was no accepted equivalent of "art." His was not the unobtainable Blue Flower of the German Romantics, but the ideal performance for actor and audience alike.

"Art" is misleading in that the English term applies to a wide variety of practices, not simply to the aesthetic. There were arts of logic and of rhetoric and even affectionate parodies of Horace's *Ars Poetica* as *The Art of Cooking*. The absence of a general term is a limitation in the vocabulary of classical Japanese poetics until the seventeenth century. Many terms exist, some of which have the value precisely of there being no European equivalents. But to signify the art of *nō*, Zeami had to take recourse to metaphor.

Zeami's flower includes the ends as well as the means of *nō*. It provides a normative expressive means (the flower as the art of *nō*) to normative affective ends (the flower abloom, as it were, in the hearts and minds of the audience). The motives behind this poetics seem clear. To have *nō* be taken seriously, as a premier art, it had to be known to have a written poetics, even if it was also known that the nature of the poetics was a closely guarded secret. It was also necessary to define *nō* in terms of the originative poetics based on lyric and certain kinds of history. Zeami's ambitions as a theorist were realized. He achieved respect for his art by enlarging and modifying the basic poetics without contravening it.

Like the mimetic poetics of Aristotle, it has highly satisfying explanatory power, given acceptance of the premises. In comparative terms, it is at once less powerful than Aristotle's *Poetics* and more adequate. It is less powerful, because it is not an originative but an adoptive and adaptive poetics. It is more adequate in its completeness, reflecting the author's

[19] For a technical description of *nō*, see Miner-Odagiri-Morrell, 1985:307–16.

status as actor, playwright, producer, and theorist. By the time he died (ca. 1443), Japan had a poetics for all three genres.

ANTIMIMETIC POETICS OF DRAMA

There is a third dramatic poetics to take account of. It offers a dissident variant on Aristotle's and, like Zeami's, an alternative view. It differs from theirs in being, not a theoretical treatise, but an implication of actual literary works. (Out of fairness to Zeami, we shall have a glimpse of one of his plays subsequently.) Its poetics is therefore implicit, and we are put on our mettle to infer the premises rightly.

Our example is Samuel Beckett's *Waiting for Godot*, subtitled "a tragicomedy in two acts." There seem to be four kinds of tragicomedy. A first is that of mixed decorums, high and low. This kind can be exemplified by Plautus's *Amphitruo*, which, as we have seen, provides the *locus classicus* for "tragicomedy." Another kind involves a happy ending of a play that had seemed headed for disaster. This disaster averted has an exemplar in Shakespeare's *Cymbeline*. There is a third kind, a kind seen less often, in which there are two plots, with the comic plot dominating the "serious." An example of this rarer kind is offered by Dryden's *Marriage A-la-mode*. The fourth kind hovers between comedy and tragedy. Often this kind of tragicomedy makes bleak reading but may be very funny on the stage; often the tone is decided only in a director's decisions. Shakespeare's "problem plays" may or may not fit the bill, as may Chekhov's *Cherry Orchard*. Jonson's *Volpone* and Dryden's *Amphitryon* seem to do so. Beckett's play certainly does.

We never learn why Estragon and Vladimir wait. We never learn who Godot is, although he appears to have a farm. The common view may be expressed in the formula: Godot = God(ot). That may be, but the French does not bear a title such as *En attendant Dieubot*. Among the things clear is the frustration of human wishes. In what Aristotle may have meant as the *mythos* of the play, and certainly in the characters, thought, and diction, even in the visible and the hearable, Beckett provides an amply underscored meaning: life is meaningless. In that respect the play is as simple as darkness itself.

It is not a play easy to summarize, since so little happens. Beckett's great genius is for comic dialogue running every conceivable variation on the negative, the adversative, the erasive. Although the plot is minimal, the play is carefully ordered. In fact, each of the two acts consists of a sequence of the same three events.

1. Estragon and Vladimir talk at cross purposes.
2. Lucky and Pozzo come in. (In the second act Pozzo is blind.)
   Exeunt Lucky and Pozzo.
3. A boy purporting to have contact with Godot enters with the
   message that Godot will not come today. Maybe tomorrow? *Exit*
   Boy. Estragon and Vladimir prose on.[20]

Repetition is a technique common to all three genres, and the effect depends of course on what is repeated. Here it emphasizes the inconsequen-
tiality (in a double sense) of human language along with the vacuity of
life, its casual cruelty, and its hopelessness.

The characters are minimalized and amnesiac. Only the pain the world
inflicts on them proves that it exists, although sometimes it seems as if
the pain is without both cause and place. Time is almost lost in repetitions, except that its shortening falsifies any hopes and brings some threat
of approaching death. The crucial words of the play are "void," "nothing," and "insignificant."

The negative mood extends from the grammar to the tone of the play.
Although it now seems strange indeed that the play was ever thought
obscure, a *reader* of it might miss Beckett's comic gifts. They are realized
in the tragifarcical action, in the skilled timing of puff and burst, and
certainly in inconsequential words. (Surely Chekhov taught him the
comic potential of dialogue without logical connection from speech to
speech.) Words make the one inheritance Beckett richly bestows on the
characters of the play. The generosity is meaningless, however, since all
that the words add up to is what Samuel Johnson called an ideal vacancy.

To no small degree Beckett founds his drama on the ruins of lyricism,
with its expressive attention to language.

Even in reading, elements of the grim comedy crackle like a persistent
dry cough, as some examples from the second act will show. Estragon
observes, "There's no lack of void"—three negatives in five words.[21]
When Estragon observes again, "I don't know why I don't know!"(p.
67), he shows he is aware of the meaninglessness but not why it should
be. Vladimir has the (non) idea: "There is nothing we can do" (p. 68). To
Vladimir's "This is becoming really insignificant," Estragon replies,
"Not enough" (ibid.; and S. D. "*Silence*"). Vladimir later recalls the most
famous soliloquy in English drama, saying "What are we doing here, *that*

[20] As is well known, Beckett insisted on taking part in the direction of his plays, and he
was much given to changing dialogue according to the language and site of a given production. But the outline just given remains in the productions I know of.

[21] Beckett, 1956:66. Further page references will be incorporated in the text.

is the question" (p. 80). For Hamlet the issue was life or suicide, and another, spiritual world existed. For Vladimir there is his own earlier remark as answer, "There's nothing to do" (p. 74). And here is the end of the play.

> VLADIMIR. Well, shall we go?
> ESTRAGON. Yes, let's go. *They do not move.* (p. 94)

The same two lines and stage direction conclude the first act; the second reverses the order of the speakers in the first.

Anyone can see the interconnections of the pessimism, the wordiness emptied of meaning, and the painful humor. The implied poetics is that of antimimesis. Like not a few other recent western writers, Beckett does not offer us unmimesis, not an affective-expressive poetics. His aim is to deny the prior premise of mimesis, philosophical realism, and to challenge mimesis itself by demoting *mythos*, character, and thought and by substituting for it the central lyric concern with language, which is of course now all but meaningless. Beckett maintains "the basic requirement of the text . . . a *writer*, a *referent*, and an *addressee*" (Valdés, 1987:32).

It should be added that, contrary to what is said about authors of literary writings by critics sharing Beckett's idea of language, Beckett is quite at home with the idea of authorship. For that matter, he differs from the critics on the issue of *representation*. Both he and they cannot let go concern with the topic, but he is as confident of his success in representing (with minimally meaningful words) as they are given to denying the possibility (with the usual exception of the present critic). These concerns show that Aristotle, man or ghost, still stalks about the European academy.

RESIDUAL MIMESIS

Many paradoxes attend mimesis and comparative poetics, including this account. Its longest chapter concerns narrative, which is the foundation genre of none of the world's poetic systems. The shortest one of its three central chapters is the present one on drama-based poetics, the originative western kind. Some explanation, some excuse, some redress is necessary, even at the cost of further paradox.

Explanation or excuse can be found in the fact that there is very little distinguished contemporary criticism of dramatic poetics. The once *nouvelle critique* of recent years has been marked by a nearly total lack of concern with drama, in spite of the fact that an Ionesco and a Beckett have more skillfully undermined the prior realist presumption of mimesis than have writers of narrative or lyric. As we shall have reason to see later, in this respect as well as certain others the American version of poststructuralist theory grows neatly out of the old New Criticism, with new "reading" replacing old "analysis." For that matter, the tendency can be traced back to Romanticism and Enlightenment critics.

And yet. By what may be the "curiousest" of the paradoxes that grow "curiouser and curiouser," western criticism has maintained a residual mimesis in the teeth of rejection of Aristotle and his ways. The signs of the mimetic survival can be found, as has already been suggested, in common critical parlance. The words of betrayal are fiction and fictionality, the world, origin and originality, literariness, plot, structure, character, unity, and above all, that shibboleth representation, *representation, Darstellung*. The telltale words point to lasting assumptions of reality and language (*res, verba*) and to semiotic systems in which signifiers point to significations of reality, the world. To hold that words do not represent reality and that signifiers fail to signify anything in the world is to argue that mimesis fails, to oppose both mimesis itself and its prior realist assumption.

Denial of mimesis provides negative affirmation rather than substitution of an alternative poetics.

The matter is partly a logical one. As Tendai Buddhist thinkers discovered long ago, the negation of reality inherent in the doctrine of Emptiness (*kū*) was inadequate, since the statement that something is not remains a positive predication. (They devised two further stages to reach the point where they felt logically disentangled from the natural predicative power of language.) The matter is also historical. We do observe again and again the attention paid to novelty, and one kind of historical taste will be satisfied with nothing less than a revolution, whether scientific, industrial, American, French, Russian, or whatever. (There is something fetching about the compulsion of the important Marxist historian, Christopher Hill, to include "revolution" in title after title of his books.) What goes unheeded is the fact that for novelty to exist and therefore to make sense there must be the prior, an inertial historical condition. Without a continuing state of scientific investigation or without the continuing existence of an entity understandable as Russia, a scientific or Russian revolution is a historical impossibility.

There is a counterpart necessity. For the scientific or the Russian revolution to exist, science and Russia must also continue: the moment of novelty entails a noninnovative prior and a sequent state. (Of course we can also think in nonrevolutionary terms of evolution, in which change and inertia exist in shifting balances.) The continuance of the preinnovated in the innovation and the postinnovated has its literary application. Once a poetic system is evolved it is, so to speak, the inertial science or the Russia for the vicissitudes that mark its history. Mimesis has had many trials, chiefly from varieties of skepticism, nominalism, and idealism. During the Middle Ages there was a period when it was all but forgot, and at times other impulses such as didacticism (to be treated in due course) posed kinds of threat. Antimimesis of the kind exhibited by the *nouvelle critique* is obviously one such challenge. But since the gauntlet is thrown on the very field of mimesis, the effort to deny is doomed to confirm the possible existence of what is said not to be.

For such reasons, the lingering survival—the daily usage—of mimetic terminology and mimetic assumption in the west should surprise no one. The talk lingers because the presumptions live on. If there be any doubt as to that, one may try writing literary criticism or theory without use of the terms mentioned earlier. A sterner test still comes with the attempt to engage with other-than-western literary theory and writing. In my experience, such encounters with the unfamiliar bring the most emancipated theorists back to their mimetic securities. Of course the same holds for those who pride themselves on emancipation from their affective-expressive heritages. Some may use familiar mimetic terms or even discuss, say, Chinese mimesis. (It is a very Chinese assumption, often shared by foreign students of China, that if something exists anywhere else it necessarily and thrivingly exists also in China.) But at what may be termed critical points, foreign matter is expelled as alien and inauthentic. That is, there is a general principle involved: being historical, literary systems undergo change, but a given literary system, which is abused so easily and with impunity, cannot be abandoned by effort. We may curse what we remember, but we cannot voluntarily forget it, and we are often given to thinking or presuming it unawares.

There is, then, nothing surprising or disgraceful about the residual mimesis of our western thought. Its absence would require explanation, as does our pretense to its absence. In tellings of the story of the emperor's new clothes, it is seldom observed that the example lacks a point unless the emperor's existence is presumed, whatever the current fashion in nonexistent clothes. So let us feel no embarrassment in reviewing versions of a dramatic subject of mimetic art.

DRAMATIC EXAMPLES

We may set against the close of Beckett's "tragicomedy" and its highly antimimetic emphasis the endings of four versions of the Amphitryon story. As was remarked earlier, in all four there is violation. Although the human response to being violated is the very being of the plays, the crucial matter for discovering difference in what is surely a just compari-

son—plays on the same subject by dramatists who knew their predecessors—is the playwrights' handling of the gods.

To Plautus, progenitor of a long series of plays about Amphitryon and
coiner of "tragicomedy," Jupiter's behavior in possessing Alcumena on a
long night is just what one might expect from an Olympian deity, and in
particular this one, stories of whose rapes of various mortal women were
and are familiar. I certainly do not know whether Titus Maccius Plautus
believed in the Olympians. But he could assume a cultural acceptance as
is possible today for Jehovah, Christ, or the Prophet, even if the individual Jew, Christian, or Muslim has little residual belief. The conclusion of
his version has, then, a degree of dignity and simplicity that would not
be possible for Christian poets. Here are his Jupiter and Amphitryon at
the play's end (Plautus, 1960:52–53).

> JUP. Be of good heart, Amphitryon, I come
> To you and yours with help. There is no need
> For fears. Dismiss the seers, the prophets, all.
> Learn the future and what passed from me—
> Above all oracles, for I am Jove.
> First to be said, I took as loan the body
> Of your Alcumena, getting her with son;
> She was pregnant with your own when you marched off,
> And at one delivery gave birth to both.
> The one of them begotten by my seed
> Will give you endless glory by his acts.
> Return to Alcumena, live in harmony
> With her. She deserves no blame from you:
> She was subject to my power. I am for the skies.
> [*Departs*]
> AMPH. I follow your will; pray hold to your promise.
> Now to my wife—enough of old Tiresias!
> [*To the audience*]
> Now, audience, good applause for highest Jove!

The estrangement here involves, beyond theatrical make-up itself, the
collision of the divine and the human, two orders of existence equal in
imputed stage reality. Engagement involves our getting used to the terms
on which the collision takes place. To a Roman audience, it was probably
necessary that Jupiter make clear that the good Roman matron Alcumena
had not committed adultery, so accounting for divine plain-speaking.
Amphitryon can do little more than acquiesce and start to enter his house
at last to comfort his abused wife—until the actor skillfully turns to the
audience to invoke Jupiter and request applause.

Molière's version drew on Plautus and, yet more fully, on the highly successful play by Jean Rotrou, *Les Sosies*. The delicate balance Molière sought can be judged by the fact that on the one hand he played his Sosie himself, and that on the other he wished to guard (as his prologue says) "la decorum de la divinité." His ending is marked by the absence of Amphitryon from the final scene. In fact, he did not allow his Alcmène back on stage after the revelation that Jupiter has spent that long night with her: he wished to avoid tragedy. As a result, a certain amount of comic irony was necessary if he was to adjust his versions of estrangement and engagement in a conclusion. The speakers are Jupiter, Sosie, and Naucratès (Molière, 1966:110).

> JUP. Alcmène is yours entirely whatever one may do;
> It must gratify your ardent desires that
>   To win your spouse's favor
> Jupiter himself in his high immortal state
> Could not shake her truth in his own guise,
>   And that what she gave him
> Was only done with eager heart for you.
> SOS. Our lord Jupiter sure knows how to coat a pill.
> JUP. Now let subside the dark tortures of your mind,
> Let calm completely the anger that so sways you.
> To you and yours will be born a son, Hercules,
> Whose deeds will resound throughout the universe
> With fame in a future abundant in every way
> And to be yours under my protection.
>   I shall bring the entire world
>   To envy your high estate.
>   Be rather bolder with the pleasure
>   Of these much happier thoughts.
>   It would be impious to doubt:
>   The decrees of Jupiter
>   Are the oracles of fate.
>   [*He disappears into the clouds.*]
> NAUC. I am overcome by such glorious distinction—
> SOS. Gentlemen, be good enough to hear my thoughts.
>   Do not by any means embark
>   On lovely congratulations:
>   It would be poor embarking,
> And for one side or the other compliments may bear
>   Phrases of some embarrassment.
> The great god Jupiter has conferred much honor,

And his bounty for us no doubt has no second;
    He promises unfailing luck,
    An abundant future in all ways,
A son to grace both us and ours with mighty courage:
    This may well impress the world,
    But I am for an end of talking
And for all of us to go quietly to our beds.
    In these affairs it's always
    The less said the sooner mended.

Molière depicts an imperial violation of human lives, and his agilely ironic comedy provides a delimited, reserved area affording some safety to the audience and himself.

Dryden's version is very different, almost no longer comedy at all. His furious, driven, and yet hilarious play becomes what it is by his conception of the gods. From that the rest follows. There is a prior issue of what that conception itself follows, and it seems to be Dryden's working out an explanation for the danger and humiliation he found himself encountering after the revolution of 1688, a position remarkably like Milton's in 1660. Milton's solution was to "justify" eternal providence on the basis of whole human history, since England alone no longer allowed for the belief. In *Amphitryon* Dryden seems to turn in fury on the heathen gods, since his piety would not allow him to question Christianity.

Basing his first scene on Molière's prologue, Dryden signals his displeasure by his violation of stage decorum. After twelve lines, the verse breaks into prose, although the speakers are two gods, Phoebus and Mercury. Jupiter's entry introduces a rugged verse style and the following casual inquiry from Mercury to the father of the gods about Jupiter's current intentions (Miner-Guffey-Zimmerman, 1976:233).

> Mine was a very homely Thought; I was considering into what form your Almighty-ship would be pleas'd to transform your self to night. Whether you wou'd fornicate in the shape of a Bull, or a Ram, or an Eagle, or a Swan: What Bird or Beast you wou'd please to honour, by transgressing your own Laws, in his likeness; or in short, whether you wou'd recreate yourself in Feathers, or in Leather?

Things like this in the play have gone down hard with many readers (it was a great success in the theater), because they went down hard with their author. The problem is that what engages is what estranges, that the comedy seems unbearable. It is significant that, unlike Molière, Dryden brings his Alcmena back on stage after the revelation of Jupiter's possessing her.

Dryden's ending has the whole cast on stage, including Amphitryon and Alcmena. When Jupiter offers his cold consolation, Mercury remarks in an aside, "*Amphitryon* and *Alcmena*, both stand mute, and know not how to take it" (ibid.: 315). Sosia also has an aside in prose modeled on Molière in verse. Jupiter then foretells the birth of Hercules, again speaking in couplets and a final triplet dissonant with the prose. What follows resembles Molière again, but with Dryden's Mercury speaking (decorously, for the gods here; indecorously otherwise) in prose in place of Molière's Sosie in verse. (Jupiter ascends to the empyrean.)

OMNES. We all congratulate *Amphitryon*.
MERC. Keep your Congratulations to your selves,
     Gentlemen: 'Tis a nice point, let me tell you that; and the less that
     is said of it the better. Upon the whole matter, if AMPHITRYON
     takes the favour of *Jupiter* in patience, as from a God, he's a good
     Heathen.   (ibid.:316)

At this, Sosia pruriently rubs his hands, counting on using the night to get his wife Bromia with child to provide Hercules with a squire. He ends with some verse as a moral, including the last two lines: "In fine, the Man who weighs the matter fully, / Wou'd rather be the Cuckold than the Cully" (ibid.). A less adequate moral could scarcely be imagined, except as coming from "a good Heathen." It was no aim of Dryden's to preserve the decorum of pagan divinity.

Kleist's passion may be no less strong than Dryden's, but it is more clinical. For him the issue is the exact psychology of his Jupiter, Amphitryon, and Alkmena. Kleist's exactitude, as his readers will recall, goes with the baffling or even calamitous—a pregnancy with no known intercourse, earthquake, rank injustice—leaving us with mystery as to the precise nature of our understanding. For that reason, it is necessary to quote at greater length from his ending than from the others. We observe that all the characters, including Amphitryon and Alkmena, Merkur, and Sosias—even the generals and a colonel—express their points of view. That is natural enough, but in the Kleistian world, there is little consistency (Kleist, 1952:218–19).

JUP. . . . Should you not be satisfied with thanks,
     All right—your dearest wish will be fulfilled;
     With my allowance you may give it voice.
AMPH. No, father Zeus, I am not satisfied!
     And my dearest wish has this to say:
     What before you did for Tyndarus do now

For Amphitryon as well—give him a son,
One as strong as the Tyndarians.

JUP. So be it! To you there will be born a son,
Whose name is Hercules; his fame will grow
So that no other hero is a rival,
Not my immortal Dioscuri themselves.
He will perform twelve mighty labors, by them
Raising an everlasting monument,
And when the pyramid is completed,
Reaching from here unto the welcoming clouds,
He shall ascend upon its steps to heaven:
On Olympus I shall conceive him as a god.

AMPH. I thank you! You won't rob me of her now?
She doesn't breathe. Just look.

JUP.   She'll stay with you.
But grant her rest if she's to stay with you. Hermes!

> [He disappears into the clouds, which meanwhile have opened
> on high, and now reveal the peak of Olympus, upon which the
> Olympians are gathered].

ALK. Amphitryon!

MERK.   I come at once, O holy one!
—At least as soon as I have told that lout
That I am weary of having to endure
His foul features, and that I shall cleanse
My Olympian cheeks with pure ambrosia;
That his beatings will be stuff for songs;
And that I am not more nor less than Hermes,
The messenger god who travels with winged feet.

SOS. If only you had left me quite unfit
To be made poetry! In all my days
I never saw such a devil with his fists.

1ST GEN. Truly, this is triumph.

2ND GEN.   Abundant fame.

1ST COL. You see us overcome.

AMPH.   Alkmena!

ALK.   Oh!

Critics have justifiably focused on Alkmena's anguished cries in this passage, and there are a few dozen interpretations that need not be added to here. Suffice it to say that Kleist's exactitude in revealing what most deeply moves us leaves us with the conviction of the cognitive, psychological separation of one person from another. This is a variety of mimesis, a variety under threat. It is not the antimimesis of Beckett, which seeks to exclude reality by means of meaningless words. To Kleist the world is real and knowable, presentable, even if what is so precisely known exceeds the words that are (with stage make-up) the basis of our knowing.

For a contrasting dramatic version, now an example from a tradition of affective-expressive poetics, we require one that will enable us to infer the implicit poetics. Our purposes will surely be best served by a piece thought representative and without special difficulties. And, as promised, it will be a *nō, Matsukaze*. It is described as a two-part dream *nō* (*fukushiki mugen nō*). Since it is a dream *nō*, the chief characters are spirits at the time of the action. Since it is a two-part play, the spirits appear in human form in the first part and in their true ghostly form in the second. The secondary role (*waki*) is as usual that of a priest, and as is often the case, the one entering at the beginning of this play is unaccompanied. The primary role (*shite*) has the spirits of two sisters: Matsukaze, meaning Wind-in-the-Pines (the *shite* proper); and Murasame, meaning Sudden-Shower (the *shitezure* or companion of the *shite*).

The priest is familiar with the story of the two sisters. When Ariwara Yukihira (?818–?893) was banished for a few years to the seacoast at Suma, he met two sisters who had the miserable task of carrying sea brine to kilns for making salt. They became his lovers, and he shed a courtier's elegance upon their lives. He left each an item of clothes as keepsake (clothes were the most common present, almost a kind of currency) and the memory, of course, of their poet-lover. Their attachment to him, or more precisely, to their memories of him, has denied their souls repose, so that the specters of the two sisters still frequent the area. On seeing a single lovely pine (the "matsu" of "Matsukaze"), the priest resolves on religious recitation. Perhaps his efforts may gain the sisters enlightenment, or at least free them from their earthly attachment.

The sisters speak of autumn and the moon, of the place, and their shame for their wretched appearance. The priest asks Murasame for a night's lodging. She reports the request to her elder sister, who says that their place is too humble. Murasame gives the message to the priest, who answers that as one who has renounced the world he would welcome the lodging, no matter how poor. Murasame reports that to Matsukaze, who thereupon agrees. The priest then remarks on how the two responded to his reciting a poem by Yukihira in exile, and he asks who they are. At this point, the active duty of the *waki* is done; the actor of the role has been sitting on the stage as if in the sisters' hut. After commenting on their tears and their spirit-like comments, he says not another word, but just sits—as is usual in *nō* at this point—as the actors playing Matsukaze and

Murasame speak the rest (when not being substituted for as speakers by the Chorus).

There is not a great deal more to summarize. Matsukaze and Murasame recall the past: Yukihira's three years with them, his giving them the elegant names by which they are known, and leaving them items of clothes as keepsakes. As a *mythos*, this is as minimal as Beckett's in *Waiting for Godot*. The issue is of course what one makes of what one has. Quotation from the ending may offer us some idea.

> Does it not blow from behind the shore,
>   The wind from the mountains?
> For along the barrier road the cocks
>   Cry with crossing voices,
> Summoning from a vanished dream
>   As the daylight breaks,
> And though a sudden shower was heard
>   In the morning light
> Only the wind in the pines remains,
> Only the wind in the pines remains. [22]

Both such verse sections and the prose sections as well are rich in imagery and allusions. There are a number of recollections of the "Suma" chapter of *The Tale of Genji*. There is a double echo of poems by Yukihira, both through recall of *The Tale of Genji* and independently. Here are the two poems by Yukihira.

> If from time to time
> Anyone should ask about me—
>   "Along the coast of Suma,
> He drips with the brine he carries,"
> Tell them, "and he suffers so."
>
> I must take my leave,
> And if I hear you long for me,
>   Long as pines on peaks
> Here in your Inaba mountains,
> I shall return to you at once. [23]

---

[22] The text used in this discussion and for translation of Zeami's play is that of Yoko-michi-Omote, 1973:57–65, here 65.

[23] Ibid.:62, 65. Although the second poem is really unconnected with Suma or this story, it is beautifully interwoven in the prose of pp. 64–65. (The place name Inaba can also mean something like "if one goes.") Whether this be a kind of pastoralism depends on definition. If sophisticated treatment of the humble is all that is required, then *Matsukaze* is pastoral. If sheep, song-contests, and other conventions are required, there is no pastoralism.

The poetic texture of *Matsukaze* contrasts with the comically reduced prose of *Waiting for Godot*. The one employs amplification, the other diminution. Beckett must hold out some degree of possibility in the world, in life, and in language to have something to subtract from, to allow for our engagement. With too little for him to play take-away, there would be nothing of sufficient interest to hold our attention. It has been said to me that Beckett really does not offer us anything, as Modernist writers did, but merely counts on our having a degree of hope, a sense of existing reality, a lingering cultural memory, for him to subtract from. From the evidence of some of his short pieces, which are unsuccessful in having no stick to whittle, I judge that he requires that something exist in order that it can be taken away.

Zeami's augmenting offers a full-scale contrast. (That includes the play's origins: an old work on the subject was adapted by Kan'ami; his work was in turn adapted by Zeami.) In social station, Matsukaze and Murasame are poorest of the poor, worse off than Estragon and Vladimir in all but spirit and imagination. Nonetheless, they appear before us on the stage as actors wearing brocades and masks that are precious heirlooms, spectacular works of art. Their verse language is a version of that of the court, its imagery resonant with centuries-old tropes. The anti-mimetic Beckett maintains a mimetic decorum between the level of his own intelligence and that of the characters representing his minimalizing purposes. *Matsukaze* has no mimetic fit between characters and theme, between human misery and its presentation. It takes no wit to decide which of the plays is that of the Flower.

Because so much of the play—and this is typical of *nō*—is spent on recollection, there is a great deal of Brecht's "narration on the stage."[24] What we hear is nonetheless also highly lyric, as no further quotation is required to show. These qualities are absent from Beckett's play, or rather we find them in touches of smeared color. As the contrast with Zeami shows, Beckett's low characters are shown decorously, mimetically low. There are none of the heirloom brocades and masks of the *nō* theater. The pain shows as obviously, as mimetically as the raw sore caused on Lucky's neck by the rope Pozzo pulls him with. Beckett employs the very mimetic presumption he rejects, which is a fundamental reason for his power and our engagement.

Zeami's narrative-lyric libretto gives the reader no sense of the appearance of the stage, of the characters, of their properties, of the delivery, of the music, or of the effect of switching between the main characters, Mat-

---

[24] Karen Brazell used to exclaim to me that *nō* is entirely narrative (Yeats's similar insight led him to call it "reminiscent"), although of course she meant to be teasingly hyperbolic.

sukaze and her sister, and the Chorus for the words or thoughts of the sisters. Of course anyone who has seen the play, or anyone who has seen other *nō* and consults a text for performance (*utaibon*, with line drawings of the actors from time to time) will know that *Matsukaze* is unquestionably dramatic. But it is not mimetic. The boot Estragon pulls off is a real boot; his and Vladimir's incongruous hats are real bowlers. The brine cart and buckets of the sisters in *Matsukaze* are, however, lovely little versions in which the sisters see imagined moonlight reflected in the imagined water.

Perhaps the best evidence for the affective-expressive nature of this kind of drama is found in the closing passage quoted above. It is part of the final unit, here what is technically called *noriji* or *ōnoriji*, a kind of cantillation in which there is one musical beat per syllable recited. It begins with Matsukaze chanting two lines of verse. Thereafter, the Chorus does the recitation, all the way to the end. In theory and in usual practice, the chorus speaks the words or thoughts of only the main character(s), the *shite*. Here are the last lines again:

> Summoning from a vanished dream
>> As the daylight breaks,
> And though a sudden shower was heard,
>> In the morning light
> Only the wind in the pines remains,
> Only the wind in the pines remains.

On the face of it, these words, these thoughts seem most appropriate to the mind of the priest, the *waki* role. Japanese critics will not allow that.[25] One possibility is that the Chorus does continue to transmit the thoughts of the sisters, who speak of themselves as if they were other people. That clearly happens in some plays. Another possibility, which is hard for westerners to grasp, is that the words of the Chorus originate from no speaker. Not "third-person" monologue, but a nonperson chorus. Consideration of the theoretical basis of such things in literature must wait for discussion of points of attention in narrative (Chapter 4). Some things are clear, however, even if we do not know which choice of speaker to make here. Whatever choice is made, it is *not* one involving either mimetic or antimimetic drama. It is a matter of expressivism founded on deeply moving affect. It is also Buddhist rather than Athenian or anti-Christian. And it is the result of Zeami's augmenting of a poetics founded on lyric.

---

[25] They do agree, however, and it is a fact to which experience attests, that the silent, motionless *waki* actor can assist or ruin a performance.

Zeami's and Beckett's plays raise other issues.[26] That of the vicissitudes of mimesis has been touched on historically before and will be discussed more theoretically in the next two sections of this chapter and toward the end of the next chapter. Two other matters concern us here. One involves the nature of tragedy and comedy, the other what will be termed echo and adaptation. We can see what Beckett meant in terming his play "a tragicomedy in two acts." On the other hand, some people might deny the existence of a tragic element in *Waiting for Godot,* on the grounds that anything tragic must have an essential dignity and a wholesome metaphysics. If tragedy must be dignified, and if it must have a metaphysics different from Beckett's, why then *Godot* is not a tragedy. There are many who hold that a Christian tragedy is impossible. If so, it is so.

It is a nice question. Aristotle allows for tragedies that end happily, although he prefers the downturn of catastrophe.[27] The only surviving Greek trilogy, the *Oresteia,* ends with the triumph of the institution of Athenian justice. *Oedipus at Colonus* suffers (if that is how to put it) from a transcendence of suffering. Must we consider Seneca, "whoso red him can" (as Chaucer says), the most tragic of playwrights? The French think the English mixture of comic scenes in tragedy gross, impure. The English think French tragedies abound in insupportably long-winded speeches and hair-split sentiments. (It *is* striking that such different plays arise from mimetic grounds.) Reflecting on these matters, I am inclined to allow as tragic plays that both treat of suffering as the central experience and that do not fundamentally redirect or distract the suffering with other elements. Of course *Waiting for Godot* is profoundly funny, comic, but the suffering is as real as its meaninglessness is comic. I accept that it is "a tragicomedy in two acts."

What about *Matsukaze?* Comedy is out of the question with nō. There is only one piece, *Sanshō,* with laughter; it is seldom performed and is never liked. (Of course the *kyōgen* interludes are comic.) In *Matsukaze,* the two humble sisters are not objects of derision but of appreciation for beauty and dignity. The presence of suffering is unquestionable: their lives consisting of harsh labor, and the one happiness they ever knew, the

---

[26] Takahashi Yasunari is engaged in a sustained comparison of nō and Beckett. His conclusions will surely be concerned with theatrical matters and differ in many respects from those reached here.

[27] R. McKeon, 1947:640 (ch. 13). Aristotle is quite clear in his own mind that "the change in the hero's fortunes must not be from misery to happiness," but that is a normative claim. A little later he praises Euripides as "the most tragic certainly of the dramatists" for following Aristotle's requirements "in his tragedies, and *giving many of them an unhappy ending*" (my emphasis). The implication as to actual practice is obvious. If it were not, there is this on p. 635 (ch. 7): the hero passes by stages "from misfortune to happiness, or from happiness to misfortune."

love by Yukihira, has now become a yearning for him that keeps their spirits from enlightenment or birth in the Western Paradise. In the revelation in the second part that the women who first appear as brine-bearers are really ghosts of the two sisters, there are even versions of the peripeteia and anagnorisis that Aristotle so esteemed.[28] What we cannot discover is antagonism.[29] As a result there is a shift from suffering itself to its beauty. I have often seen tears at *kabuki* performances and have felt them myself, but never at *nō* performances. Nothing is there for tears. But I must inquire: how much do audiences weep at performances of tragedies by Sophocles, Shakespeare, or Racine?

These are issues people will decide differently. My own decision will be given indirectly, by discussion of the ending of another play, *Kumagai Jin'ya* (which, properly speaking, is but part of *Ichinotani Futaba Gunki*). The puppet theater version must, in this case, yield to the *kabuki* version. The renowned warrior Kumagai has been charged to capture a son of the Taira enemy, Atsumori, and bring his head for the ritual verification. The head-showing involves three principal characters on stage: Kumagai, his wife, and his lord. When the lid of the basket is removed, the wife and the lord discover to their horror the head of Kumagai's own son. He had captured Atsumori, but a deep indebtedness to the boy's mother led him to his hideous substitution as a resolution of contrary claims. There is a *kabuki* "quick change," and Kumagai enters again, now with the shaven head, robes, and staff of a priest. He advances slowly along the stage ramp running diagonally through audience left to an exit door. He pauses when he hears war-horns sound on stage, reminding him (and us) of his martial code and vanished heroic glory. Musing, he turns to look back in the direction of the sounds, only to see his wife sobbing uncontrollably over his killing of their son and now her loss of her husband. As he turns away in pain, a temple bell sounds in the closing light of evening, summoning him to austerity and devotions. He has only one brief speech: "Oh, it's a dream—those days bygone." Having seen two different but excellent productions of this play, I have no doubt but that it is one of the great tragic moments in the theater.

The tragic nature of *Kumagai Jin'ya* seems to me to depend not only on the obvious suffering, and not only on the extraordinary anagnorisis-peripeteia. There is also an important antagonism, which seems to me the finer for existing within the character of the hero. Although the play has beauty, it differs in kind from that of *Matsukaze*. The *kabuki* has the

[28] R. McKeon, 1947:632–33 (ch. 6) and 644–46 (ch. 16), for example.
[29] Konishi, 1984:12–13. He takes "the lack of an opponent and systematic oppositions" to be a major characteristic of all Japanese literature. That seems too sweeping, but it holds for *nō*.

beauty of the expression of human agonies, whereas the nō transforms the agonies into refinement. I regard *Kumagai Jin'ya* as tragedy in a full sense. I cannot say that of *Matsukaze*—not that nō is a failed attempt to be tragic. Here is Zeami's presentation of his father's ideas in *Teachings on Style and the Flower*: "a successful play of the first rank is based on an authentic source, reveals something unusual in aesthetic qualities, has an appropriate climax, and shows Grace" (Rimer-Yamazaki, 1984:44 [*Fūshikaden*]). The criteria are entirely appropriate for great drama. But here I must agree with Aristotle on the importance of suffering in tragedy (R. McKeon, 1947:638 [ch. 12]).

Both *Matsukaze* and *Kumagai Jin'ya* show a kind of echo not uncommon in drama: the drawing upon earlier plays on the same subject. The Don Juan plays and the Amphitryon plays are reminders of that. Yet it is more common, especially in traditional drama, that the echo involve not plays but nondramatic sources. *Matsukaze* shows this in the use it makes of *The Tale of Genji* as well as of poems by Yukihira and others.[30] Athenian drama was also based on nondramatic sources, and somewhat the same is true, if in decreasing degree, of Renaissance and Restoration drama. This tendency for drama to draw more frequently on nondramatic than dramatic sources seems to be usual, regardless of culture. Who does not know of Shakespeare's use of Plutarch for his Roman plays and of Tudor historians for his history plays?

The striking thing is that narrative so seldom draws on drama in a complementary fashion. It appears easier for drama to estrange, say, a narrative source and yet preserve our engagement. It also appears that the greater estrangement of drama precludes narrative's drawing on plays in any direct way. Most accounts in novels of the performance of plays treat the enterprise as some kind of comic disaster, suggesting an inability to take drama into narrative "straight."

The adaptation by drama is another matter. Here the chief objects to adapt are other plays of the time. Of course we must also think of stage traditions and conventions, along with the revival of old plays. But plays are normally *composed* in the context of what is being acted in theaters these days, along with some alteration to heighten the familiar, some difference to attract audiences with a novel touch to what has recently proved would take on stage. There are few departures as marked as Gay's *Beggar's Opera*, unless we take the special case of foreign imports and recall the sensation that Ibsen's *Doll's House* created in Asia or nō in Europe. This dramatic adaptation for the drama reverses the main pattern for

---

[30] Soon to be published work by Janet Goff has revealed that those who wrote nō adapted *The Tale of Genji* by suggestions and practices formulated for use in composing linked poetry (*renga*), an interesting if unusual example of echo.

echo. Another "revenge tragedy," another "romance," another "absurd-ist" play will engage audiences because they offer what is familiar, pop-ular. Conversely the departures will offer estrangement of the known and expected.

There is another kind of adaptation different in nature and effect: that of the author in an age and culture. *Waiting for Godot* can only be of our time and from western Europe or North America. From the evidence of his other plays and of his novels, we understand that *Godot* reflects Beck-ett's abiding concerns with the manifold indignities culminating with three score and ten. Various specific Irish matters have been traced through his work. But his general attitude is more important: a ten-foot pole is by no means too long for dealing with life. If in his novels he uses the written or thought words of his characters as the means of telling, in his plays the general narratorial voice is necessarily absent. A related dis-tinction holds for his composition in two languages. As we all know, the distance provided us by a second or third language enables us to talk of things that reveal too much in one's native tongue. To rewrite the plays and stories into English in France has much the same distancing effect. All this combines to make an *oeuvre* of an elusive author distinctive, rec-ognizable. Zeami's plays are equally distinctive (Konishi, 1986B:522–33). Great as the other differences may be, there is no appreciable difference, by age or culture, in an author's adaptation for the theater.

There is a last difference to mention in the comparison of Zeami and Beckett. The western playwright uses radically fictional resources. This contrasts with the idea held by Kan'ami and Zeami that first of all "a successful play is based on an authentic source" (Rimer-Yamazaki, 1984:44). *Matsukaze* has its origin in the historical exile of Yukihira, as *Kumagai Jin'ya* is based on Japanese history in an age of wars. The *nō* is also greatly indebted to *The Tale of Genji*, which was by then thought an "authentic source" equal to history. And by the time Kumagai's story was reshown in *kabuki*, his and Atsumori's stories had been so often told (apart as well as together) that it is difficult to separate fact from fiction.[31]

Aristotle addresses the fact-fiction issue in his fashion in speaking on the subject of "names" in tragedy; he prefers the historical: "In Tragedy, however, they still adhere to the historic names; and for this reason: what convinces is the possible; now whereas we are not sure as to the possibil-ity of that which has not happened, that which has happened is manifestly possible, else it would not have come to pass." His preference is clear, although the very next sentence has a large admission: "Nevertheless,

---

[31] At Suma Temple near modern Kobe, there are real or purported relics of Atsumori, including his famous flute.

even in Tragedy there are some plays with but one or two known names in them, the rest being inventions; and there are some without a single known name, e.g. Agathon's *Antheus*, in which both incidents and names are of the poet's invention; and it is no less delightful on that account" (R. McKeon, 1947:636 [ch. 9]). The rigorous concern with the fictional or factual status of literary matters reflects some of Plato's concerns in a new way, and the concern will become stronger and stronger after Aristotle. This contrasts with the much more relaxed view in east Asia, where it was assumed that something was a fact in the absence of evidence to the contrary. "An authentic source" could be factual or fictional. Of course the most authentic source will become fictional when played on a stage. For that reason, the fact-fiction distinction is a *differentia* for drama, as it is not for lyric and narrative.

THE TRIALS OF PRESUMED REALITY

The authors of the plays on Amphitryon and Don Juan shared with the authors of *Matsukaze* and *Kumagai Jin'ya* a presumption that there is a reality to which they had access and which they shared with those who saw their plays. It is clear, however, that the western and Japanese playwrights made very different assumptions about the role of art in representing (in the one case) or expressing (in the other) what was presumed. This difference is one that is at the heart of this study, but in a sense it is no greater a difference than that between either group mentioned and the Samuel Becketts. To deny the presumption of reality is a radical act in itself and, if successful, undoes mimesis. The presumption of the reality of the world and people is an obviously necessary premise of mimesis (as also of affective-expressivism).

One may play with conventions all one wishes: the ramp through the audience that Kumagai takes for his exit performance is said to be the ancestor of the ramp in a burlesque theater. The toying with conventions, the desire to innovate, the naughty players' delight in shocking audiences are all easily accepted, understood. And thereafter further innovation is required. As long as the audience may continue to presume reality, mimesis is secure.

Beckett's "void" may not entirely fill his plays, but the degree of its dominance is such that the presumption of reality is no longer feasible. Beckett apparently feels the pain of the loss but is led by a conviction beyond a desire to innovate, a conviction that reality is lost to art, because it cannot be presumed in the world. At least that is what I think much of the time. It is possible that the trees, the rope, and the bowler hats may allow later critics to assimilate him into mimetic presumptions of an imitable reality. For the fact is that in these matters not everything is dependent on the author or on the readers of one or more generations.

As an example, let us take the first portion of *Gargantua and Pantagruel* that Rabelais wrote and published. The episode became book two, chapter thirty-two, and the foundation for "The World in Pantagruel's Mouth." In writing that chapter of *Mimesis*, Erich Auerbach was struck by the way in which this extraordinary fancy maintained a correspondence between the world inside the mouth and the world around Pantagruel (Auerbach, 1971:ch. 11). Reality is presumed. With his classical and renaissance training, Auerbach was no doubt aware that Rabelais was playing on an old trope: *mundus alter et idem*, to use the version of Joseph Hall's composition (1605). The German translation differs somewhat: *Die heutige neue alte Welt*. And so does the English: *Discovery of a New World*. In other words, the trope Rabelais used would continue to be employed in Latin and the vernaculars for centuries, just as it had been known to the Prester Johns long before. *The Tempest, Paradise Lost, Gulliver's Travels*, Jules Verne, and many, many other works follow the line with differing emphases but recognizable family resemblances.

Yet, what if a *reader* doubts the prior premise of mimesis? What if the reader does not choose to presume that there is any sense talking about reality, truth, fiction, and other outmoded concepts? What if Rabelais does not show a world different yet the same but the disorder of a carnival? Whether Mikhail Bakhtin himself went as far as readers have taken his idea of carnival is not really the issue (Bakhtin, 1984). The point is that they can read the same things that the Auerbachs read and derive differing consequences. And in the process they can convince themselves as readily as Auerbach did otherwise that Rabelais willy-nilly wrote as they say.

Perhaps the only difference is that Auerbach did not need to take out the exemption for himself that more recent critics have had to, when they have assumed the unreality, unreliability, indeterminacy of all writing (with the one exception). Or is it that, without Beckett's strong measures, it is in the nature of natural human language to be arbitrary and to signify? These issues can be better dealt with on grounds smaller than those of the "overwhelming question" whether the presumed reality is real or whether the presumption that it is not real is what is real. (As we have observed, how to postulate unreality or rather emptiness, *śūnyatā*, exercised the wits of Buddhist metaphysicians.) In turning to a particular version of the issue, we advance toward lyric.

REPRESENTATION VS. LANGUAGE

Literary differentiation, like other kinds, requires ruling in and ruling out, including and excluding. Such differentiation must be pursued in the close of this discussion of drama and its poetics. We have been considering both the basic features of drama and the mimetic poetics founded on drama. Because there is drama in other poetic traditions whose foundation genre was not drama, the basic features of drama and those of a poetics based on drama need not have common foundations.

Drama is founded everywhere on conventions of what I have been calling estrangement and engagement. Those features will also be found in lyric and narrative, which is to say in literature as a whole. Yet drama remains the special instance of estrangement and engagement. It in turn (as a variety of literature) shares in the essential properties of lyric and narrative, although it does not possess those properties as essential, differentiating features. The make-up of drama—from cosmetics and costumes to fictionality—gives its fearsome and entrancing energies a status different from the distinguishing characteristics of lyric and narrative.

To found a systematic poetics on those specially dramatic features is to do something very special, in fact unique to the "west" among the world's literary cultures. That is, Aristotle used drama as the basis of his understanding, not merely of drama, but of all literature and some visual art by way of comparison. Attention to drama led to a *Poetics*. His extraordinary attempt to demote Homer and his all but complete indifference to lyrics cannot conceal the fact that Homer continued to seem definitive and that the Greek tragedies themselves featured choral odes.

The *Poetics* was lost early in antiquity and recovered by the Alexandrians. There have been those centuries when it could not be understood, because readers (in Islamic countries, in the Middle Ages until quite late) had no living drama. By the Renaissance, Aristotle's treatise had become golden rules, even if critics found it necessary to incorporate Horatian principles with those based on drama. Horace made the task at least seem easier by writing generously about drama.

On other grounds, the space he devotes to drama is peculiar, since drama was not highly esteemed by the Romans. (See note 11, above.) Only supposition attaches to the life of Plautus, except that he died in 185 B.C., author of twenty-one surviving plays. Much more is known about Terence (d. 159 B.C.), who is known for only six plays. He was a freed slave and in fact the western world's first important black writer (Publius Terentius *Afer*). He was not terribly successful, and jealous rumor held that Laelius improved what Terence had written less well. The tragedian Seneca, who lived after Horace, left behind compositions that are not true plays but meant to be endured in reading. Nero's antic disposition also manifested itself after Horace wrote. This does not sound like Aeschylus, Sophocles, Euripides, Aristophanes, and Menander.

In their usual syncretic way, renaissance writers endeavored to assimilate not only Aristotle with Horace but Roman with Greek dramatists, as if they were held in the same respect by their respective communities. They also added from their own ideological needs what had been more aesthetic than social in Horace's *Ars Poetica* itself: the grand doctrine of decorum. In fact, that doctrine owed more to the rhetoricians than to sources we would term literary. Yet it was on decorum that the two great renaissance literary debates turned, as the assumptions that characterize the renascence were as much born (as reborn) in a neoclassicism (alias, humanism or classicism), in Italy and moving north and west. Wrath fell on Tasso and later on Corneille for plays not sufficiently observant of decorum. Tasso mingled the low decorum of the pastoral with other, higher ones in *Il Pastor Fido*, and Corneille introduced elements not as dignified as tragedy in *Le Cid*.

The fabric of history is to be found in that dialectic between what was inherited or echoed and the need to adapt. We must also consider the specifically typical and synchronic features that enable us to speak of a mimetic poetic system, one ever subject to chance, challenge, and adaptation, but one with inertial sameness as well. For these purposes we turn to the sceptered isle and the tradition of English mimesis, especially in the versions by Sidney (who wrote before Corneille) and Dryden (the Frenchman's younger contemporary).

The entry into Sidney's golden world is inevitably that point at which he speaks of the object of mimesis, which equally ineluctably is *nature*. "There is no Arte [study, *Wissenschaft*] delivered to mankinde that hath not the workes of Nature for his [its] principall object, without which they [arts] could not consist, and on which they so depend, as they become Actors and Players, as it were, of what Nature will have set foorth."[32] Mimesis depends on a world, a reality—"the workes of Nature"—for its "principall object."

The simile into which he glides betrays the dramatic basis of mimesis. That is so, in spite of the fact that Sidney had no adequate English drama to base his theory on: his laudatory reference to *Gorbuduc* is notorious (196–97). If there were any question that this simile and talk of Nature have origins in Aristotle (with whatever intermediaries such as Antonio Sebastiano Minturno and Julius Caesar Scaliger) it would be dispelled when Sidney next speaks of the art of poesy: "Poesie therefore is an arte of imitation, for so *Aristotle* termeth it in his word *Mimesis*, that is to say a representing, counterfetting, or figuring foorth: to speak metaphorically, a speaking picture: with this end, to teach and delight" (158). With his

[32] G. G. Smith, 1904:1, 155. I have normalized "u" and "v," "i" and "j." Further references to this volume will be given by page number in the text.

"representing," Sidney uses a term central to the mimetic legacy to this day. It is not only Auerbach's *Mimesis: The Representation of Reality in Western Literature* but the *Representations* associated with the "New Historicism." It will be observed how like the two passages are, how necessary to each other. Each shifts into figurative language: the first with the arts as players and Nature the playwright; the second with literature as painting and specific Horatianism (the *ut pictura poesis* and the *dulce et utile*).

Renaissance critics were as assimilative and almost as given to taking exception as we are. Their great task was to assimilate Horatian affectivism-expressivism to Aristotelian mimesis. The usual cheerful way was to say teaching and delight are the ends, and imitation the means, of poesy. There were some points at which syncretism became impossible, however, and a side had to be taken.

One major strand of Horatian affectivism developed during the Middle Ages, when Aristotle was all but lost or rendered affective-expressive by those Arabic commentators who tried to make sense of the *Poetics* without a knowledge of the theater, of drama. This strand was didacticism. The moral dimension of *utile* is easily read into Horace's *Ars Poetica*, and it was so read for serious, respectable literature. The *dulce* was variously treated, whether as bran to the kernel or the province of popular literature. Horatian *imitatio* was never mimesis, and as didacticism rose in prominence, the imitation was guided by a moral affectivism based on select texts, including the Bible. Aristotle posited moral goodness as the chief distinction between characters in plays and, no doubt, Athenian citizens. But affective didacticism simply lay out of his purview.

It is striking how eagerly mimetic theory was welcomed when it was recovered along with drama in the Renaissance. That would seem to be because Horatian affectivism itself presumed mimesis (about a third of the *Ars Poetica* concerns drama). Also the realism of the prior presumption of mimesis has been a matter of great comfort to most readers of literature. That hypothesis gains strength from a comparison. Once the didactic was introduced—and justified by the Horatian *locus classicus* of *utile*—it could flourish periodically thereafter, sharing as it does the prior realist assumption.

The intermittent nominalism in western thought has not had nearly the same effect, being seemingly as distasteful to readers as to writers. The reason appears to be that nominalism puts at hazard the prior presumption of both mimetic and affective-expressive poetics. Otherwise, there is nothing in principle to make nominalism inconsistent with those two poetic systems.

As we shall have reason to see in the next chapter, Horace celebrated words, language. English renaissance critics mostly sided with Aristotle against Horace on the issue. As is well known, Aristotle prized *mythos* as the soul of tragedy. Characters and thought came next, and then diction, before such other yet lesser parts as thought, spectacle, and melody (or, *melis*; R. McKeon, 1947:632 [ch. 6]). Sidney is actually harsher than Aristotle: "Now for the out-side of it [poesy], which is words, or (as I may terme it) *Diction*, it is even well worse. So is that honny-flowing Matron Eloquence apparalled, or rather disguised, in a Curtizan-like painted affection: one time with so far fette words, they may seeme Monsters, but must seeme straungers to any poore English man" (202). Pace Horace, words are mere "out-side," mere harlotry.[33]

Dryden's acquaintance with Sidney included at least the *Defence* and one or both of the *Arcadias*. And he too glides, from Aristotle to Horace, although so gradually that it seems a single point is being made. Actually, he raises the stakes to include truth and ethics:

> The imitation of nature is therefore justly constituted as the general, and indeed the only, rule of pleasing, both in poetry and painting. . . . Truth is the object of our understanding, as good is of our will, and the understanding can no more be delighted with a lie than the will can choose an apparent [glaring] evil. As truth is the end of our speculations, so the discovery of it is the pleasure of them. And since a true knowledge of nature gives us pleasure, a lively imitation of it, either in poetry or painting, must of necessity produce a much greater. For both these arts, as I said before, are not only true imitations of nature, but of the best nature, of that which is wrought up to a nobler pitch. (Miner, 1985A:484–85)

Here is the high point of English attempts to synthesize Aristotle and Horace (even if at the end neo-Platonism and its idealized *belle nature* prove necessary).

Dryden's synthesis has the same reservation that we found in Sidney. His final consideration of poetry and painting involves a comparison between "colouring" (cf. *colores*) and "all that belongs to words" (ibid., 495). More than that, Dryden cheerfully follows his source, follows Sidney, and follows the tradition all three knew of verbal harlotry, "The adulteries of art," in Ben Jonson's phrase. "Our author calls colouring 'lena sororis' [the lenient sister], in plain English, the bawd of her sister, the design or drawing; she clothes, she dresses her up, she paints her, she makes her appear more lovely than naturally she is, she procures for the

---

[33] Compare Milton's rejection of the style of Greek literature in *Paradise Regained*, 4:434–44: "their swelling Epithetes thick laid / As varnish on a Harlot's cheek" (Milton, 1931:2, 2, 471).

design and makes lovers for her. For the design of itself is only so many naked lines" (495). As late as his preface to *Fables*, Dryden found occasion to insist that poetic language was the last to be considered. He is criticizing Hobbes's discussion of Homer. Hobbes

> begins the praise of Homer where he should have ended it. He tells us that the first beauty of an epic poem consists in diction, that is, in the choice of words and harmony of numbers [versification]. Now, the words are the colouring [*sic*] of the work, which in the ordering of nature [*sic*] is the last to be considered. The design [*mythos*], the disposition, the manners [habitual moral conduct], and the thoughts [*dianoia*] are all before it. (523)

Dryden's is a summa of humanist (or, neoclassicist) conceptions of mimesis, in which nature and imitation of it (representation) are paramount, and in which language is given no pride of place. Yet there are genuine contradictions in all this, as there are between the sources, Aristotle and Horace. Both Sidney and Dryden were poets, and we do not have to look very closely to find them praising well-handled diction, particularly when Horace rather than Aristotle is being followed or when they speak of their own work.

In the next two centuries, critics altered renaissance priorities. In the Romantics' insistence that Shakespeare's *words* had to be read, because no players could adequately represent the bard's genius, we discover a flight from true drama. In Wordsworth's attention to diction in the preface to the second edition of *Lyrical [sic] Ballads*, we find what was being moved to. The subsequent critical debate has involved attempts to do away with the mimetic and the romantic legacies. One or both, again, again, and again. And still they return: representation and words. To all appearance, the linguistic hammer taken to shatter the mirror of nature has grown ever weightier, and the blows culminating in antimimesis have taken on increasing strength. Yet the premise that the glass should be shivered has existed with a belief that art involves mimesis. We can hear such notes, even in the song of Deconstruction. Writing of "Ariadne's Thread," J. Hillis Miller necessarily enters a world like Sidney's and Dryden's when they deal with words. Of course today we encounter "an inescapable *aporia*." Yet, on at least another hand, "Mimesis in a 'realistic' novel is a detour from the real world which mirrors that world and in one way or another, in the cultural or psychic economy of production and consumption, leads the reader back to it."[34]

---

[34] J. H. Miller, 1976:69, 72. (See also n. 10.) I must confess to difficulty in understanding the antecedents of the "which" beginning the second clause and of the "it" closing the sentence. And I am not presenting Miller as a Sidney or Dryden *malgre lui*. But talk of mimesis,

This great present contest betokened by words and the looking glass is a clash between incompatibles that calls for another *Hudibras*, another play of the absurd. In this essay the subject will be raised again in different guises and in relation to the other two genres. Our next flight, then, is in the direction of Goethe's Ganges, "On wings of song."

mirroring, and the real world allegorizes the deconstructionist's irony so that that which has been so carefully excluded breaks through like a line of cheerful sunshine.

❏

CHAPTER 3

Lyric

What in the heart is intent is poetry
when emitted in words.

—Classic of Poetry

Is there any living thing not given to
song?

—Kokinshū, Preface

. . . internal difference,
Where the meanings are.

—Dickinson

BECAUSE singing so obviously differs from talking, and because typical
lyrics are so plainly not set in downright prose, the lyric shares in the
estrangement of drama. It remains evident, however, that lyric is special
in being the most familiar to us of the literary genres, whether in formal
concerts, in broadcasts, in what we hear from a passing automobile, or in
what we sing as we go about some daily task. Evidently that preference
supplies the explanation for the poetic systems most often devised. For,
as I have repeatedly emphasized, only the western systematic poetics
emerged with drama as its foundation genre. And, for complex reasons,
mimesis required Horace's use of affective—lyric and satiric—poems to
render an adequate account of the reader and the reader's poem, so to
complete the five immediate factors of literature discussed toward the end
of the first chapter.

Since poetic systems founded on lyric have not required further enlargement to account for the five factors, it would seem that they have an
inherent justice in them. What else could explain the fact that all poetic
systems other than the western seem to be founded on lyric?[1] It is per-

---

[1] "Seem to be founded." Some reservation must be expressed. Neither Arabic nor Persian
literature has an originative poetics *per se*. But they obviously establish a lyric tradition, and
the highly developed rhetorical studies seem to serve as surrogates for poetics. See Miner,
1979B:351–52. In a separate article I hope to show that Indian poetics is—in result—affective-expressive like a lyric-based poetics, even if the actual development is unusually complex.

fectly evident that Homer and Hesiod and other writers of narrative preceded the dramatists on whom Aristotle based his poetics. He does not refer in any full way to earlier Greek lyrics. But they must have existed, since it is far easier to imagine that poetic practice began with shorter units which then were amalgamated into longer ones than to imagine that lengthy poetic productions came first and smaller units thereafter, especially given that Greek literature was oral in origin.

This supposition is greatly strengthened by evidence from modern "primitive" cultures. The first step consists of nonsense sounds; later there are repetitions; a prosody is worked out and song is born.[2] Lyric seems to be the most pristine, most basic art (Welsh, 1978). There is often a point before what we think of as lyrics gained the necessary autonomy to be taken as lyrics, as literature. The Book of Psalms has no such name in the book itself or in the rest of the Hebrew Bible. (The Greek *psalmos* appears in the New Testament and the Septuagint.) These "Songs of David" were cited repeatedly in the Renaissance as a justification for poesy.[3] They were the central model for sequences on the vicissitudes of the Christian soul (Miner, 1969:231–46). In short, lyric is remarkable less for its estrangement than for its powerful force of engagement, excelling drama and narrative alike in that respect.

The long debate whether epic or tragedy is the highest example of literary art introduces those normative concerns that it seems we cannot, no doubt ought not, exclude from a general discussion of poetics. Yet the debate belongs to the western parish, where it is assumed that great issues can be decided only on wide champaigns. In other parishes, the earthly paradise is a garden of song in which long continuance would constitute not only bad taste but redundancy. Of course there are numerous complexities. The lyric-based poetics of east Asia also included histories of certain kinds. And in the still widely influential Romantic turn to lyricism for its expressive properties, the poets were often unfaithful, or faithful in their fashion.

In English Romanticism alone there are grand infidelities, including that epic of the poet's mind, Wordsworth's *Prelude*. All the same, the example of Keats is instructive. His most successful narrative, *The Eve of St. Agnes*, is inspired by Spenserism. His attempt to appropriate Miltonism was, however, a dallying with false surmise, bringing him the disappointments Miltonism almost always did. Keats freed himself to write

[2] See Konishi, 1984:index, under "primitives, modern" for a wealth of details taken from anthropological and other sources. See also Welsh, 1978 on early stages of poetry. A range of essays more or less based on recent literary theories will be found in Hošek-Parker, 1985.

[3] See Sidney, *Defence*, as in G. G. Smith, 1904:1, 154–55; Puttenham, 1968:8; Davenant, 1971:27 (bk. 2, cto. 5, st. 66), also Postscript.

what the world considers his finest work only by turning to the example of Dryden's odes. No wonder that there is inescapable lyric in the Romantic heart. And no wonder, also, why that being so and their being western poets, they felt the need to justify themselves. Wordsworth's "Preface" to the second edition of *Lyrical Ballads*—a title whose oxymoron itself is revealing—goes on at length, but the opening of one of his sonnets says it all: "Scorn not the sonnet, friend." Western poets and critics have been living ever since with this ill-sorted *florilegium*, this self-doubting *anthologia* with its lovely *Fleurs du mal*.

LYRIC IN ASIAN POETICS

To turn away from the Romantic quest seems impossible unless we depart the west with its troubled flowers. But we do not necessarily leave the organic metaphor. We may recall the centrality of the "Flower" to Zeami's writings on drama. And here, translated, is the opening of Ki no Tsurayuki's preface to the *Kokinshū* (ca. 910):

> The poetry of Japan has as its seed the human heart and flourishes in the countless leaves of words. Because human beings possess interests of so many kinds, it is in poetry that they give expression to the meditations of their hearts in terms of the sights appearing before their eyes and the sounds coming to their ears. Hearing the warbler sing among the plum blossoms and the frog that lives in the waters—is there any living thing not given to song? It is poetry that, without exertion, moves heaven and earth, stirs the feelings of gods and spirits invisible to the eye, softens the relations between men and women, calms the hearts of fierce warriors.[4]

The word translated "heart" (*kokoro*) may also mean "mind" and "spirit." "Leaves of words" (*koto no ha*) involves wordplay that sustains the organic imagery. "Seed" (*tane*) also means "cause." And as mentioned before, Tsurayuki later adds as a criterion *sama*: style or convention, poetic coding in descriptive and normative terms.

In themselves, however, these opening sentences offer a view of poetry accounting for the five basic factors: the poet, the (poet's) work, the text, the (reader's) poem, and the reader. They also take account of the world (with a premise of philosophical realism) and, to some degree, the production of poetry. The heart (mind, spirit) of the poet is moved to words, as are the hearts also of the warbler and the frog. Those words of song

---

[4] Miner, 1968:18, slightly revised. Properly speaking the title of the collection is *Kokin-wakashū*, but since all twenty-one royal collections have the *waka* in their titles, it is common to omit those syllables (meaning "Japanese poetry").

affect others, and not simply other people, but the whole of things, including heaven and earth and spirits we cannot see. In brief, it is a poetics based on the moved poet, the poet's words, and upon moved hearers. It is the affective-expressive theory that, in one version or another, characterizes the poetics of all civilizations but one.

As is well known, in the back of Tsurayuki's mind was the opening of another preface, "The Great Preface" to the Chinese *Classic of Poetry* (*Shijing*):

> Poetry is where the intent of the heart/mind (*xin*) goes. What in the heart is intent is poetry when emitted in words. An emotion moves within and takes form in words. If words do not suffice, then one sighs; if sighing does not suffice, then one unconsciously dances it with hands and feet.
>
> Emotions are emitted in sounds, and when sounds form a pattern, they are called tones. The tones of a well-governed world are peaceful and lead to joy, its government harmonious; the tones of a chaotic world are resentful and [angry], its government perverse; the tones of a defeated state are mournful to induce longing, its people in difficulty. Thus in regulating success and failure, moving heaven and earth, and causing spirits and gods to respond, nothing comes closer than poetry.[5]

The second paragraph just given is obviously a model for the close of the passage quoted from Tsurayuki. The stress on feelings—thoughts and words—is the major link between these two poetics based on lyrics (and on certain canonical histories). There are also differences. Tsurayuki conceives of a graded, harmonious world running from frog and bird to spirit and divinity. His emphasis is Shinto, therefore, and Buddhist (in his concern with causation). The Chinese preface begins with an emphasis on intent (*zhi*) and goes on to the Confucian concern with a well-ordered state. Neither the intentionalism nor the politics weighs on Tsurayuki's mind, although there is a political dimension to the plan of this first royal collection (Miner, 1985B:44–53).

As these prefaces are recalled through the centuries, the echoes reverberate somewhat differently, but always sustaining the affective-expressive poetics. Its prior premise of philosophical realism might be challenged by extreme versions of Daoism or Buddhism, just as in the west there might be challenges from extreme idealism or nominalism or reli-

---

[5] Yu, 1987:31–32. She comments, "Although frequently printed separately from the anthology [*The Classic of Poetry*] as part of the so-called Great Preface, this passage also appears as part of the Little Preface to the first poem in the anthology" in certain editions (32). For all of both prefaces and a text of the collection itself (in Chinese and antiquated English), see Legge, 1970.

gion, just as in Islam the challenge came from extreme religionism. But the example of Zen Buddhism is highly illustrative. Founded with no small philosophical basis in Confucianism, it held to a kind of heresy that writings were unnecessary, even the sutras. Yet the Zen monks were prodigious writers, not only poets themselves but the cause of poetry in others. Wang Wei (699–759) is the conspicuous Buddhist poet in China. Although Japan is yet more thoroughly Buddhist, even Bo Juyi (or Bai Juyi; 772–846) could summon his prose art to give his secular poetry religious point: "I have long cherished one desire, that my deeds on this earth and the faults occasioned by my wild words and fancy language shall be transformed, for worlds to come, into a factor extolling the Law and a link to the preaching of the Buddha's word. May the myriad Buddhas of the Three Worlds take heed."[6]

Once again: the affected poet, the expressive words, and the hoped-for effect upon superior spirits. In effect, his "wild words and fancy language" will be, he hopes, an equivalent of the Buddha's expedients (Skt. *upāya*) to bring enlightenment to all sentient creatures. In an affective-expressive poetics, this is the reach of lyric with no middle flight to things never written in unlyric rhyme or prose.

Yet what is this wondrous thing that moves gods and spirits? Or rather, what qualities, conditions, or nature do we attribute to writing we readily recognize as lyric and yet find difficult to describe, much less to define? In the terms posited in this essay, the task is to distinguish it from drama and narrative. To speak, as I have been speaking, of it as the foundation genre for affective-expressive poetics says something the mere word does not imply. But to propose that as a definition is tautological. What we seek are simple bases of discrimination to explain the ease of our recognition, for example, of a lyric passage in a play or a novel. And beyond that lie the distinctions between the three genres. Let us start beyond.

The distinguishing of lyric from drama presents no great difficulties, for reasons given in the last chapter. Drama is the sole genre *represented* by players on the boards. Of course, people writing in the western tradition commonly talk of representation, *Darstellung*, in lyrics or narratives. When they do so, they use the word out of inherited mimetic habit, or loosely, as we all do, *Avec Privilège du Roy*, as those old French books stated. The far harder task is to distinguish lyric from narrative. I suspect that many of us have moods of quiet desperation when we realize that we can recognize a lyric with ease but seem analytically able to conclude no more than that lyrics are shorter and narratives are longer.

[6] Konishi, 1984:218. This passage was given currency in Japan about 840, when it was added to the collection of Bo's writings, *Hakushi Monjū* (pt. 71).

It would be somewhat helpful to infer from Chinese and Japanese gross assumptions that lyrics are in verse and narratives in prose, but that does not work for their practice any more than for that in other languages. Quite apart from the evidence of *dramatis personae*, it will not do to say that lyrics have speakers or *personae* and that narratives have narrators. That simply sets the problem at one remove. Nor can we say that lyrics *tend* to deal with feelings, since that sells both it and the other two genres short. (There is also a *Tendenzroman*.) As usual, there are in addition troublesome marginal examples like the Chinese *pian wen* and *fu*. The former is a kind of elaborated prose written in highly parallel four- and six-character couplets, with odd measures from time to time. The latter even uses rhyme, and the subjects range very widely. As so often in these investigations, we can get lost at the margins of the map. Let us try to find a center.

Sometimes it is useful to begin in hope where we ended in desperation. Surely something can be salvaged from the gross assumption we entertain that lyrics are brief and narratives extensive.[7] Marginal examples are never of more than heuristic use, but that is what we presently seek, a little suggestiveness. Three Romans uttered what might be taken as the most concise of narratives. Scipio reported to the Senate, "Carthage is eradicated" (*"Karthago delenda est"*). To the same body, Caesar of course alliterated (in the Latin), "I came, I saw, I conquered" (*"Veni, vidi, vinci"*). And Cicero reported the execution of Catiline with "He has lived" (*"Vixit"*). The terseness on what might have been occasions for long relations possesses obvious rhetorical force. Some in the Senate may have turned over in memory the long course of the Punis wars when Scipio spoke. A story of many ups and downs, including Hannibal's. On the other hand, those in the Senate who attended to the clipped nature of those reports may have taken a lyric satisfaction in the celebration of the moment. In a double sense, is lyric not of moment?

PRESENCE AND INTENSIFICATION

In short, as seems to be the spirit of lyric, I shall take lyric to be literature of radical presence and narrative literature of radical continuance. If the root of lyric is presence, its means must necessarily be—not those of getting and staying on but—those of being and therefore of intensification.[8] Caesar's *"Veni, vidi, vinci"* seems the more lyric to us for employ-

---

[7] See Killy, 1972:"Kürze," 154–69. Hardy, 1977:2–4, deals with brevity also: "Lyric poetry thrives, then, on exclusions" (2).

[8] Hardy, 1977, is among those who have remarked on lyric intensity: "Lyric poetry isolates feeling in small compass [brevity again] and so renders it at its most intense" (1). Only

ing three schemes distinguished by the rhetoricians (we do not need their terms). The schemes are identical initial sounds, identical terminal sounds, and identical terminal grammatical inflections. Cicero's *"Vixit"* intensifies by the device of substitution, saying the opposite of what was expected (but meaning it), "He has died" or "He has paid for his crimes."

It is very appropriate that Indian critics should have devised the concept of *rasa*, codified emotions (Ingalls, 1972:11–12; Gerow, 1977:245–58, 284–88). The *rasa* of happiness and the *rasa* of love might not go together, although that of sadness could accompany that of love. Songs of love are sad songs, as the song says. The *rasa* inheres in the poet's conception, in the line or poem, and then in the hearer or reader.

Some examples are needed of poems as purely lyric as is easily imagined while yet being normal within their literatures. They are needed to show that they are marked by presence of moment and by means of intensification, means varying with culture, age, and poet. We may begin with two rigorously parallel Chinese couplets:

月照水澄澄
風吹草獵獵
凋梅雪作花
杌木雲充葉

The moon shines, waters brighten, brighten
the wind blows, grasses whip, whip
on the shrunken plum tree snow makes blossoms
on the limbless tree clouds burgeon leaves.

Although in western terms parallelism is one of many forms of repetition, it is essential that the constitutive properties differ while the formal features are the same: "The moon shines . . . / The wind blows." In terms of Chinese thought and practice, this has been described as "yoked similarity and difference," "interpenetration and complementarity," and "nondialectical treatment of existential duality."[9]

Various kinds of intensification other than parallelism may make a lyric of moment. One of Tennyson's songs from *The Princess* provides a good example.

---

her first chapter meditates on the nature of lyric, emphasizing feeling. That emphasis will also be found, in different terms, in Sun, 1983.

[9] Plaks, 1987. He also quotes a Chinese folk song in five lines of five characters. Each line is the same except for its last character, which successively designates the five Chinese points: center, east, west, south, north. Plaks terms this "zero degree of parallelistic import." Perhaps it is insufficiency by overlikeness.

Now sleeps the crimson petal, now the white;
Nor waves the cypress in the palace walk;
Nor winks the gold fin in the porphyry font:
The fire-fly wakens: waken thou with me.

5   Now droops the milkwhite peacock like a ghost,
And like a ghost she glimmers on to me.

Now lies the earth all Danaë to the stars,
And all thy heart lies open on to me.
Now slides the silent meteor on, and leaves
10 A shining furrow, as thy thoughts in me.

Now folds the lily all her sweetness up,
And slips into the bosom of the lake:
So fold thyself, my dearest, thou, and slip
Into my bosom and be lost in me.

The repeated "Now" and the present tense, like the repetition of local and floral imagery, assist in creating stillness and stasis. In what seems to be heavily charged eroticism, things are as unclear as they are intense. Perhaps the confusion is deliberate Victorian smoke to hide what is being risked. One wonders what a Chinese would make of the parallelism in 5-6 between a ghostly male bird and a ghostly female person. This seems a heady but purposefully obscured version of a seventeenth-century "persuasion to enjoy" or "seduction poem." The sexuality is a trifle odd: the woman addressed is to drown herself in his bosom as the lily did herself in "the bosom of the lake." Of course, there is the Tennysonian verbal magic. Its lyric character is also caught by the famous closing lines of the next (and last) song from *The Princess*: "The moan of doves in immemorial elms, / And murmuring of innumerable bees."

The two songs have dramatic and narrative contexts in *The Princess*. As the Princess watches out the night by her wounded Prince, she reads the songs aloud. Each should be set in quotation marks, as being read aloud by her, and the last song in double quotation marks, as being sung in the first instance by a shepherd. (The eroticism gets more and more gauze veils.) The Princess must take herself as being addressed, since her love for the Prince and these invitations (although read aloud to herself) lead her to break her resolve to isolate herself from the world. It is no accident that these songs are anthology pieces. It is also understandable that "Now sleeps the crimson petal" was added only in the third publication of the poem. It added a lyric moment, one also quasi-dramatic in role-playing, to the narrative. But it is so intensely lyric that the drama and narrative are arrested. It is especially no accident that anthologies omit the narrative.

Poems by Dickinson often succeed in being clear and finally baffling. Here is one (Dickinson, 1960:118–19) whose means of intensification at least may be pointed to.

> There's a certain Slant of light,
> Winter Afternoons——
> That oppresses, like the Heft
> Of cathedral Tunes——
>
> 5 Heavenly Hurt, it gives us——
> We can find no scar,
> But internal difference,
> Where the Meanings, are——
>
> None may teach it——Any——
> 10 'Tis the Seal Despair——
> An imperial affliction
> Sent us of the Air——
>
> When it comes, the Landscape listens——
> Shadows——hold their breath——
> 15 When it goes, 'tis like the Distance
> On the look of Death.

Beginning with an image in the first line, by line three the poet gives us personification, simile, and metaphor. There is the seeming oxymoron of "Heavenly Hurt" in the fifth line. And the last stanza has a personification in each line as well as a simile in the fifteenth and a metaphor in the sixteenth. Those are only my schoolboy comments, and a subtle critic would want to dwell on the connection between the "Tunes" in the fourth line and "the Air" of the twelfth. Like many others of her poems, this one gives us momentous understanding of the providential dispensation of misery and a close glimpse of the Grim Reaper.

Two poems by Fujiwara Teika (1162–1241) will transport us to poems of other moment and other place. One is an autumn poem that seems very like a love poem (*Shinkokinshū* 4:420).

> Samushiro ya   Her strawmat bedding—
> Matsu yo no aki no   In the waiting autumn night
> Kaze fukete   The wind grows late,
> Tsuki o katashiku   As she folds back the moonlight,
> Uji no hashihime.   The Lady of the Uji Bridge.

Teika works here by unexpected substitutions or repositionings of words that belong in the poem but, if a verb, with a different noun. Instead of spreading out her garments for bedcovers, the Lady spreads out moonlight, so giving momentary magic to what starts as a humble scene. The night rather than the Lady is said to wait (for her nonattending lover), and the wind rather than that night grows late. The most daring gesture occurs in the second word of the third line: *fukete* means "grows late and," whereas the natural verb to expect with *kaze* (the wind) is the almost identical word *fukite*, "blows and." Legends and allusion to an old poem add to the heightening, and given the role of substitution in the poem, it is quite fair that Teika should make an autumn poem out of a love situation.

The other poem is a spring poem (ibid. 1:38).

Haru no yo no	The bridge of dreams
Yume no ukihashi	Floating on the brief spring night
Todaeshite	Collapses wholly,
Mine ni wakaruru	And from the peak a cloudbank
Yokogumo no sora.	Takes leave into the empty sky.

The first three lines seem to be describing a scene. But the scene is a metaphor of someone's waking up after a proverbially brief spring night. Perhaps the dream is that of love, but it is not clear from the details whether the speaker is a man or a woman. The last two lines depict a human action, taking leave, bidding farewell, and parting. But the action is taken by a cloudbank. A great deal more is involved. The second line comes from the title of the last chapter of *The Tale of Genji*, exactly "Yume no Ukihashi," an image of boats aligned and planked over to form a bridge, here breaking apart metaphorically as if a dream.

Certain matters are more easily discussed than decided. In my view, Teika's allusion to *The Tale of Genji* is quite precise. The heroine of the last ten books, Ukifune, is recalled by the first three lines, and the hero, Kaoru, who meanders into well-meant solipsism, by the last two lines. The only poem in "Yume no Ukihashi" is by him, features a mountain as here, and addresses or apostrophizes a priest on Kaoru's going astray in the mountains. That is one reason why, in my translation, I have added "empty" to "sky." But the Chinese character for sky may also signify Emptiness, one of Tendai Buddhism's three related principles to convey the illusion of even the nonbeing of phenomena.

The central question posed to interpreters is whether the person who wakes up from dreams wakens to the reality of enlightenment or to further illusion. My guess is that Teika felt Ukifune awoke to reality and Kaoru to illusion. But the problem with so glossing the poem is that it has made the secondary primary. The primary emphasis of this poem is on spring, and the allusions should be taken as a strengthening rather than as a diminution of the vernal character of the poem.

Symbolism, figuralism, metaphor, imagery—these are familiar means of lyric intensification, along with various kinds of repetition. But they are not necessary means. Pushkin is famous for the nonfigurative nature of his poetry. Some Japanese wrote intense, image-free love poetry (Miner, 1968:127–36). It is debated whether Chinese poetry is metaphorical at all. To one view, the elements or images in Chinese poetry cohere, as it were, as members of nondistinguished classes. There is not that otherness of meaning required by metaphor but rather a single semantic, cognitive field for which "description" is a better word than "metaphor." To another view, we must find Chinese metaphor not in words or in images but in elements constituting a distinction central in Chinese poetics. That is, the *jing* (the scene, nature, the observed world) arouses and corresponds to the *qing* (the affective human response).[10]

As all know, the concept of metaphor in the west derives from the rhetoricians. There is no oratory in east Asia, none at least that resembles what is described in Aristotle's *Rhetoric* or Quintilian's *Institutes*. We who know rhetoric less well than our forebears may be unaware that the rhetoricians distinguished two kinds of figures: tropes and schemes. (The distinction is also made by use of other terms.) Tropes were distinguished as abuses (manipulations) of words, and schemes as abuses of syntax.

If we accept the distinction, then parallelism is a scheme, not a trope like metaphor or synecdoche. If so, and perhaps on other grounds, one could hold that Chinese poetry does not indeed use metaphor, although it uses schemes: the words are not abused.[11] On the other hand, we have no special obligation to think tropes are abuses of words. It can be held natural or traditional in a culture to make associations that would seem farfetched or perhaps fresh in another culture: the word for hill or mountain in east Asian countries often means temple, and "original mountain" means "main temple." We could investigate the Chinese concept of *bi* or comparison (Yu, 1987, index, under "*fu, bi, xing*"), but then we would find we had left one problem to take up another. In the end what happens in a language and a literature is more important than the labels, although we find it difficult to say what happens without using our customary tokens. One thing is clear: the dominant Chinese lyric tradition employs

---

[10] For the first view, see Yu, 1981 as also 1987, ch. 1 and index. For the second view, see Sun, 1985. It will be observed that both accounts may be true in description, and that a decision may rest on the definition of metaphor.

[11] Plaks, 1987, seems to come to conclusions similar to Yu's on the basis of his analysis of parallelism.

means of intensification, whether or not those are the same as the means used outside China.

In these technical matters, Japanese poetry seems to occupy a third position. In early poetry, especially in that of one of Japan's greatest poets, Kakinomoto Hitomaro (d. 708–15, ca. aet. 50?), we discover ample use of the most directive, indicative of tropes, the simile, and the most directive of schemes, parallelism. Although both figures continued to be employed in prose, they all but disappear from poetry. Whatever the historical basis of the shift, the cognitive basis is definable. Japanese have their polarities, like every other people. Among those not derived from the continent, some few, like *omote* and *ura* (front and back) are richer than their English counterparts. But Japanese do not much take to the clearcut oppositions, or rather distinctions, that are required for parallelism and simile. It is no accident that in the opening of his preface to the *Kokinshū* Tsurayuki depicts a harmonious world ranging from warbler and frog to human beings of various kinds to spirits and heaven itself. "Is there any living being not given to song?"

It is also relevant that it was in Japan that there grew up the belief—perhaps a heresy—that the Buddha's Original Vow to make enlightenment open to all sentient creatures extended to plants, trees, and the land itself.[12] The Shinto animistic heritage clearly affected the way Japanese understood Buddhism. A passage from the *Nihon Shoki* (*The Chronicles of Japan*, an early history of sorts) will make early Japanese beliefs clear. Here are words of the principal divinity, Amaterasu, the sun goddess, readying her grandson to descend to rule Japan: " 'And what is more, in that land there are many gods who sparkle like fireflies, as well as wicked gods, noisy as a swarm of summer flies. And even the grasses and trees have the power of speech' " (Konishi, 1984:101).

We may well wonder, then, why Japanese poetry clearly (as Chinese poetry debatedly) employs metaphor, as the examples of Teika's two poems show. The best answer seems to be that in Japanese usage the signifier and signified are not taken to be different so much as versions of each other in another aspect: hence my retreat from reading Teika's floating bridge of dreams poem too much as allusion and not enough as what it is, a spring poem that absorbs *The Tale of Genji* without ceasing to be a poem about spring. The distinction between signifier and signified in western thought is thereby blurred: the two terms merge. And Japanese find that natural.[13] Once again we observe that a poetic tradition (Japa-

---

[12] See Miner-Odagiri-Morrell, 1985:299, under "Sōmoku kokudo shikkai jōbutsu."

[13] My discussion is indebted to Konishi, 1973. He is one of the very few scholars of Japanese literature in Japan acquainted with western literature and criticism. I disagree with

nese) used figurative language to intensify lyric presence. And yet again, we find that the familiar assumptions we bear about the matter require alienation to be workable. We may pursue the comparative point a bit farther.

Place names and conventionalizing of nature are common to literatures around the world, and they are often used to intensify lyric presence. With those conditions to constitute our formal identity, we may enter an implicit comparison by seeing how similarly and yet how differently one of the world's lyric traditions uses the two features. The evidence will be Japanese and brief.

To Japanese, names of familiar places have special resonance, as do the distant, canorous ones that Milton liked so much (rejecting certain names because he could not abide their sound). One of my favorite Japanese examples is a very early "Song for an Eastern Dance" (*Azumaasobiuta*, 8):

Ōhire ya	O Great Hire!
Ohire no yama wa	And little Hire Mountain too,
Ya	Ya!
Yorite koso	Just come close up!
Yorite koso	Just come close up!
Yama wa yora nare	How splendid are these mountains!
Ya	Ya!
Tōme wa aredo.	Though not much seen from afar.

Until the bathetic last line, all is intensification: we do like our hills! (*Yama* may mean hills, as the outcome of this song seems to suggest.) And we have two with almost the same name. "Ya!" Parnassus, Arcady, Guilin— how many are the places rich in associations!

Japanese practice is distinguished by the early codification of place names among other "poetic pillows."[14] In Japan, these place names as poetic pillows were to be deployed by aspiring poets, who learned that Miyagi to the far north was famous for bush clover in autumn, although they never dreamt of going so far themselves. It became next to impossible to write a poem mentioning Miyagi at any season other than autumn. Well after Mount Fuji ceased to be a visibly active volcano, judges at poetry matches would fault a poet who did not mention the smoke that no longer rose from its cone.

In other words, there are mere places and there are special places in Japanese practice, and it is not always evident why some get special status

---

him to this extent: I think the conception of figurative language he develops antedated the introduction of Zen Buddhism.

[14] For an account with examples, see Miner-Odagiri-Morrell, 1985:433–41.

and others do not. There are three islands in one stretch of the Uji River south of Kyoto: Maki no Shima, Tachibana no Kojima, and Ume no Shima. Each name means Island or Isle of a tree, respectively Black Pines, Oranges, and Plums. In spite of the fact that the plum was the favorite flower of the court in its heyday, the Island of Plums failed to get classification as a poetic pillow (*utamakura*). To attain such an honor, a place had to have been celebrated by some well-known poet or be otherwise familiar by respected attestation.

Matters are yet more complicated. One of the poetic pillows is Mount Makimuku (Makimukuyama). There are also pillow-words (*makurakotoba*)—not to be confused with place-name poetic pillows, although in some usages they are one species of poetic pillows, and sometimes are used as "epithets" for place names. Pillow-words are evocative prefixes, something like Homeric epithets, although the meanings of some old ones are irrecoverable. One of the pillow words is "Makimuku no"—the place name just mentioned and a possessive particle. Like the Homeric epithets, pillow-words attach to a given word, or commonly to a given set of words. Here are the beginnings of two poems:

> Makimuku no   In Makimuku
> Hishiro no miya wa   The Hishiro palace . . .

and

> Tsu no kuni no   In Tsu Province
> Naniwa no haru wa   At Naniwa the spring . . .

The Japanese is almost identical: place name, possessive particle, place name, possessive particle, feature, topic particle. Of the four place names, "Makimuko no" is always thought a pillow-word, and "Tsu no kuni no" is so accounted in some lists and not others. "Naniwa" is a poetic place name, or poetic pillow, whereas "Hishiro" is not. What began as an aid to the novice ended as a complex verbal armory. The linked poetry (*renga*) master Sōgi saw a shoreline in Kyushu that he thought superlatively beautiful, but he did not give it a second look because, as he said, it had not been celebrated by any poet of note. It was not a matter of indifference at all: Sōgi compiled a collection of poetic places.

Such attitudes do not give unalloyed joy to the would-be translator, but they are part of the same way of thought that produced the codification of nature. What came to be known as essential nature (*hon'i*) has counterparts in western lyricism. For example, love in springtime ("Hey nonny no, / Sweet lovers love the spring") is a fine thing. Japanese simply go farther. Travel (*tabi*) is deemed so important a poetic subject that the twenty-book royal collections devote one book entirely to poems on the subject. But travel was essentially by nature, or poetic nature, always away from the capital or between other points. One did not travel—one returned—to the capital. With rare exceptions, love came to mean loving someone, longing for someone, not being loved. By the time of the hand-books for linked poetry (*renga*; from about 1400), very many things were classified for their essential nature, often making explicit what had been implicit in earlier practice. Konkū's *renga* treatise, *Ubuginu*, has this to say about a well-known topic of lyrics:

> The essential meaning of love is to love a person passionately, but un-successfully, unrequitedly. The essential character involves the expiration of the loving person in body and spirit. It holds the same meaning for men and women alike. To write of being loved by somebody is neither love nor the essential character of love. The matter is the same as longing in vain to hear the hototogisu sing. (Miner, 1979C:84)

Similarly, the spring wind is a gentle breeze. Nights are best in summer. The moon is an autumn moon. Unnamed flowers are plum blossoms early on and cherry blossoms after the thirteenth or fourteenth century. That is the essential poetic nature of those phenomena. In another, down-right prosaic nature, strong winds may blow in a Japanese spring, as else-where in the northern hemisphere. Of course there are lovely nights out-side of summer and unlovely ones then. The moon may be beautiful in any season or clouded over in autumn. (One could write about moons at other seasons than autumn, but then one had to specify the season.)

The disadvantages and advantages in this codifying are those of all con-ventions. They enable the half-talented to observe the rules without get-ting any farther. They also free the genuinely talented by offering a "lan-guage," a "code," in which to express what is important. And if you are a lyric poet, the shorthand they provide is a great aid in securing a pres-ence and an intensification that educated readers recognize at once. Like Tsurayuki's *sama*, lyric coding is at once arbitrary (another also arbitrary code might have been used), descriptive (it defines what is lyric), and normative (it offers a standard for excellence). Because of the arbitrari-ness, the grounds of the normative differ from culture to culture or even from age to age in a single culture. But the fact of a coding's being de-scriptive also reveals what we know on other grounds to be true: there is no such thing as art without conventions. It is also true that observation of conventions is not sufficient in itself for us, again because the conven-tions are arbitrary. Lyric conventions also differ from those of drama and narrative.

LYRIC JOINED WITH DRAMA
AND NARRATIVE

The special character of lyric emerges when we compare its uses of the other genres with their uses of it. Of course a lyric (lyric passage) may occur in drama or narrative, and it may incorporate elements of them. At the close of the first chapter, various distinctions were drawn, including the possibility of drama and narrative entering as it were a second stage (drama within drama or metadrama, narrative within narrative or meta-narrative). The most familiar examples for readers of drama in English are surely the visiting players in *Hamlet,* by whom the Prince hopes to catch the conscious of Claudius (*Hamlet*, 3, 2) and the miserable performance of "Pyramus and Thisbe" (*A Midsummer Night's Dream*, 5, 2). Narrative examples may be less prominent in our memory, but there are many. Fielding's story by the Man of the Hill (*Tom Jones*, 8:11–14) is but the longest of many narrative interruptions in that novel. Dickens' "Story of the Bagman's Uncle" (*The Pickwick Papers*, 2:21) provides another example. Sterne's *Tristram Shandy* is founded on what might be termed uninterrupted self-interruption. *The Arabian Nights' Entertainments* is one sustained interruption by Scheherazade. Something similar is true of the *Decameron,* the *Heptameron, The Canterbury Tales,* and certain other "framed" narratives. Such simple, clear, and radical examples cannot be given for lyric. What may be termed the generic presence of lyric disallows "self-interruption," testifying to its intensification as a major difference from drama and narrative.[15]

There is a second set of evidence, somewhat more complicated and qualified, involving lyric incorporation of attributive versions of drama and lyric. It will be recalled that "attributive" designates what we mean when we say that a poem in one genre has features of another without becoming that other. A song in a play is not attributively lyric but simply lyric, so abating or interrupting the drama. A poem like Donne's "The Sun Rising"—"Busy old fool, unruly sun"—is an example of lyric with an attributive version of drama. It is not simple drama, because it is not really being acted. Dryden's "To the Memory of Mr. Oldham" exemplifies the incorporation of an attributive version of narrative into lyric. Although finer distinctions will follow in this and the next chapter, it is significant that in the examples from Donne and Dryden the lyric is un-

[15] The relation of lyric to the present is a major thesis in Staiger, 1939; and distinctions between the "foundation genres" similar to those made here are made by Kayser, 1962:ch. 11. Or again, the necessary temporality of narrative is of a kind setting it off from lyric: see Ricoeur, 1984–85:vol. 3:sec. 2.

abated, uninterrupted by the other genres. The power, the radical of lyric presence is simply too strong.

These matters can be understood better from example, and two poems follow by George Herbert. The first is "Vertue," one of his most purely lyric poems.

> Sweet day, so cool, so calm, so bright,
> The bridall of the earth and skie:
> The dew shall weep thy fall tonight;
>   For thou must die.
>
> 5 Sweet rose, whose hue angrie and brave
> Bids the rash gazer wipe his eye:
> Thy root is ever in its grave,
>   And thou must die.
>
> Sweet spring, full of sweet dayes and roses,
> 10 A box where sweets compacted lie;
> My musick shows ye have your closes,
>   And all must die.
>
> Onely a sweet and vertuous soul,
> Like season'd timber never gives;
> 15 But though the whole world turn to coal,
>   Then chiefly lives.

Perhaps there is a touch of narrative in the final line or two, moving from the present to the future. But it is doubtful that readers much notice it. What strikes us more are the repetitions, beginning with the first line, developed in the apostrophes to the day, rose, spring, and (in a manner) soul, along with the play on the refrain line. If this be not lyric, where is lyric to be found?

Herbert also has other poems the world thinks lyrics but that, unlike "Vertue," have dramatic or narrative elements or both. A familiar poem, one of the anthology pieces, is "The Collar." What follows are the first nine and the last eight lines.

> I struck the board and cry'd, "No more.
>   I will abroad.
> My lines and life are free; free as the rode,
>   Loose as the winde, as large as store.
> 5   Shall I be still in suit?
>   Have I no harvest but a thorn
>   To let me blood, and not restore
> What I have lost with cordial fruit? . . .

Call in thy deaths head there: tie up thy fears.
30   He that forebears
To suit and serve his need,
    Deserves his load."
But as I rav'd and grew more fierce and wilde
    At every word,
35 Methoughts I heard one calling, "Child:"
And I reply'd, "My Lord."[16]

The momentary rebellion of the normally devout Christian speaker surely exemplifies in its initial outbursts what we mean when we say that a lyric is dramatic. Narrative also appears at times. "I struck the board and cried" is an example of narrative past tense. So is the induction to the remarkable drama of the ending: "But as I raved and grew more fierce and wild." Clear, indisputable as the dramatic and narrative elements are, neither interrupts, neither abates a lyric, as a lyric does them. Our point about lyric presence is confirmed yet again.

Numerous other examples could be given from any century of English poetry. Browning's monologue poems such as "The Bishop Orders His Tomb" are textbook examples of lyric incorporation of drama. Shelley's "Chorus" from *Hellas* ("The world's great age begins anew") offers a narrative of cyclical history. Like "The Collar," Browning's "My Last Duchess" incorporates both drama and narrative.

Some qualification is necessary. The most dramatic lyric is not played on a stage. It only has some of the qualities of stage presentation: a greater degree of estrangement than usual in a lyric and greater emphasis on a speaking personality. It is not surprising that, in cultural traditions other than western, it is rarer for lyrics to incorporate drama than narrative. In fact, if we inspect Japanese poetic history closely, we discover that in the centuries before Tsurayuki defined Japanese poetics out of lyric, incorporation of drama into lyric was much more common than it was afterward. Yamanoe Okura (?660–?733) wrote an elegy on the death of his son, Furuhi. Here is its envoy (*Man'yōshū* 5:905):

Wakakereba	Since he is so young,
Michiyuki shiraji	He will not know the road to take.
Mai wa sen	I will pay your fee.
Shitabe no tsukai	O courier from the realms below,
Oite tōrase.	Bear him there upon your back!

[16] Patrides, 1974:103 ("Vertue") and 161–62 ("The Collar"). I have added quotation marks and deleted italics in the latter.

The address in exclamation and choppy syntax has obvious dramatic effect, as dialogue might have in other early poems.

It is striking that, from the time of Tsurayuki, lyric is more congenial with narrative, which—as a nonperformed genre—it more closely resembles. As we shall see in the next chapter, there are Japanese examples that some will insist are lyric and some narrative. *That* is a very different thing from the use of narrative and lyric that we found in *Matsukaze* (see Chapter 2).

Of course no poem of any length will remain wholly pure in genre. (This in no way militates against a concept of genre: we are able to identify the narrative and dramatic elements in a lyric, and so forth for narrative and drama.) There will always be some conversion of other genres to the dominant genre, and occasionally even conversion to co-generic status, an equality. The conversion is no simple thing, since it may involve differing literary phenomena, of which a given one may have differing effects, depending on context. Songs have delighted theater audiences whenever well performed, and stage narratives are at least as old as the messenger figure in Greek tragedy. But narrative enters drama by other means as well. One of the chief means, because so crucial to audience understanding, is dramatic exposition. For this, characters—major or minor—recall and relate those events from the past that are necessary to the audience's understanding of the present state of things.

The Tempest will serve as a useful example. Ariel's songs provide the play with attractive lyrics. Prospero's narrative exposition, hectoring Miranda to attend (1, 2), on the other hand, is often cut to reduce its tedium. It is telling that a parody of this scene has more dramatic effect than the original. In 1675 there appeared Thomas Duffet's play, *The Mock-Tempest: or the Enchanted Castle*. In this precursor of Gay's *Beggar's Opera*, the castle is a prison. And the slatternly Miranda now has a yet messier sister at home in refuse ("dust"), to judge by this little exchange:

PRO. *Miranda*, where's your Sister?
MIR. I left her on the Dust-Cart top, gaping at the huge noyse that
  went by.[17]

Songs and narratives in plays are not fully converted to drama, and because they lack an inseparable identity with the drama, they are most subject to deletion. If a player has a part requiring singing and does not have the necessary voice, the song will be cut or some device be found to give it to someone who can sing. Interpolations of lyrics or narratives

---

[17] Duffet, 1675:9. He also has a parody of another well-known or notorious scene in the play, the noise-making to represent a storm in the first scene.

abate the action of the play, whether we take action to be Aristotle's *my-thos* or what the players usually do—act, as opposed to sing or narrate.

There are also uses of other genres that involve true conversion, al-though the effect may vary. The last act of *A Midsummer Night's Dream* contains both the ineffable "Pyramus and Thisbe" by Bottom and his fel-low mechanicals and, after a speech by Theseus, a very masque-like close featuring the fairies. Here are two quite different kinds of drama inserted into yet a third variety, that of the general comedy of the high-born peo-ple. As we have seen, that "self-interruptibility" is possible for drama and narrative but not for lyric. The removal to another level of drama requires some difference, if only of tone or stage area, in order that inserted drama and the drama into which that has been inserted retain their distinguish-able integrities. The distinguishable takes priority over the integral on the stage. It must be differently "marked." "Pyramus and Thisbe" (though much interrupted by the giggling sarcasm of the nobility) and the fairies' songs of benison are at once integral and distinguishable, separate. Both scenes are marked (in the linguistic sense), the former by parody, the lat-ter by lyricism.

The masque in *The Tempest* (4, 1) is similarly integral and distinguish-able; it is also similarly marked by lyricism. The value of lyric presence takes precedence over the progress of the main action. As distinguished from the songs of Juno and Ceres, the masque at large converts to its ends a lyric element that, because of the full conversion, does not abate the action (of the masque, that is). The masque takes on, even while contin-uing as a dramatic action, an attributive or co-generic version of lyric. It becomes lyric drama. Leaving opera aside, attributive lyricism (or narra-tion) may, then, be either an interruptive force, because not fully con-verted, or an attributive feature of the dramatic genre. As the example of *Matsukaze* may have suggested in the last chapter, the extensive generic conversion of the other genres to drama renders *nō* almost co-generically dramatic-lyric-narrative. And with poor acting, especially in a long piece like *Teika*, the incorporation of lyric and narrative can have the effect of being countergeneric, antidramatic. It is no accident that, around the world, plays are more often cut than added to.

Lyric adaptation of narrative differs from lyric adaptation of drama. As we have seen, a lyric may convert drama only to the point of its being an attributive version of drama. It is not really drama as played in a theater. And what of narrative? "I struck the board." Is that not narrative in full version? "I struck the board and cried." Surely still full narrative. But thereafter we move to self-quotation and shift first to the future and then to the poem's dominant present tense. The seemingly full narrative sud-denly evaporates—only to reappear with the past tenses and its account of events (with dialogue) in the last four lines. By then the lyric character of the poem (with an attributive dramatic quality) has been sustained for thirty lines, the bulk of the poem.

Is it not true that what starts by seeming to be full (rather than attributive) narrative only seems so, because it is at the beginning of the poem? If we need proof, we need only look at the end of the poem, where the lyric dominates and the narrative in fact has a lesser attributive role than the dramatic does. On the other hand, the lyric speaker and narrative narrator make these two genres far more alike than either is like drama, whose essence is staging: with players and without speaker or narrator (except to interrupt drama).

Let us see if we find anything different in a poem by the seventeenth-century master of dramatic lyrics, Herbert's friend, John Donne. "The Indifferent" is certainly lyric, and equally certainly it uses an attributive version of drama. It opens with a male speaker who seems to be addressing womankind at large (Smith, 1975:61):

> I can love both fair and brown,
> Her whom abundance melts, and her whom want betrays,
> 3 Her who loves loneness best, and her who masks and plays . . .
> I can love her and her and you, and you,
> 9 I can love any, so she be not true.

Usual expectations are overturned. We expect a man to be particular about the kind of woman he would love and to wish his beloved would be true to him.

In the next stanza he bursts forth, speaking of a vice, which turns out to be fidelity in love, something (he says) the mothers of today's young women never fell into:

> 10 Will no other vice content you?
> Will it not serve your turn to do, as did your mothers?
> Or have you old vices spent, and now would find out others? . . .
> Must I, who came to travail thorough you,
> 18 Grow your fixed subject, because you are true?

With its attributive dramatic cast, the lyric moves wittily along.

With the beginning of the third and last stanza, however, we encounter something entirely new:

> Venus heard me sigh this song,
> 20 And by love's sweetest part, variety, she swore,
> She heard not this till now; and that it should be so no more.

> She went, examined, and returned ere long,
> And said, "Alas, some two or three
> Poor heretics in love there be,
> 25 Which think to establish dangerous constancy.
> But I have told them, 'Since you will be true,
> You shall be true to them who are false to you.' "

What happens in this remarkable third stanza is rare in Donne and different from what happens in "The Collar." With "Venus heard me sigh this song" we get not an attributive form of narrative but real narrative, real and strong enough to take on co-generic status. (The descriptive, theoretical grounds for saying "This is narrative" are something we may leave to our own cognitive grasp for the present, reserving discussion of "the nature of narrative" to the next chapter. It is enough to point to the shift in verb tense and the addition of another character who does something.) Meanwhile the words spoken by the eavesdropping Venus retain the attributive drama.

Yet the poem is a lyric, something that it were tedious to set out to prove. So I shall point only to the stanzaic character of the poem, with the final words of the closing couplet of each stanza: you, true; you, true; true, you.

Before proceeding to other matters, we may pause here to reflect on some highly significant features of lyric. To begin negatively, there is no "metalyric." One portion of a lyric may be more intense than the rest, but lyric does not interrupt itself as do drama and narrative in their "meta" versions. To put these matters positively, lyric draws on drama and narrative freely, easily, subjecting them to its sway. In fact, it makes them means of intensifying the fundamental lyric presence itself. Lyric uses the other genres, as it were, to become more lyrical. It is remarkable that the genre normally briefest should exercise such sway over its bulkier fellows. Other inferences can be drawn later as further issues are raised. But given what we have seen, it is hardly a historical or cultural accident that all but one of the world's poetic systems are affective-expressive.

It follows that, in those conversions of lyric, in those visions and revisions of genres, two manipulations take place: of generic codes and of their cognitive elements. The distinction between codes of knowing and things known may seem to belie our total experience of the poem, but it is useful for formal purposes, and in particular for getting at conventions of the lyric code. A major feature of that code is, as we have been seeing, presence. One of the conventions of the code is brevity. Dilation is feasible and desirable as long as it involves ebb and flow rather than a narrative continuum to some entelechy, some end. We see the dilating to and fro in the (varied) repetitions of Herbert's "Vertue" as well as in the middle thirty lines of "The Collar." We see it also in the first two stanzas of Donne's poem. Each change rung is not so much change at all as another variation referable to the speaker *now*, whenever that now is. And all we know, really, is that it is now, whether at the moment of rebellion in "The Collar" or before Venus and narrative enter "The Indifferent." Of course there is also art at the exclamatory moment of the overflow of powerful feeling.

Another convention of the code of presence is rhythm. It is no accident that the lyrical is thought of in terms of song and verse, or that it is more often expressed in verse than are narrative and drama. Prose has its rhythms, but verse requires language used most rhythmically, for even if there are not a fixed prosody and stanzas, there are lines—units at once aural, visual, and conceptual. With that formal recurrence there goes another kind involving the syntactic and cognitive in ways special to a given poem: fair and brown, wealthy and poor, reclusive and gregarious, and so forth, in the first stanzas of "The Indifferent." We do not so much march off to some goal as join in song on the spot, the temporal point, the now that is lyric: "Now sleeps the crimson petal, now the white."

A third convention of the code of presence is reduction of active characters, the most important constituent of narrative, as we shall see. Three, more often two, are and very often only one is enough to sustain a lyric—and to prevent, if prevention is desired—an interaction suggestive of drama or a motion to other things suggestive of narrative. Donne so seldom uses narrative because his approach typically employs the monologue or, if a woman or God is being addressed, it is very apt to remain a "dialogue of one" ("The Ecstasy," l. 74). Unlike Browning's dramatic monologues, Donne's give us no account of intrigue in a Spanish cloister, no account of a last Duchess culminating in her murder ("All smiles ceased"). By such omission, Donne maintains the attributive drama of his lyrics, whereas Herbert's tendency to recall more often brings attributive narrative, even if to join attributive drama.

We have just observed certain conventions of presence. They include repetition as emphasis on brevity (the same thing is recurred to rather than new matter added, as with a plot), the rhythmic singing at a temporal point, and the use of attributive versions of drama and narrative. These are clearly conventions of intensification as well. Yet other conventions of intensification involve choices whose nature is the stuff of literary history. The Tudor "courtly makers"—including most of the sonneteers, but not only they—played minute changes on a set of motifs sometimes designated Petrarchanism. Some readers sigh (and not the lover's tempests), wondering whether yet another poet's suffering from the disdain of his fair mistress represents a deliberate effort to be unoriginal. Here the historical conventions of lyric at the time represent social conventions, a ritualistic use of language necessary at the Tudor court for poets to convince themselves and others that they possessed saving bonds to each other in a court atmosphere of intrigue and overreaching.

Spenser, I ween, may intensify with a language of Chaucerisms. Others delight in copia or conceits or both. Donne and Jonson respond to those conventions with a new one, each of them introducing a language far closer to that of natural speech. Donne retains the Petrarchanism for his astonishing exaggerations and parody. Jonson rejects it, drawing instead on classical poets, especially Horace. Lyric presence has, then, more constant features in its code, whereas the conventions of intensification are more apt to change as renovation is required. The constancy lies in the requirement for intensification rather than in a particular means of fulfilling it.

Changes in means of intensification are basic to the accounts of styles from one Chinese dynasty to the next and within a dynasty, marking stages of the Six Dynasties; marking Early, High, and Late Tang; marking Northern and Southern Sung. There are also means of intensification peculiar to a language or culture. The kinds of prosody provide one example, and rhyme another, of cultural kinds. Arabic poetry is quantitative (like but different from Greek and Roman), and poets writing in it and related languages frequently write poems with one rhyme, something natural to very few languages. Japanese poets use syllable (or, rather, morae) count as the basis of prosody (fives and sevens and sevens and fives being the major traditional combinations), and rhyme is absent.

In addition, individual poets have their own styles of intensification. As we saw with Teika's poem on the Lady of the Uji Bridge, he might displace words from their natural connections, creating an air of ethereal mystery and beauty. Horace will begin a line with the word (if perhaps in different inflection) that ended the preceding line. It would take a lot of noise and a tin ear to prevent distinguishing either Teika or Horace from the Tennyson of "Now sleeps the crimson petal." By "Horace's style" or "Teika's style" we mean characteristic ways of thought, characteristic human situations, and characteristic ranges of idea and feeling. But we also mean characteristic means of their intensification of lyrics.

There are other differences that either participate with one of the two mentioned or lie between. Although, as has been said, Japanese and Chinese poets do not use dramatic elements as much or as strikingly as do a Donne and Herbert, east Asian poetry, especially Japanese, seems to have an extraordinary affinity for, or common cause with, narrative prose. In Chinese we also find exchanges of poems between friends, as we do from time to time in other languages. But where else is there the stated convention of using the friend's rhymes? For that matter, "rhyme" does not signify the same thing in Chinese, Arabic, and English. In Chinese it is a distinction between level and deflected *tones*. In Arabic it involves a final consonant. Yet again, intensification may involve fiction (or fact) and allegory (or allegoresis).

Since, as allegoresis shows, these matters necessarily involve readers, we may reflect that the others also have implied readers as well as authors. We are concerned now with the poet's relation to the work, the reader's to the poem, each to other, and reader to reader. It is through this forest of forests that we must now pass for comparative evidence about the nature and range of principal features of the lyric code.

At the margin of the forest there is a thicket of issues and disputes. As I feel well qualified to testify, anybody with even superficial knowledge of Chinese poetry knows the first poem in *The Classic of Poetry* (*Shijing*), or at least its seemingly obvious first line, "*Guan, guan* cry the ospreys." On the other hand, nothing has been simple about the poem for two millennia or more. One interpretation holds that the birds cry "Fair, fair" in allusion to the woman at the center of the poem. A learned account by another critic holds that the birds are not, could not, be ospreys. If there could be such a thing as an innocent eye, to it the poem would look like some manner of amatory appreciation of the woman.

The *Classic of Poetry* was not, however, simply a book of importance. It was one of the Five Classics, which were followed in importance by the Four Books and Three Histories in the first and long enduring panoply of Chinese learning. We see here the autonomy for poetry necessary for a systematic poetics. To obtain such exalted status from Confucians (the compiling was traditionally but wrongly attributed to Confucius himself, or to an immediate disciple), *The Classic of Poetry* had to have a moral import making it powerful enough, on right reading, to order lives and the state, as well as suitable for quotation on diplomatic missions. That first poem is not long, so we may have it all:

關關雎鳩
在河之洲
窈窕淑女
君子好逑

5   參差荇菜
左右流之
窈窕淑女
寤寐求之

求之不得
10 寤寐思服
悠哉悠哉
輾轉反側

參差荇菜
左右采之
15 窈窕淑女
琴瑟友之

參差荇菜
左右芼之
窈窕淑女
20 鐘鼓樂之

Guan guan cry the ospreys
On the islet of the river.
The beautiful and good young lady
Is a fine mate for the lord.

5 Varied in length are the water plants;
Left and right we catch them.
The beautiful and good young lady—
Waking and sleeping he wished for her.

He wished for her without getting her.
10 Waking and sleeping he thought of her:
Longingly, longingly,
He tossed and turned from side to side.

Varied in length are the water plants;
Left and right we gather them.
15 The beautiful and good young lady—
Zithers and lutes greet her as a friend.

Varied in length are the water plants—
Left and right we cull them.
The beautiful and good young lady—
20 Bells and drums delight her.   (Yu, 1987:47)

These twenty lines have probably been more discussed, and read as with
a difference, than the whole Song of Songs. Confucius was said to have
praised the poem's morality. Some said it criticized King Kang, others
that it praises the queen of King Wen. And so on.[18] Through the colored

---

[18] See Yu, 1987:47–55 for the translation (adapted from one by Bernhard Karlgren) and

lenses of the moralist, the poem presents exemplary history. To plain eye-sight, it looks like an anonymous song. To blue eyes, it looks fictional. To dark but unspectacled Han eyes, it is factual, dealing with what some-one now unknown spoke of on a real occasion. Yet to any pair of eyes, this is a lyric, not a narrative or a drama.

Scratched as we may be by this thicket, we emerge with the under-standing that, in the absence of evidence to the contrary, Chinese think that poetry is factual.[19] Of course east Asian readers recognize that certain poems are fictional. But the assumption that poetry is essentially factual is very strong, especially in China and Korea. This assumption is of such importance that no amount of iteration is sufficient for westerners until they cease to identify literature with fiction.

A poem by Du Fu may assist in making the point. It is "The Lovely Lady" or "The Fine Lady" ("Jiaren").

佳人
絕代有佳人
幽居在空谷
自云良家子
零落依草木
5 關中昔喪亂
兄弟遭殺戮
官高何足論
不得收骨肉

世情惡衰歇
10 萬事隨轉燭
夫婿輕薄兒
新人美如玉
合昏尚知時
鴛鴦不獨宿
15 但見新人笑
那聞舊人哭

discussion. The use of the seemingly unrelated water grasses—repeated and juxtaposed without comment—was called *xing* ("stimulus") and identified as one of six features and one of three techniques in *The Classic of Poetry*. Yu remarks on the passage quoted from the "Great Preface" that it "also appears as part of the Little Preface to the first poem in the anthology" (p. 32), giving some sense of the importance attached to this obscure poem.

[19] See Yu, 1987:ix, 14–16, 35, 81. Paul de Man (Hošek-Parker, 1985) considered apostro-phe the basis of lyric, but as the example just given (and numerous others) would show, that is not the case, although it might be argued that often the speaker-reader connection in lyric has a special quality. The argument offered by de Man is further vexed by his seeming equation of apostrophe and prosopopoeia and giving the latter an idiosyncratic meaning.

在山泉水清
出山泉水濁
侍婢賣珠迴
20 牽蘿補茅屋
摘花不插髮
采柏動盈掬
天寒翠袖薄
日暮倚修竹

    Unrivalled in her time the beauty
    now lives obscurely in a desolate valley;
    her own words tell of her high family
    if now dependent on plants and trees;
5   in the capital long since seized by rebels
    her brothers met death on the gibbet
    their high offices giving no protection
    and she could not inter their flesh and bones;
    the world feels hate for what has seen its time
10 its ways as inconstant as a flickering wick;
    her husband has proved unfaithful
    for a new woman he prizes as his gem;
    even a tree is sensitive to time
    and mandarin ducks dwell in conjugal pairs
15 but he has eyes only for the new one's smiles
    and no ears at all for the old one's crying;
    water housed in the mountain is thought pure
    but once ejected it is thought to run dirty;

    her serving woman comes back from selling pearls
20 and they try to mend holes in their roof;
    she gathers flowers not meant for her hair
    and breaks off bitter cypress by the handfuls;
    in the cold her fine blue clothes are thin
    and as sun sets she rests against large bamboos.[20]

A political upheaval has thrown the once privileged lady into a harsh world. She seems now to have a few jewels left and one attendant. Du Fu delicately implies that the flowers she picks are meant to be sold for some pittance. Once so elegant, her bright clothes are pitiably thin for the

[20] The translation follows the interpretation by D. Hawkes, 1967:poem 12, with some departures. His title is "A Fine Lady," suggesting her high birth.

weather that has come on. Her brothers killed and her husband unfaithful, she has lost all support and will not last long in her newly hostile world.

There are many Chinese poems about, or as if spoken by, women abandoned to misfortune. Many of them were written by men under circumstances showing that the poems express the resentment of a literatus-official for loss of office or support by a king or high minister. Is that true of this poem? Presuming that it is, is the poem an allegory?

In fact, it has proved difficult to describe just what goes on in Chinese poems that mean something else. James J. Y. Liu devoted an important passage to the matter, which involves "Guan Guan" as well as "The Lovely Lady."

> Encouraged by Confucius' example, later Chinese scholars and critics interpreted the poems [in *The Classic of Poetry*] in such a way as to make them yield moral lessons. Such interpretations, which are often far-fetched, have been called by many Western scholars "allegorical interpretations." However, as Pauline Yu has demonstrated, these interpretations differ radically from Western allegoresis but rather resemble Dante's "tropological" level of interpretation: instead of using the particular and concrete to represent the universal and abstract, these interpretations sought to relate each poem to particular historical persons and events. [See Yu, 1982; also 1987:index, "allegoresis," "allegory."]
>
> At the same time, Mencius' dictum that one should encounter the author's intent with one's own mind gave critics confidence in claiming to recover what the author intended to mean. The combination of Confucian moralism and Mencian intentionalism led to the historico-biographico-tropological approach, which has remained the dominant mode of literary interpretation down to the present day. On the one hand, poems are generally assumed to be biographical, and great pains are taken to pin every poem down to a precise date. On the other hand, when the speaker of a poem is clearly not the historical author, such as when a male poet assumes a female persona, or when a poem appears to be concerned with erotic love, then critics will resort to ingenious and far-fetched interpretations to uncover supposedly hidden references to contemporary political events or to the poet's personal circumstances. In other words, what may be quite innocently love poems or not too innocently symbolic poems are all treated as *poèmes à clef*. However, it must be admitted that some Chinese poets did write and read poems in this manner, and the tropological mode of interpretation cannot be totally ignored. (Liu, 1988:96–97)

A more cogent account is probably infeasible, and although the main lines are clear, it is plain that Liu himself is not wholly comfortable with traditional interpretation and yet must close by acknowledging that some "poets did write and read *in this manner*." It is another issue what that manner is. Both Yu and Liu are far better acquainted with western assumptions and practice than their counterparts in European literatures are of Chinese practice. They are certainly motivated by uneasiness over the western premise that allegory relates to another, transcendental realm, something rare in Chinese literature. They attribute, however, more consistency to western terms and practice than is deserved. Because of Liu's reference to tropology, we may take recourse to another cogent account, this time the second of two definitions of "allegory" from Richard A. Lanham's *Handlist of Rhetorical Terms* (Lanham, 1968):

> One of four levels of interpretation common in medieval and Renaissance interpretation. Allegorizing of this sort had begun with Greek commentary on Homer and by the Middle Ages was common in reading [the Bible and] Virgil as well: (*a*) Literal; (*b*) Allegorical; (*c*) Moral or Tropological; (*d*) Anagogical or Spiritual. Or, as the medieval catchverse has it:
>
> > Littera gesta docet,
> > Quid credas, allegoria,
> > Moralia, quid agas,
> > Quo tendas, anagogia.   (Lanham, 1968:3)
>
> (The Literal teaches you what happened,
> The Allegorical what you should believe,
> The Moral what you ought to do,
> The Anagogical where you head.)

(There were other catchverses, and the two middle terms are not stable.)

On this western account, the additional and fuller or better meanings of Chinese poetry are properly allegorical ("Allegory" is the entry in Lanham) in the third sense of the moral or tropological, what one is to do, an ethical issue highly congenial to Chinese. There are also features of the western system that are inapplicable to China—what make Liu and Yu nervous about "allegory." Chinese were of course interested in the literal sense (which is not really allegorical at all but the necessary basis for an allegory). But matters of faith (Lanham's Allegorical)—which allowed Christians to take over the Hebrew Bible as their Old Testament—held no interest to Chinese. Nor did the Anagogical to a people who did not believe in a Christian kind of afterlife. Equally to the point, western allegoresis is largely confined to the Bible and narrative, whereas the Chinese are most concerned with lyrics. One can see why Yu and Liu are so uneasy with the phrase "allegorical interpretation" in accounting for Chinese composition and interpreting of poetry. But properly understood, as these two critics direct us, "allegory" may be used to describe the writing by some Chinese poets, and "allegoresis" (also properly understood) describes traditional modes of interpretation.

To return, then, to Du Fu and his "Lovely Lady." Because of the tradition of writing allegorically, particularly of using the figure of the woman abandoned, and because Du Fu has many poems critical of his time, the traditional, "moral" interpretation is intrinsically possible. But modern interpreters tend to reject the "moral" interpretation of this poem. David Hawkes is one of them. "Some Chinese commentators used to understand this poem as an allegory (the lady standing for an out-of-office statesman and the philandering husband for his Emperor), but I find this quite impossible to believe. There is no reason at all why we shouldn't think of it as a faithful record of real encounter" (D. Hawkes, 1967:81). How very unwestern, how exquisitely Chinese our choice is! Either we can follow the traditional commentators and find an allegory in a lyric, or we can take the poem "as a faithful record of a real encounter." Ultimate fictionality is *not* an interpretive option. One way or another—by moral allegory or by literal factuality—Du Fu was writing about what had really happened, facts.

This assumption about the poet and about assurance in interpretation derives from a firm belief in intentionalism. As the "Great Preface" begins by saying, "Poetry is where the intent of the heart/mind goes." Like the belief in factuality, the assumption of intentionalism is not only old but strong. James J. Y. Liu credits Mencius with initiating interpretive intentionalism in remarking: One who interprets *The Classic of Poetry* "should not let the words damage the phrases, or the phrases the intent [*zhi*]. To encounter [the author's] intent with [one's own] idea [*yi*]: this is the way to get to it" (Liu, 1988:98; the brackets are Liu's). The belief in intentionalism is long-lasting. Grace S. Fong quotes "the *shi yan zhi* 'poetry expresses intent' dictum," and she quotes a late Song (Sung) writer about the poetic kind called *ci*: "*ci* should be elegant and proper; it is where the heart's intent goes," an obvious recollection of the first sentence of the "Great Preface" (Fong, 1987:103).

The Chinese poet is presumed to have a moral purpose that requires dealing with facts. It is presumed that the poet's intention is based on facts and is clear in the poem. As for modern critics like Hawkes, Liu, and Yu, my guess is that their stand is what it is because it is the more economical, parsimonious as scientists say. It allows for factuality without the need of allegory—of Dante's or a Bunyan's kind. It also allows us to identify the speaker of the poem with the poet. I find it delicious to consider that, on such Chinese grounds, the allegory of the woman abandoned would be a more acceptable interpretation of Du Fu's poem if the poet had written as if *he* were the woman abandoned, rather than of the woman he saw abandoned, making Hawkes's assumption. Needless to say, this long line of intentionalism has not reduced, over the centuries, Chinese poems to a single interpretation each.

Japanese lyricism both resembles and differs from Sino-Korean and western practice. Until ca. 950–1000, it was assumed with the Chinese that poems are factual in the absence of gainsaying evidence. Exceptions had to be made for some poems in the *Man'yōshū* (last datable poem 759). For example, Yamanoe Okura has a "Dialogue on Poverty" in which first a poor man and then a destitute man speak (*Man'yōshū* 5:892–93). It is impossible for him to be both. In fact, the dialogue speakers are considered to be fictional (in 892), while the speaker of the generalizing envoy (893) is taken to be Okura. In *The Records of Ancient Matters* (*Kojiki*; after 672) and the very similar *Chronicles of Japan* (*Nihon Shoki* or *Nihongi*)—similar except in Chinese—there are many poems attributed to various individuals, divine or human. Because of the lack of apparent connection between what transpired in the prose and what the poems seem to be about, it was formerly held that work songs, children's songs, or other primitive pieces had been drawn on rather imperfectly to give expression to an individual's emotions when those became too intense for prose to convey. In recent years it has been shown that some of the songs, perhaps all, make perfect sense in their contexts, once we understand various ritual and social practices in early Japan (Konishi, 1984:111–35).

The drive to discover fact is strong enough to have led to convincing discovery. Many of the songs in question are attributed, however, to individuals who did not exist—divinities, for example. In other words, the poems involved are fictional because the speakers to whom they are attributed are fictional, even while they are expressive of realities of the human world in archaic Japan. Indeed, these records of ancient matters are sometimes fabulous and sometimes historical, and the more that is learned from archaeological and other sources, the more genuine the songs seem to be—including some grim actions by the royal houses. Efforts to discover evidence of the real existence of some early monarchs have led historians back to A.D. 239 (Konishi, 1984:189–94).

The fictionalizing of Japanese poetry really takes on scale with the generation of the compilers of the *Kokinshū* (ca. 910). Tsurayuki himself, who accounted for Japanese poetry as that which has the human heart as seed or cause, participated in two activities involving clearly fictional poetry. One was writing poems to go with pictures as ornaments on screens. Another was writing poems for poetry matches. Since, in his day, a low-ranking nobleman like himself wrote for matches as a stand-in for a high lord, the poems were clearly fictional, and in any event, composing poems on topics set by others produces fictional writing. Chinese would have been shocked, and westerners are apt to draw too hasty conclusions.

This is another dense place in the woods. Tsurayuki's fictional poems for screens or poetry matches do not really differ from those he composed on factual occasions: the same conceptual and stylistic conventions prevail. Without the headnotes, nobody could say whether this poem is fictional or factual. One could infer that his statements in the Japanese preface to the *Kokinshū* represent an ideal to which he did not live up. One could similarly assume that he passes on traditional ideas that are now out of touch with the realities of his age. One might also infer to the contrary, as I do, that on whatever occasion he wrote, whether on actually visiting a temple or writing a poem for a screen, he sought to write as if the experience were genuine, as if he were truly moved by the occasion, whether factual or fictional. I infer that whichever of those choices may be correct, his descriptive and normative conception of conventional style (*sama*) was a lyric code governing factual and fictional alike.

Japanese poetry grew increasingly fictional as composition more and more focused on poetry matches and sequences of a hundred or other number of poems. Factual, immediate poems continued to be written and exchanged but it was the formal, fictional kind on which one's reputation was based and which therefore evoked a poet's strongest efforts. The major exceptions to the rule that formal poetry was fictional came in certain books of the normal twenty of a royal collection. The most important poetry traditionally was that on the four seasons and next that on love. Those were now usually fictional. But factual poems continued to be composed regularly on occasions of congratulation, lament, complaint (usually for being passed over for promotion), and books on Shinto and Buddhist topics. Sometimes allegory was used as a recognized means to convey a fact of personal situation or religious verities. Sometimes we cannot be sure whether something is factual or fictional. *The Diary of Izumi Shikibu (Izumi Shikibu Nikki)* may or may not be by her. A minority of scholars think it is made up by a later hand from known events and poems in her personal collections. On the other hand, most of those poems are presumed to be factual. The majority view is that Izumi Shikibu is indeed the author, and that the prose and poetry alike are factual—with one exception. That involves the author composing a poem for her lover to send to another woman. The chief basis for assuming Izumi Shikibu the author is pretty much opposite to the logic of western assumptions: it must be factual in the absence of sufficient evidence to prove anything else.

By the time the eighth royal collection, the *Shinkokinshū*, was commissioned in 1201, the main line of poetic composition was fictional, with whatever exceptions. But the best poets had, as poets often do, their contrary moods. Some composed factual poetry for themselves, in defiance of fictional domination. The most remarkable effort to reconvert the fictional, however, is exemplified by the theory and practice of Fujiwara Shunzei (1114–1204) and his yet more gifted son, Teika. Following the meditative practices of Tendai Buddhism, they sought to concentrate on the fictional topic so profoundly that, in their view, the object and their contemplation of it became one. A symptom of this desire to defictionalize can be found in the headnotes to poems. Where before the topics (e.g., at a poetry match) specified with a poem might be "Travel" (*Tabi*) or "Waiting Love" (*Matsu Koi*), they would now be "On the Spirit of Travel" (*Tabi no Kokoro o*) or "On the Spirit of Waiting Love" (*Matsu Koi no Kokoro o*). That *kokoro* is none other than Tsurayuki's word as part of the phrase for "the human heart" (also mind, spirit). It now means something like "the essential conception." However successful this new seriousness was—Teika's two poems quoted earlier in this chapter may be reexamined—the result was not exactly fact. It seems more accurate to say that a Shunzei or a Teika strove to discover (spiritual) truth in fictional topics. Once again, this is not the place to review possible truth statuses of literature, but surely something may be fictional and yet true *about* something. It must also be said that Shunzei and Teika succeeded in something else: in reidentifying the poet with the speaker of the poem. Can there be such a thing as a factual poet-speaker of a fictional poem? They would have thought so.

A poem by a later poet, Fushimi (r. 1287–98), may offer some clarification. It appears to be a factual account of the poet's situation on a rainy night (*Fūgashū* 18:2057):

Mado no to ni	On the windowframe
Shitataru ame o	The raindrops patter tapping,
Kiku nabe ni	And as I listen
Kabe ni somukeru	I have turned against the wall
Yowa no tomoshibi.	The lamp that burns at midnight.

A contemporary reader would know that this is an allegorical poem, because the eighteenth book of the collection contains Buddhist poems, even if there is nothing in the poem itself to give a literal religious sense.

Of course Fushimi was not seeking mystification; he provided a head-note: "On the Topic, 'The Three Dogmas Are Not One Dogma, Nor Are They Three Dogmas.' " The dogmas are those of the Empty, the Phenomenal, and the Mean, alluded to earlier in this chapter.[21]

It is wholly impossible to say whether the scene described was a real one that led Fushimi to his religious significance, or whether the religious topic came first and he composed a fictional nature poem to embody the religious matter. If the latter is the case, the "literal" sense is fictional and the allegorical is true. If the former is the case, then the natural scene is factual and the allegorical is still true. The truth is of course that of religion in each case. Whether we take the literal sense to be factual or fictional, the most economical way to account for the existence of this poem is to hold that Fushimi is its speaker.

To those who think that the actual poet cannot be speaker of a poem, I must say two things. They hold an assumption held by me for many years. I no longer hold to it as a necessary one, because it now seems to me that there are too many instances in which it is simpler to hold the poet a speaker, or when holding otherwise trivializes a poem, something especially true of religious poetry. And once started there, one cannot declare a *cordon sanitaire* for all else. I also think that holding the poet to be the speaker is neither the overwhelming possibility that east Asians sometimes think or the zero possibility westerners sometimes think. When I explicitly write about my thoughts, as I am at this moment, there is no reason to think that the statement represents all I think, or all of me. The act of expression requires a self-stylizing based on the conventions of the kind that writing holds in a given culture at a given time, and based also on the writer's purpose and audience.

St. Augustine's Pauline *Confessions* has engendered a religious genre concerning God's grace to the chief of sinners lasting from his time, through saints' lives, through Puritan autobiography, through revival-tent scenes I witnessed as a boy, and into our own time.[22] Shunzei, Teika, and Fushimi deserve our taking them seriously—whether in fiction, fact, or an allegory mediating between the two—because it is only by taking them seriously that we take ourselves seriously. And there is no possible way of taking them seriously if we ignore what they were serious about or, for that matter, if we ignore what we are serious about. If we do not come out in the same place, it is good to know so and to set about to see what can be done. (The last chapter will touch on some of these matters.)

---

[21] See Nakamura, 1962:under *sangan*. This specific formula is a Tendai one, but the idea is common in various versions.

[22] The account offered by Starr, 1965, gives some of the literary implications of the tradition.

The east Asian evidence we have been examining also shows, as does the Augustinian tradition, that the historical moralizing and intentionalism of the Chinese and the religious meditation of the Japanese require for the very possibility of expression Tsurayuki's conventionalizing *sama*. To put that another way, no matter how we express ourselves we necessarily stylize ourselves. We might pick up five pieces of our writing for different purposes, subjects, and audiences and remark on the differences in the selves of each, and a given two might seem inconsistent. To deny, however, that a given stylizing is a stylizing of *ourselves* is to trivialize ourselves in the act of writing or reading, and with lyrics not least of all. The east Asian tradition may go too far in the direction of identifying, especially in the full sense of that word, the poet and the speaker. There is no need to be so intentionally and reflexively earnest as the Confucianists. But westerners are afraid of going far enough.

If these reflections are at all correct, there is some reason for another look at lyric poets we considered earlier, Herbert and Donne. In his "Life of Mr. George Herbert," Izaak Walton tells of a conversation Herbert held, not long before his death, with a Duncan or Duncon concerning the manuscript of *The Temple*: "Sir, I pray deliver this little Book to my dear brother Farrer [Nicholas Ferrar of Little Gidding], and tell him, he shall find in it a picture of the many spiritual Conflicts that have past betwixt God and my Soul, before I could subject mine to the will of Jesus my Master; in whose service I have now found perfect freedom."[23] Walton's factual purpose and his hagiography are not opposed camps at moments like this. Simple identity of Herbert with a speaker reported at two removes seems too credulous. With the poems, we have the speaker firsthand, self-stylized and stylized by conventions of meditative poetry.

There is no reason to insist that "The Collar" represents an autobiographically real outburst of rebellion by Herbert. But to dissociate the poem entirely from Herbert, to hold that there is no connection between its speaker and Herbert is to take away what may be termed the self-authority that characterizes *The Temple*. A deeply committed, a self-authorized and self-stylized, poet projecting a speaker as a version of himself—that makes the greater lyric and therefore also human sense.

The same may be said of the Donne of the divine poems and of a prose work like *Devotions Upon Emergent Occasions*. But what of "The Indifferent" or "The Flea"? Nobody would think that although the poems are fictional, we may still think of Donne as their speaker after the manner of some east Asian poems. The speakers are fictional, as is that rarest of

---

[23] Walton, 1962:314; I have removed the heavy italicizing. The passage is also quoted in Hutchinson, 1953:xxxvii, but without acknowledgment of its origin.

characters in a Donnean poem, a classical goddess, Venus in "The Indifferent." Where, then, shall we find Tsurayuki's lyric cause, the human heart? Where does John Donne stand? Must we go and catch a falling star?

The answer is indicated by posing another question: why should Donne have needed to take recourse to the fictional in his amatory lyrics? The brief answer is that he had a strong emotional and veracious need to expose the false fictionality of earlier and still current views about the nature of the amorous. His fictions are offered as truer than others. We must recall that in a Germanic language like English the comparative degree of the adjective may be less extensive than the mere positive: a collection of "longer" (or "truer") poems includes poems shorter ("less true") than "long" ("true") poems. The poems in Donne's *Songs and Sonnets* claim a truth in their truerness that he found wanting in English Petrarchanism and the other conventional sets he so wittingly exploits. Not only that. Among the other witty young men less interested in law at the Inns of Court than a stepstone to court, Donne shows revulsion over current cant and even distrust if not revulsion over his own motives.[24]

Donne's self-styled "evaporations of wit" are fictional, but they also deal with what matters to him. Some are more fictional than others, because those less fictional include material on features of society in his time. To Donne, the fictional was often a necessity, and for some evident reasons. One is self-protection. Poems like some of his had been burnt by episcopal order. He also needed protection in the fall from those mighty gyrations and leaps of wit to sober earth. In his secular poems, Donne means seriously—with a discount for wit—what he says fictionally.

Some poetry is necessarily fictional, and often it would be naive to identify the poet with the lyric speaker. That view has arisen in the west, because it accords with practice, and not only in the west. Yet it is not a full explanation. It is not surprising that in a culture that prizes lyric above all—the Arabic—it should be assumed that the poet and speaker are one unless there are grounds for thinking otherwise. Of course, in so highly developed a rhetorical tradition, discounts would be made for flights in panegyrics, and indirections might be necessary when speaking of erotic love in the culture of the Prophet. There as well as in Donne, self-stylizing enters in, but the connection assumed between poet and speaker is

---

[24] See Ellrodt, 1960:vol 3. Ch. 1 concerns "Les origines sociales de l'esprit nouveau: le réalisme et les 'Inns of Court' "; and for what I have termed revulsion, see ch. 2 with its Sartrean subtitle, "La Nausée." In vol. 1, see ch. 6, "De la sincérité a l'humour" on the matters being discussed, and in the same volume, ch. 1, "Présence" for an argument agreeable with that offered in this chapter.

very different from what seems natural to a culture like the western, which has been so strongly influenced by a drama-based poetics.

There is a corollary to the lyric-inspired close connection of the poet and speaker: because the poetic expression conveys the ideas and feelings of an actual person, it will also move readers. As we might expect, that view finds particularly strong support in Japan, where it is assumed that people of all classes, even illiterates, may be poets. What was true for the unlettered and unkempt was all the truer of those who dedicated themselves to the way or vocation (*michi*) of poetry. As we have seen, one such was Shunzei. The fifteenth-century monk (later, archbishop) and poet both in court poetry and linked poetry, Shinkei, passes on this sentimental picture of the old poet.

> Very late at night he would sit by his bed in front of an oil lamp so dim that it was difficult to tell whether it was burning or not, and with a tattered court robe thrown over his shoulders and an old court cap pulled down to his ears, he would lean on an armrest, hugging a wooden brazier for warmth, while he recited verse to himself in an undertone. Deep into the night, when everybody else was asleep, he would sit there bent over, weeping softly. (Miner, 1968:34)

Shinkei is passing on a story he heard from Shunzei's Reizei descendants, with whom he studied court poetry. It is one of those things that ought to be true, whether it is or not, and especially in that culture, where the anxiety of not using the past was so heavy a burden. The point is that any civilized person could be expected to recite appealing poems, honoring the great poets of times bygone and defining one's own acute sensibility in relation to them and the Way of Poetry; it therefore stood to reason that a great poet like Shunzei would make it his purpose to know more poems than others did and was bound to recall them with unusual feeling.

That this is not mere sentimentality we know from Shunzei's comments on 196 poems he chose as models for his *Notes on Poetic Style Through the Ages* (*Korai Fūteishō*). This collection of exemplary poems is as much a fact as Shinkei's account of his reciting his favorite poems is an unproved legend. But it is precisely the kind of legend that occurs in a culture whose poetics is defined chiefly by lyric. It is not one likely for dramatists or writers of narrative. Nor would we expect Aristotle to compile an exemplary collection for readers and poets, or reader-poets. Perhaps after all, Shinkei's account arose from one of Shunzei's poems (*Shinkokinshū* 3:201) on a bird whose long-awaited first song finds the poet deep in reflections on other days.

Mukashi omou	Longing for the past
Kusa no iori no	Here in my grass-thatched cottage
Yoru no ame ni	In the rain at night—
Namida na soe so	Do not bring me to tears again,
Yamahototogisu.	Hototogisu in the hills.[25]

LYRIC RADICALS AND REVISIONISM

Like any other really important poet, Shunzei represents salient features of his culture and of his art. His art was lyric and, taken together, his poem and Shinkei's story verify that affective and expressive theory which Tsurayuki had originated for Japanese poetry. Shunzei was also the most esteemed judge of poetry in his time, participating with that function in many poetry matches. He was also a poet-critic in a sense recognized more readily in the west—someone who writes pronouncements. His most famous slogan urged poets to employ "old words and new conceptions" (kotoba furuku, kokoro atarashi—drawing on Tsurayuki's central terms). Some conservatives rejected the second half as no longer possible for an age of spiritual decline and defined the first half as the language of the first three royal collections.

In short we have identified three radicals of lyric: the poet, the reader, and language.

As we have seen, in cultures with affective-expressive poetics, the poet tends to be identified with the speaker of the poem, and the reader is presumed also to be stirred so much as to be likely to turn to lyric expression. Moreover, the expressive implications of lyricism lead the author of the Chinese Great Preface and Tsurayuki in his preface to the Koninshū to emphasize words, language. For comparable western evidence, no poet-critic is more suitable than the owner of the Sabine farm.

Horace's odes provide the basis in his own poems for his poetics, which brought affectivism and the reader into western poetics as major differentiae. It will not be amiss to run through the first ten of the first book as a reminder of the nature of his lyrics (following the Loeb edition).

1. To Maecenas.
2. To Augustus.
3. To Virgil.
4. Spring brings thoughts of death. To Sestius.

---

[25] The hototogisu is the gray-headed Asian cuckoo, *cuculus poliocephalus*. Its egg-laying habits differ from the western cuckoo. Its song is a sustained series of notes rather than but two (cuc-koo), and the legends about it differ greatly from those of cuckoldry in the west. For that reason, I have kept the Japanese name. See further Konishi, 1986A:62.

5. To Pyrrha faithless in love.
6. To Agrippa.
7. In praise of Tibur. To Plancus.
8. To Lydia, who has infatuated Sybaris.
9. Winter thoughts. To Thaliarchus.
10. To Mercury.

Ode 10 has a divine addressee, but only Odes 5 and 8 stand out as being likely candidates for fictionality. It is possible that real individuals are meant by Pyrrha and the rest; it is barely conceivable that Horace gives their actual names—although "Sybaris" surely is a fictional type of the young man devoted to creaturely delight. In conservative terms, seven out of the ten odes are addressed to real people who could only have read them as real people—however stylized by the poet's version of them and by social as well as literary conventions.

Is Horace, Quintus Horatius Flaccus, the speaker of those seven (or eight) poems? A Chinese or Japanese would say, of course. If we allow for authorial stylizing, I think them right. Classicists take the first three books as a unit and, among other things, the following emerge. In their initial poems, the first book is dedicated to Maecenas and the second to Pollio. The opening poem of the third book is dedicated to no one, but is on the poet *himself*, as the last (3:30) is on his immortal art, so repeating the pattern of the last poem in book 2 (20). Horace is felt to be present, because it is crucial to him and his lyric art that he be present. Without arguing that everything said is exactly true in Horace's lyrics to and about his contemporaries and himself, we can assume that apart from omissions and exaggerations contemporaries recognized the poet and themselves. Serious divagations would have become notorious.

The so-called conversion ode (1:34) is a good example. Hearing thunder from a clear blue sky: "A doubtful and infrequent worshipper of the gods, / Devoted to a wisdom discordant with reason" (Parcus deorum cultor et infrequens, / insanientis dum sapientiae consultus), he thinks of the power of Zeus the Thunderer. It is surely an overinterpretation either to think that this recounts a sudden conversion of an Epicurean to Stoicism or to insist that this must be fictional. The idea that the poet is not present in the poet's work is not an idea held by poets, particularly lyric poets.

The affective side of Horace is doubly clear. He writes as a person moved: even in 1:5 and 8 Horace addresses the no doubt fictional characters in the tones he uses for actual people. And when he writes to Maecenas or Virgil he writes out of this or that feeling. Of course he needs to draw on the *sama* identified by Tsurayuki, the lyrical conventions inherited from Greece. No other Roman poet draws upon Greek lyric measures with the fullness and ease of Horace. But technique is both consistent with art and essential to it whether in extreme factuality or extreme fictionality. Similarly, Horace's relations with the great men of his time can only imply that they were moved by his poems, finding nothing in them that seriously violated the facts of themselves and other Romans. It was on the basis of these odes in particular that Horace could say that poetry should offer the delightful and useful (*dulce et utile*). If Horace had broken with essential fact in writing of his friends and acquaintances, there would have been a shock not felt in such a satire as that on the town mouse and the country mouse. Because that satire is an obvious fiction.

Much of Martial is also factual, although he had to take out some insurance for his contemporaries with the plaintive joke that his life was chaste even if his Muse was jocund.

Horace is also at one with Asian poets in the attention he devotes to words in his writing about poetry; that is, he shares their expressivism. Toward the end of the last chapter we observed how critics in the mimetic tradition—Aristotle, Sidney, Dryden—belittled language, extolling instead the version of the world embodied in the action of a play. By contrast, Horace dwells on words and language in his *Ars Poetica*. In the first hundred of its 476 lines, the following expressions occur at the line indicated (and elsewhere in repetitions):

    41 facundia; 47 verbum; 52 verba; 59 nomen;
    61 verborum; 69 sermonum; 72 norma loquendi;
    86 colores; 95 sermone; 97 verba.

In the ensuing lines the same words are often recalled and a few others are added; 111 lingua; 112 dicta; 390 vox (318 voces); and the double example of verbo verborum in 133. It is a virtuoso feat to find so many words for words.

Such an extent of agreement between the Horatian and the east Asian poetics testifies to the common lyric base by which the poetics were originated. Put another way, the comparative evidence shows that language, identification of poet and speaker, and affectivism are signs of lyric premises. He also has much to say about drama and an *imitatio* largely redefining Aristotle's mimesis: in *Ars Poetica*, lyricism constitutes a revisionist poetics. And as was observed in the first chapter, the history of Japanese poetics can be considered as a series of adaptations of other genres to lyric along with the enlargement but not breakage of that lyric-based poetics (Miner, 1979B). We may now consider some later western revisions.

Wordsworth's preface to the second edition of *Lyrical Ballads* (1800, and with alterations in 1802 and 1850) does not represent total English romantic thinking and certainly not total European romantic thought.

But it is heuristic, suggestive of the way generic revision can be undertaken. Viewed one way, "Lyrical Ballads" is a label for disparate things, Wordsworth's lyrics and Coleridge's narrative, notably *The Rime of the Ancient Mariner*. But Coleridge also wrote lyrics, and I think the title more nearly redundant than contradictory. "Ballads" conveyed singing, recalled Sidney's love of them, were songs gathered by eighteenth-century antiquaries. Above all, they could be idealized as a native strain of language held as authentic. The word "ballad" was a shibboleth to show the falseness of the language of most poetry from Pope to Gray, a touchstone for the genuineness of a selection of the ordinary language people use.

There had been similar ideas about poetic language earlier. Donne and Jonson had led the effort to bring poetic language closer to the natural tongue than the Petrarchans and Spenserians had allowed. Dryden did the same in the wake of Milton. But, as we saw in the last chapter, language was not yet considered a central principle of poetics. The poets and critics mentioned may be important in other ways, but they were not important in Wordsworth's way.

There is another feature of English Romanticism that is better known, more fully understood. As Coleridge's remarks on imagination show, and as is confirmed by that epic of the growth of the poet's mind, Wordsworth's *Prelude*, Romanticism introduced a degree of expressionism thitherto not made a prime basis in English poetics. The remarkable thing about this expressionism founded on lyricism is not its late date nor its indifference to Horace, but its omission of an affectivism complementary in strength. To omit full affectivism in a lyric-based poetics, and after centuries of importance of Horace's affective-expressive theory, is to make a change that has to reflect a revisionist definition on the basis of more than lyric alone. The obvious explanation is a hidden agenda of narrative. This is easy to show in any of the poets but easiest of all with Scott. When he stopped writing lyrico-narrative poetry, he turned to novels. "Lyrical Ballads" thus has narrative as yet another implication.

The legacy of official lyric and of narrative longings continues to Eliot, Pound, Aiken, Crane, Williams, and others. The dialectic between the acknowledged and the unacknowledged led the Romantics to their strange omission of affectivism and the reader. And the spirit of that decision would subsequently inform even those movements nominally opposed to Romanticism.

The old Anglo-American New Criticism provides a conspicuous example. As with the Romantics, their revisionism was founded on lyricism, and in particular that of the Metaphysical poets. It is a kind of sour jest that, except for some of Keats, Romantic poetry was unacceptable to the New Critics. In a sense they did the Romantics one better, or worse. As the Romantics with their official lyric ideal nonetheless largely omitted affectivism in practice, the New Critics omitted it in principle, and expressivism along with it. The affective and the genetic became fallacies. It was wrong to consider either the poet or the reader in relation to the poem. The poem was an "object," "a verbal icon," "a well-wrought urn," an "autotelic" entity. Affected readers were also dismissed—Shelley could always be summoned to warn readers not to fall upon the thorns of life and bleed. There were the verbal object and the Critic, who did not read but analyzed. And we believed that, then.

Once again we must pause to stress certain implications of what we have been seeing. We have now discovered that a genre may be not only the founding genre of a poetics, so reflecting poetic practice and assumptions about what poetry is. Genres may also be stressed—or hidden—as bases for historical alterations in poetic practice and ideas about poetry. Finally, genres may also be used, which is also to say adapted and even misused, as bases for critical as distinguished from poetic systems. The preface to *Lyrical Ballads* has been the example from which these inferences are drawn, but there is no lack of other evidence.

Lyric conceptions of literature have often played a hidden role in criticism of writing in other genres. Only in Japan have varieties of narrative and drama been harmoniously related to lyric—because the lyric assumptions were not held dogmatically and yielded or were modified in the presence of distinguished practice in other genres. Or, it may be said that ways were found to define narrative and drama in terms particularly hospitable to lyric.

Otherwise, it is in principle a problem for affective-expressive poetics to account adequately for narrative and drama. Just as it is a problem for mimetic poetics to account adequately for narrative and lyric.

There are examples near us. It has been the strength and the weakness—the exciting misfit—of many recent discussions of narrative that they have used theories based on language. Since literature, including narrative, obviously uses words as its medium, attention to language can hardly be deemed perverse. But to base a theory radically upon language is, as we have seen, to make lyric presumptions. The *nouvelle critique*, now no longer new, has been many things. Particularly as practiced in North America and specifically as exemplified by Deconstruction in its varieties, it has shown itself more and more a kind of language-based Formalism that grew out of Anglo-American New Criticism, which it fought every inch of the field. "Reading" is the legitimate though unfilial child of "Analysis" and, *mutatis mutandis*, French versions have involved a similar revolt against the Academy while yet employing, as "all the world" knows, an advanced model of that familiar tool, *explication de texte.*

Those are obvious and now historical features. For a wider view of this lyric-based critical revisionism with narrative as object, we must step back from the concerns of the last generation, seeking to grasp issues in a comparative way that is at once theoretical and historical. This requires intercultural evidence, rather than the simply intracultural, Eurocentric understandings.

Until recently, our metaphors for narrative were dominantly diachronic. They still are for many people, and the fact is that studies of narrative far more often concern time than space. We may *proclaim* that narrative is linguistically or textually synchronic. But when we come to write about it in detail, we cannot avoid temporalities. For time is like a river, as they said tirelessly in the Renaissance, and the course of narrative resembles the temporal current. Efforts to catch that flow in the net of language have yielded many a fish to fry, but meanwhile the narrative river has taken its own unimpeded course through the mesh.

The extolling of written language in recent criticism is devout and yet in bad faith. The rejection of a supposedly poisonous "logocentricism," or devotion to speech, appropriates from two sources that had to be denied or overlooked. One source is Ferdinand de Saussure, the linguist whose synchronic semiotics was appropriated by the *nouvelle critique* but whose belief in the priority of spoken language had to be rejected. The other source is lyricism. It too must be placed under erasure, lest its positive assumptions be allowed to brighten forth.

To use the twisted semiotics and the twisted lyricism upon narrative is to presume failure. It involves suspicion, of any agency other than the suspector. What is analytically appropriate to a semiotics of lyric meaning is analytically distorting when it is used with the presumption of (particularly) narrative meaninglessness. Language has been rendered into the perpetually deferred meaninglessness of "textuality." What is analytically appropriate to the intensification of moment in lyric is analytically distorting when applied to the larger, looser, less consistent narrative continuum.

This leads to suspicion of the author, who cannot be trusted either to say what is meant or to mean what is said. This is a legacy widely, bountifully derived from Deconstruction. It adds to the Cretan paradox another conundrum: Trust me—trust nobody. The cream of the jest is that whereas the author is impotent and guilty, the "reader" is potent and bears no responsibility. The "reader" does not trust the author, but as author of a "reading" the reader requires trust. As the Australian writer Michael Wilding puts it, to some of us there are "preferred ironies and negativities and all those safe doubts."[26] This passion, and the death of a dear friend. . . .

In addition to the lyric-based concern with language, many recent discussions of narrative have been getting at something far more basic and long-standing in western thought about literature. This can be termed the practices by which narrative "represents" or questions about its ability to "represent." The dispute has been whether narrative can or cannot convey such things as people, the world, meaning. We have learned a great deal in the course of these discussions, especially about literary conventionalism, about "realism" as a period-bound style, for example. But the issue of representation was not suddenly born twenty or thirty years ago. It has been in western poetics, with its base in drama, from the beginning.

In terms of comparative poetics, the question whether narrative represents or fails to represent requires a prior question. Why should narrative be expected to represent at all? Why should it submit to radicals of drama any more than to those of lyric?

There is one important (if insufficient) reason. It involves the prior assumption of traditional poetics of all kinds, that philosophically realist position holding that the world and people in it are not only real but knowable, susceptible to aesthetic as well as other cognition. The anti-realist position in western literature and criticism has aggregated many theorists, especially those whose premise has been that language is the basis of all understanding, or rather of inherent human misunderstanding.

There are two dilemmas here. The first was the strong suit of that recent criticism. There is simply no way to show that what is postulated in language has referential truth status, unless one starts from a prior premise. Even someone willing to entertain that premise must admit that we can know only as our minds are equipped to know. In another world, if it exists and if it somewhat resembles our own, creatures like ourselves may mow the grass, not to keep it in trim, but to keep it from singing too loudly.

That very constraint sets the second, more serious dilemma. As Buddhists, who have really questioned the real, recognized, to say that all is illusion applies to the very statement itself, and two further stages of dialectic were required to get things right. (See note 21.) As a simplistic classroom statement, to say that literature is indeterminate means merely that interpretations will differ.

To say, however, with anything approaching logical rigor that literature is indeterminate is to hold that we have nothing to discuss. Criticism,

---

[26] Wilding, 1975:171. Not inappropriately, he is also a critic of Milton and—*Hudibras*.

theory, and literary history all have no ground for existence. Nothing whatsoever can be determined logically or practically *about* what cannot be determined. And to say that literature is indeterminate because it is based on language, and above all to say "Language is indeterminate," falsifies the very statement about language being made in language.

Any assertion, any predication—any sentence, article, or book—rests on the presumption that a declaration is sufficiently true. Some shrink from that in words but not in what they say. Even the pragmatist, asserting that the best we can hope for is what will be useful for our purposes, makes an assertion resting not at all on utility but entirely on the truth of the predication that utility suffices.

It cannot be said often enough that we know only as we are able to know, whatever the adequacy of that knowing is, whatever the unknowable degree of correspondence with what is outside our minds. But we must also remind ourselves that that ability to know is all that we are given, that others of our race talk as if they know in the same way we do, that in practice we necessarily act as if our knowledge is sufficient, and that one of those actions is what we say, as another is what we write. Besides those vast spaces that terrified Pascal and symbolize what I do not know, much of what I know is wrong, or if right, often right for the wrong reasons. Since, like others, I tend to judge those others by myself, I find it surprising that the pessimistic critics of the recent past often found so many problems with important writers and so seldom problems within their own fence. It also puzzles me that many of those who sought to break down so many familiar distinctions yet held that language and writing are separated from life. Where else we are to situate them remains unknown. It is literature *and the rest of life* with which we are concerned.

LYRIC AS MATRIX AND SURROGATE GENRE

Let us return to the fundamental historical premise of the first chapter. With one exception lyric is the foundation genre of the world's explicit poetic systems and is the implicit basis of others. Why narrative never serves as a foundation genre is something of a mystery. There is that semi-exception in Japan, for which the evidence will be given in the next chapter. What requires attention here is the role of lyric in the absence, abeyance, or dormancy of the other genres.

We have already observed that Aristotle's *Poetics* was lost rather early, recovered by the Alexandrians, and acquired by the Arabs. Lacking a drama of their own, the Arabs naturally lyricized Aristotle, the version they made available to the rest of the west in Latin. It should not be thought that all the essentials of mimesis were lost. As the Miltons were fond of pointing out, the only biblical reference to poets (Acts 17:23) referred to Greek dramatists. And a version of drama was conceived of in terms of the Ciceronian or, more generally, the Academic dialogue (Behrens, 1940). Above all, the prior premise of mimesis remained unshaken. The realist assumption of the reality, knowability, and describability of the world and the people in it is as traditional in lyric- as in drama-based poetics.

There is, however, another line of literary practice that cannot be so explained. This is didactic literature, which achieves some dominance (in the west) during the Middle Ages and appears intermittently thereafter. The purpose of didactic writing is less to say how things and people are than how they ought to be. When mimesis was fully recovered in the Renaissance, didacticism was harmonized with it by Neoplatonic means. Other means were devised later: the *belle nature* of French classicism, the party line of socialist realism, and so forth. But there was a period of centuries in the west when didacticism was *not* harmonized with mimesis. There was a time when that which was not conducive to proper teaching was frowned upon as mere entertainment or repressed as immoral writing.

Recognition that didacticism could be accommodated to revived mimesis, and in part on realist grounds, does not identify the poetics of didacticism. A distinction must be drawn between literary and nonliterary didacticism in the west. The nonliterary versions originate of course in religious, philosophical, and occasionally scientific writings. We shall return to this in a moment. Literary didacticism is easily accounted for: it is founded on lyric affectivism. We need go no farther than the central affective-expressive pronouncement in western poetics: Horace's *Ars Poetica*. We need only take his *utile* as the standard. We need only take his own didactic account as a model.

Long before Horace, the Chinese had developed moral or didactic affectivism into a serious and supple hermeneutics of literature, including the kinds of history considered part of *wen*.[27] Moreover, this didacticism participated in philosophical and what was for the Chinese scientific principle, particularly the *dao*, the way of heaven or the sages. The Chinese counterpart of Horace is Lu Qi (261–303), whose *Wen Fu* is worth a glance. "Wen" is the word most closely corresponding to "literature" or "Dichtung." "Fu" is that kind of verse that is prose or prose that is verse. (See Levy, 1988, for the distinction between the fu principle and practice

[27] This is not a simple matter, as earlier discussion has indicated; see Yu, 1987:19–30, 45–46.

of the fu.) James J. Y. Liu offered a number of English paraphrases but settled on "exposition," so translating Lu's title as *Exposition on Literature*. From this "exposition" he rendered four lines near the end:

As for the functions of literature:
It is the means by which all principles are known;
It expands over ten thousand ages so that no obstacles remain,
And spans over a million years to form a bridge.   (Liu, 1975:20–21)

Literature combines with the loftiest philosophical ideas, including the bases of morality and science. And again, as with Horace, Lu's own work exemplifies the very didacticism that he attributes to literature. In a special emphasis of its affectivism, lyricism is the matrix of didacticism.

A similar conjunction occurred in the western Middle Ages, when biblical interpretation was brought to bear on pagan literature—on Virgil and, most stronghandedly because most necessarily, on Ovid. Various numbers of senses of Scripture were devised, along with various names for them. But the kind most favored until the Reformation was the moral ("moralia," i.e., "quid agas," what you should do, how you should behave). By these means the *Aeneid* became the model of a human life span, and Ovid's sordid tale of Myrrha and her father became a warning against incest.

It was not *difficult* to reconcile the moral biblical interpretation with Horatian affectivism. It was necessary. The same urge is evident in Lu Qi and could be shown from Korean evidence. Japan provides a limiting case, for as has already been mentioned, Japanese affectivism is marked by its involvement both of the poet and the reader and by its remarkable reluctance to feature morality in its affectivism. Significantly, there is no Japanese didactic literature of importance except for Buddhist writing and writing in Chinese. There is no *Ars Poetica* or *Wen Fu*. Downright prose is the medium for such ends.

In short, when didacticism was necessary, its poetic was provided by lyric affectivism. When mimesis was fully recovered, didacticism was harmonized with it, although the lyric always existed as a means of support, as it remained throughout the centuries in China and Korea. Given the fact that didacticism, like mimesis and affective-expressive poetics, rested on the prior realist premise, and given the fact that it was indebted to lyric poetics and compatible with mimesis, and given finally the fact of the intercultural nature of the evidence, there is no need to find a separate compartment for the view of literature as *docta*.

We may now turn to a contrasting issue, that of the absence of a poetics based on narrative. Here it is not the presence of practice that calls for explanation, but the absence of explanation of narrative itself. As it happens, there is a particularly striking western example of a narrative poet devising a poetics that is fully integrated into the plot. In the next chapter we shall see something similar in Japanese literature, albeit with remarkably different results.

One of the world's great narrative achievements is all too little recognized. Middle High German epic poetry is skillful, varied, remarkably intelligent, and very moving. Two of the greatest of these poets were also arch-rivals. Wolfram von Eschenbach may be represented by his *Niebelungenlied* and Gottfried von Straussburg by his *Tristan*. Each narrative (each lyric, drama) deserves a poetics doing it justice, and one of the surprising things about Gottfried is that he supplies it in a so-called excursus on literature.

A whole episode is devoted to Tristan's investiture as a knight.[28] After an allegory of certain virtues as tailors of the knightly clothes, Gottfried turns to dyers, that is, to epic poets. He names Heinrich von Veldeke(n), Hartmann von Aue, and Bligger von Steinach; he either does refer to (Hatto, 1967:105; 367–68) or probably does not refer to (Closs, 1944:4636 n.) his enemy, Wolfram von Eschenbach. (Recent opinion is better represented by Hatto.) Hartmann is mentioned first, as one who "dyes and adorns his tale through with words and sense" (Hatto:105; "mit worten und mit sinnen / durchvärwet und durchzieret!"—4622–23). Later we hear that there are "other dyers" (p. 106; "värwaere meer"—4689), with Bligger and Heinrich mentioned.

Gottfried does not stop with the dyers but goes on to include the nightingales (p. 106; "nahtegalen"—4749), naming Reinmar von Hagenau and Walther von der Vogelweide as examples, of course, of lyric poets. Nobody has any difficulty in understanding why a poet of lyrics, especially lyrics set to music, should be called a nightingale. But even if the term "dyers" participates in some sense in the allegory of the tailors, it is not immediately apparent why Gottfried should apply the name of so humble a craft to his own art of narrative.

The word itself, "värwaere," is the Middle High German ancestor of modern "Färber," which is obviously derived as a noun of agency from the verb "färben," derived in turn from the noun "Farbe," or "color." The concepts of dyers and colors are crucial to Gottfried's poetics and therefore require some account.

---

[28] "Episode" refers to ll.4587–5038. I cannot enter into matters of text. Many older editions omit the "episode" or do not distinguish it as a separate entity. I follow Closs, 1944:30–43 and Hatto, 1967:104–10. My remarks will also fail to honor the complexity of the episode, but my sense of the ironic context is owed to Michael Curschmann. In the text, Closs is cited by line number and Hatto by page number.

Gottfried "was well read in Latin, French, and German literature" (Hatto, 1967:11), so it is natural to connect his metaphor of the dyers to the *colores* of Latin usage. These "colors"—styles, tones, choice words, embellishments—feature repeatedly in Roman rhetoric.[29] Quintilian offers a locus classicus for "color" in the rhetorical sense: "No single style serves the exordium, statement of fact [narrationis], arguments, digression, and peroration" ("non unus color . . . servabitur"; *Institutes*, 12, 10, 71). Gottfried is far from being an orator, eloquent though he may become. But he "had a subtle, scathing wit, and we shall never plumb the depths of his irony" (Hatto, 12). It is difficult to think of anything further that he needed to learn of rhetoric.

Let us return to the passage involved, to Tristan's investiture. One critic has envisioned the scene in rather fanciful pictorial terms. In a flanking left-hand panel are the busy tailors, balanced to the right by Cassandra weaving clothes and Vulcan making armor.

Now the great central fresco (cf. *Tristan* 4261–4895). In the foreground we see a procession of poets—two groups, one approaching from the left, the other from the right. Both stand in a lavish landscape, the trees heavy with flowers and foliage. On the left are four figures, the narrative poets: the first is Hartmann von Aue. He is crowned with a laurel wreath and carries in his arms cloth representing poetry, which he has colored and dyed through and through. . . . The second is not a member of the procession, but skulks in his own private wasteland surrounded by emblems of the charlatan [a hostile reference to Wolfram]. The third is Blicker von Steinach. He stands at a magic well where fairies are making the garments of which he will make the words of his poems. The fourth, Heinrich von Veldeke, is depicted as a tailor of meanings . . . , carefully trimming them to fit his poems, and behind him the winged horse, Pegasus, the guiding spirit of his inspiration, rises up. In the group on the right, two dominant figures precede a host of sketchily drawn followers. The first is Reinmar von Hagenau. He carries the lyre of Orpheus. The second, Walther von der Vogelweide, carries a banner with a nightingale, the emblem of lyric poets. . . .[30]

---

[29] On the general topic of Gottfried's knowledge and use of rhetoric, see Christ, 1977, especially "Rhetorik als Instrument einer Wirkungspoetik zu Gottsfrieds 'Tristan' " (pp. 14–16) and all of the second chapter, "Gottfried und die Rhetorik, Poetik und Dichtung des Mittelalters" (pp. 17–50), particularly "Die 'artes poeticae' des Mittelalters" (pp. 34–41).

[30] Jaeger, 1977:139–40, part of a chapter on "The Two-fold Invocation" (of Jupiter and the Christian God) in this episode. Jaeger's chapter as a whole is not as fanciful as the scene described in the quotation. The scene is premised on an earlier discussion (pp. 49–62) holding that this episode on "literary excursus" is based on a sustained allegory of tailors. In my view that is overdone (some details in the "fresco" are inaccurate). We do have *fabric* detail

One matter stands out: there are two kinds of poets, those dyers who color narratives and those nightingales who sing lyrics. (Roswitha and her comedies seem unknown to Gottfried.) It may well be that the nightingales "are connected with the narrative poets through the images of sources of inspiration" (Jaeger, 1977:55), but the question is why they are there at all.

To deal with that, we must take recourse to what has been dealt with earlier in this chapter. That is, the answer lies in repeated diction ignored by the commentators. Once again, here are the two lines on Hartmann's dyeing:

> mit worten und mit sinnen,
> durchvärwet und durchzieret! (4622–23)
>
> (With words and with meanings
> he thoroughly dyes and adorns!)

The range of significance of "sinne" is not easily limited, any more than for its modern German counterpart. But it obviously refers to matters of thought and feeling. In the whole passage, there are numerous uses of expressions for verbal means (e.g., "worten," as above) and for conceptions or conceptual powers ("sinnen," as above). Including variants, here is a brief accounting. First, "worten" and related terms with the number of occurrences in this episode of investiture.

worten 15	bluome 8
zunge 8	ris (sprays) 2
stimme 2	vogelsanc 1
sprechen 1	

There are somewhat fewer, but still conspicuously clustered and repeated, terms for conceptual matters.

sinnen 12	wiisheit 5
herz 4	

The climactic passage for joining items in both sets of terms is that celebrating the last-named "dyer," Heinrich (ll. 4736–58). His is the glory of being first in German narrative:

> the glory of having grafted the first slip [riis] on the tree of German poetry [in tiutescher zungen]. From this have sprouted branches whence the blossoms [bluomen] came from which they [Heinrich and ensuing narrative poets] drew the cunning of their masterly inventions. And now this skill has spread its boughs so far and has been so diversely

---

from tailors to dyers, but the dyeing is the central image for narrative poets, as that of nightingales is for the lyric poets, with no attention to tailors (or dyers) whatsoever.

trained that all who are now writing break blossoms [bluomen] and sprays [riisen] to their hearts' content [wunsch], in words [worten] and melodies [wiisen]. (Hatto, 1967:107)[31]

In its central terms and in its botanical metaphor, this passage is uncannily like the opening of the preface to the *Kokinshū*. The two sets of terms also remind us of a succession of lyric-based poetics: Horace's *Ars Poetica*, the great preface to *The Classic of Poetry*, the preface to the *Kokinshū* once again, and the preface to *Lyrical Ballads*.

Without questioning that Gottfried knew of the *colores* of Cicero and Quintilian, it can be pointed out that Horace also provides a locus classicus for the Latin term (*Ars Poetica*, ll. 86–87):

Descriptas servare vices operumque colores
cur ego si nequeo ignoroque poeta salutor?

(If from ignorance I fail to observe the distinctions
of performance and style, why am I hailed as a poet?)[32]

The remarkable thing about the inclusion of the nightingales with the dyers is that those lyric birds were necessary if the dyeing poets of narrative were to have any poetics. Rhetoric (whence we derive our word "narration") helps Gottfried explain his dyers but was insufficient to found his poetics of narrative. For that a version of the affective-expressive or lyric poetics had to be devised, and the Horatian model (with perhaps a hint from Walther von der *Vogel*weide?) was to hand. It is indeed very striking that a poet so magnificently gifted should explain his narrative art in the terms of lyric. So far is it true that when the going grows hard—and for some reason basing a poetics on narrative has proven hardest of all—lyric is drawn on as a surrogate.

Questions arise. Is Gottfried's "excursus" an originative poetics? Is this the much-sought-after poetic system founded on narrative? The answer to both is clearly negative. Gottfried adapts Horatian affectivism and expressivism, and to do so he must include the nightingales with the dyers. His "excursus" really explains lyric rather than narrative poetry. In a sense the passage is a profound disappointment to a reader seeing in it a missed chance, an eluded opportunity. But it is certainly one reader's guess that the ironic Gottfried knew perfectly well what he was up to.

[31] Closs, 1944, glosses "bluomen" in line 4644 to mean "colores, rhetorical figures," and refers to the usage in this longer passage.

[32] Horace's phrase, "operumque colores" is a hard one. Here is a sample of renderings: "well marked shifts and shades of poetic forms" (Loeb); "subject and shades of style" (Modern Library); "form and tone" (Smith Palmer Bowie); and "clear-cut distinctions and poetic genres" (Walter Jackson Bate).

There are a few simple but useful corollaries. Talk of "representation," "referent," or "fiction" presumes a mimetic legacy based on drama. Talk of "language" or of Gottfried's "sinne" and "herz" presumes an affective-expressive legacy based on lyric. If song betrays Gottfried's dyer's hand, it does so with an increment. Like Einstein's "Herr Gott," Gottfried is devious ("raffiniert") enough, but he is not evil ("boshaft") in his use of lyric to explain narrative. In that he stands in contrast to many contemporary students of narrative, to those at least who have used their vision of untrustworthy language to prove narrative unstable, unreliable. Is there no choice, then, in studying narrative but to apply or misapply either a mimetic poetics based on drama or an affective-expressive poetics based on lyric?

We may recall Shinkei's sentimental, respectful account of Shunzei's staying up late at night to recite the words of lyrics that moved him. That is a brief narrative about the affective experience of attending to lyric expression. The lyric texts were all encoded in Shunzei's capacious mind, and his apostrophe to the bird he fearfully longed to hear in his poem about thinking of the past shows how the intense presence of lyric may run through past, present, and future with all the speed of thought. To value the intense present moment of thinking of the past offers the character of lyric. It is another enduring human tendency to ask what happened next after Shunzei heard the bird sing. That would take us, in Japanese terms, to a *Shunzei Monogatari, The Story of Shunzei*. It takes us to narrative.

❏ _____

CHAPTER 4

Narrative

The Chronicles of Japan and [other his-
tories] are a mere fragment of the
whole truth. It is your [*monogatari*]
that fill in the details.

— Murasaki Shikibu

An end to art is conceivable only
when humankind is no longer able to
distinguish true and false, good and
evil, beauty and ugliness, present and
future.

— Herbert Marcuse

AS OPPOSED to a "dramatic" incident or a "lyric" moment, the getting
on of "narrative," its movement to an end, seems to be no great thing.
Compared to the allure of the "dramatic" and "lyric," mere narrative
seems to tell us little these days, if we rely on reports, except how we rub
on in life. The excitement lately seems to have derived more from writing
about how little excitement there is. It is true that one hears, well, a different story when the novelists talk. It seems to be agreed that there were
once giants in the earth but not whether that was only once upon a time.
From time to time someone reminds us that "story" once was ambiguous
as to whether it meant literary narrative or history, as in Italian and Spanish still.

Given this basically realist view and the challenges to it, it is hardly
surprising that recent questions about where, what, and if we *are* should
involve doubts in western and in some other literary practice as well as in
some literary theories. Once reality, ordinary sense to our lives, becomes
the issue, narrative wonderfully concentrates the mind.

The clenched mind soon discovers hazards and their attending excite-
ments. On comparative grounds, this third genre is harder to get at, because there is no generative poetics based on it. We do not have the guides
that drama offers—the estrangement and engagement of representation
in the theater. Nor do we have the bases in language and affectivism at-

tested to by poetic systems founded on lyric. And yet—how much has been written on old narrative this while!

FULFILLED CONTINUITY

The effort to separate literature from the rest of life has required the recent battle to prove that narrative fails to make sense. The effort is not one that shows much chance of success, judging by the evidence of a comparative nature. In principle, that should involve all three east Asian countries, since in their originative poetics narrative history was included with lyricism. Lyric was the senior partner, however, as is shown by the fact that all lyrics written by Chinese literati were considered part of literature (or *wen*; Kor. *mun*; J. *bun*), whereas only certain kinds of history were. We do have, however, that remarkable fact of Japanese literary history: in a century after the foundation of a generative poetics using lyric, there appeared the greatest work in the literature, *The Tale of Genji* (*Genji Monogatari*). Not only is it great narrative and by a woman, the latter unique among the works thought greatest in their languages, but it contains discussions about art as perfectly natural episodes in the narrative.

One of the discussions concerns the art of *monogatari* or narrative itself. The hero, Radiant Genji, has managed to rescue the daughter of his oldest friend by a woman each had had as a lover—first the friend, then Genji—from what had promised to be disaster for someone so sensitive and gifted. Now that she is established in his palace as a long-lost daughter, Genji is having difficulty keeping his amorous hands from her. To avoid that, and to lull away the monsoon season, she—Tamakazura—has immersed herself in *monogatari*, what the translation that follows calls "romances." Readers acquainted with the work will recall the second chapter, in just the same close and damp monsoon season, in which four young men discuss women. Such contexts help explain Genji's gamesome air.

What follows is not set forth in the method of an Aristotle or a Kant. It is rather the part of this *monogatari* that is about the art of *monogatari*, and in comparative terms it is the closest thing we possess to an originative poetics founded on narrative. I shall omit the first half, in which Genji teases Tamakazura by calling *monogatari* deceitful, trivial, even if we can find in them "real emotions and plausible chains of events." After that teasing, he justifies literary narrative in terms she could not have envisioned and that are truly extraordinary.

> He laughed. "I have been rude and unfair to your romances, haven't I? They have set down and preserved happenings from the age of the

gods to our own. *The Chronicles of Japan* and the rest are a mere fragment of the whole truth. It is your romances that fill in the details.

"We are not told of things that happened to specific people exactly
as they happened; but the beginning is when there are good things and
bad things, things that happen in this life which one never tires of seeing and hearing about, things which one cannot bear not to tell of and
must pass on for all generations. If the storyteller wishes to speak well,
then he chooses the good things; and if he wishes to hold the reader's
attention he chooses bad things, extraordinarily bad things. Good and
bad things alike, they are things of this world and no other.

"Writers in other countries approach the matter differently. Old stories in our own are different from new. There are differences in the
degree of seriousness. But to dismiss them as lies is itself to depart from
the truth. Even in the writ which the Buddha drew from his noble
heart are parables, devices for pointing obliquely at the truth. The
Greater Vehicle is full of them, but the general burden is always the
same. The difference between enlightenment and confusion is of about
the same order as the difference between the good and the bad in a
romance. If one takes the generous view, then nothing is empty and
useless."[1]

"Things of this world and no other"—Murasaki Shikibu does not take
the net of language to her narrative river.

In the first paragraph of the translation quoted, Genji associates *monogatari* with *The Chronicles of Japan* (*Nihon Shoki* or *Nihongi*), then the most
valued work of Japanese history. The realist premise emerges very clearly.
In the next paragraph ("We are not told . . .") Genji associates narrative
with the largely lyric based affective-expressive poetics. Interestingly
enough, narrative requires a *moral* affectivism that Tsurayuki's lyric-
founded poetics did not mention.

Why should narrative require a basis in moral distinctions that lyric
does not? The answer surely lies in the assumption of the relation between
narrative not simply with lyric to the one side but with history to the
other. The presumption can be found in other terms in modern neo-
Marxist writing. As Jürgen Habermas writes: "In sociological textbooks
a distribution into subsystems—into economics and politics, into society
and culture, into science, art, and religion—receives too easily the bless-
ing of eternity: it allows us to forget that within itself a constellation of
'spheres of value' is reflected, a constellation which, as Max Weber well

---

[1] The translation is Edward Seidensticker's in Murasaki Shikibu, 1976: vol. 1:437–38. The
chapter is the twenty-fifth, "Fireflies" ("Hotaru"), for those who have Waley's less accurate
translation.

knew, has only a historically defined significance" (Habermas, 1978:7). Herbert Marcuse put it somewhat more apocalyptically: "An end to art is conceivable only when humankind is no longer able to distinguish true and false, good and evil, beauty and ugliness, present and future. That would be the state of complete barbarity at the zenith of civilization."[2] The implications of using or not using historical assumptions are very great, and no wise person will relinquish the assumptions without consideration of the cost of giving them up.

Murasaki Shikibu understood such things, as is shown by what follows ("Writers in other countries . . ."). We first observe that the earlier concern with history here leads to a relativism that is astonishing so early. (In English it does not appear till Dryden.) There is also cultural relativism: writers in other countries have approached narrative somewhat differently. What Murasaki Shikibu knew about Korea is itself unknown, at least to me. But it is clear that she knew some Chinese classics and, unlike Tamakazura, could have read *The Chronicles of Japan*, which were written in Chinese. It is not clear whether she read any Chinese stories. There were a few shorter ones that had been brought back from China by earlier embassies (some since lost in China). But she would have known of their low repute in China and could hardly have taken them very seriously. (The first great work of Chinese prose narrative—*The Journey to the West* or *Xiyuji*—did not appear until five centuries later.) It is certain that she would have had Chinese historiography in mind, and just possibly some Six Dynasties tales. The relativism extends to Japan: we write differently now from before.

We recognize the stakes involved when Genji turns from history to relate *monogatari* to the Buddhist scriptures. There are two main interpretations of this passage. The one followed in the translation treats *monogatari* as expedients like the parables in the *Lotus Sutra*, the idea being that the merciful Buddha uses every possible means to make enlightenment available to all sentient creatures. From his initial jests about deceptions and silly writing, Genji comes to associate *monogatari* successively with the most esteemed work of Japanese history, with Chinese historiography, with earlier Japanese *monogatari*, and with the sutras. It is an impressive pedigree.

Reflecting on this episode, we observe not only that it fits into and expands the affective-expressive poetics that Murasaki Shikibu inherited. More importantly for comparative purposes, it also assumes that fictional prose narrative possesses the philosophical realism of history (even while allowing for historical and cultural relativism) and by analogy no little of

[2] Quoted but not cited in Habermas, 1978:98.

the truth of the Buddha's teaching. As this suggests, accounting for the
fictionality of her *monogatari* seems to have been the author's chief aim in
this episode. In a passage just before that quoted, she has Genji begin with
teasing Tamakazura unmercifully over the frivolous deceits of *monogatari*.
In the passage, Genji uses two words for lies, seeming to distinguish between them in order to use one to mean fiction. But as the account continues, there is not only the claim to truth in fiction that writers (if not
critics) are given to make but, even more, the astonishing claim that the
fictional is factual to the degree that history is.

We hear nothing of Aristotle's sense of truth in art on the basis of probability or necessity, and there is nothing like his opposition between history with details and literature with universals. (Murasaki Shikibu's universals derive both from her lyric-based poetics and from religion.) We
must be clear that Murasaki Shikibu does *not* say that history resembles
monogatari in being fictional, but that *monogatari* has the essential properties of history.

The unquoted conclusion to this episode brilliantly stresses the connection between narrative and history. Genji couches a proposal to make love
in terms of his and Tamakazura's creating together a *monogatari* of an un-
exampled kind ("tagui naki monogatari"). Not only would there then be
written *monogatari* in her chamber but an enacted one. This of course relates to the close of the remarks about Buddhism and the analogy of literature to expedients for enlightenment. Significantly enough, Genji uses
a *poem* to accuse Tamakazura for being unfilial, and she decisively fends
him off with a poem accusing him of being unparental. Both say that
their accusation is founded on evidence of *historical* research. Even lyric,
the trump card in the culture, is made to sort with history in this discussion, as indeed it does in the culture. Sooner or later, anyone interested in
narrative must deal with the claims and issues raised by this first poetics
of the art.

Other matters that seem to me to get to the heart of narrative can be
found in this monsoon day's monologue. For a comparative theory of
narrative, the most important passage involves three consecutive sentences. After conceding to Tamakazura that he has been unfair to her
much loved *monogatari*, Genji says of them: "They have set down and
preserved happenings from the age of the gods to our own. *The Chronicles
of Japan* and the rest are a mere fragment of the whole truth. It is your
[*monogatari*] that fill in details." The first sentence assumes that narrative
involves continuity, and the next two that it involves fulfillment. *The
Chronicles of Japan* does no less than deal with the native pantheon, incorporate various legends from peoples vanquished by the dominant people,
tell a national foundation myth, and relate the history of various reigns

from mythical to historical monarchs. As we have seen in an earlier chapter, the then-reigning monarch, Ichijō, remarked that the author of *The Tale of Genji* was learned and had read the *Chronicles*.

In the next two sentences Murasaki Shikibu has Genji claim that *monogatari* should continue that continuum, fulfilling history. *Monogatari* not only continue, he says, but also fill out history, giving it wholeness, completeness.

From this passage, but not only from it, we may derive the simple description of narrative as fulfilled continuity. We may speak of narrative movement—moving, and moving us, by continuing to a replete fulfillment. Narrative has its values as well as its motion, being moved as well as moving. Certainly that will be argued here. Of the two terms, fulfillment and continuum, the latter is so much the more complex that it seems reasonable to discuss fulfillment first.[3]

In his comparison of *monogatari* with Buddhist scriptures, Genji refers to "The Greater Vehicle," which is to say Mahāyāna Buddhism, that kind—as opposed to Hinayāna (the Lesser Vehicle)—which was followed in southern and southeastern Asia. The Hinayāna scriptures were taken as a former stage of teaching that was developed and fulfilled by the Mahāyāna, with which they would finally become one Teaching. Buddhist enlightenment is of course the point, the end sought, as salvation is by Christians.

These remarks that the author gives her hero involve a kind of literal anagogy, an unallegorical spiritual meaning of the fulfillment *monogatari* offers. That is to say that an end, an entelechy is posited. In terms specified by the various medieval catchverses concerning allegory, or more precisely allegoretic interpretation of the Bible, Murasaki Shikibu deals with the *Quo tendit* or *Quo tendas* sense of scripture: where things lead, where we go to, the heavenly telos. The difference for *monogatari* here, as also for a theory of narrative, is that there is no need to think fulfillment or end allegorical.

Of course allegorical narratives do exist, and our tendency has been to assume that, like *The Faerie Queene* and *The Pilgrim's Progress*, those allegories represent distinct worlds, one apparent, seeming (to use Spenser's favorite verb) and the other metaphysical, far beyond. It has been argued with great learning that a Chinese *xiaoshuo* ("the classical Chinese novel")

---

[3] Two well-known studies deal in their ways with what I term fulfillment. B. H. Smith, 1968, may be concerned with lyric, but much of what she has to say applies to narrative and drama as well. Kermode, 1967, is mainly concerned with narrative. In the kind of topics I raise, my debt will be clear, as will my effort to seek out comparative evidence beyond the Eurocentric.

may also be allegorical, if on *other* grounds.[4] Yet, allegorical or not, a narrative must tend to some end. Talking about drama, Aristotle thought an end necessary (with a beginning and middle or middles) to assure wholeness.

There is an apparent paradox here. It is exceedingly difficult to think of plays or lyrics we think important that are incomplete for reasons other than textual fragmentation or the person from Porlock, whereas our narratives (particularly in verse) are often incomplete, stopped. That paradox can be raised a degree. The requirement of mimesis for completion has left behind nonetheless such abbreviated and yet important works as the *Pharsalia*, the *Heptameron*, and *The Faerie Queene*—not to mention many glorious Romantic ruins. On the other hand, it is difficult to think of Asian counterparts. Not all of a work may be extant, but from the oldest literature of all, the Sanskrit, we have narratives seemingly like the world, without end but completed. A Chinese narrative may be left incomplete, and then be completed by another hand. Such at least is generally believed to be the case with the most highly esteemed narrative, *The Dream of the Red Chamber* (*Hongloumeng*).[5] That is an exception to prove something of a Chinese rule, and it is extremely difficult to think of a Japanese narrative left incomplete.

The paradox can be resolved. The western burden of an ending has simply proved onerous, the weight of formalized mimesis too great. When the obligation is too great, it will be resisted or honored in the breach. More importantly it is a justification for many, many western works that it is simpleminded to equate the entelechy, the *quo tendit*, with a happily-ever-after or other neat completion. The wonderfully perverse genius of *Tristram Shandy* and of each of the novels in Beckett's trilogy is evident. Beckett's strong measures to spoil the endings of each novel confirm the entelechy we had discovered long before. A dark comic defiance is aimed at the very genius of narrative he finds intolerable because ineluctable in his unavailing void.

Moreover, if we inquire into the endings of Asian narratives, we shall see that the end of the *Bhagavad Gītā* or *The Tale of Genji* offers no neat, clear resolution. Indic and Japanese Buddhist thought assumes continuing

[4] Plaks, 1976, argues the case for *The Dream of the Red Chamber* (*Hungloumeng*). Anybody with an interest in allegory should study his comparative evidence. The *xiaoshuo* ("little talk") is a long Chinese narrative in prose ("the classic Chinese novel"), traditionally in 120 chapters.

[5] See the introduction by David Hawkes, Cao, 1973–86:1, 15–19, 34–42. *The Story of the Stone* (*Shitouji*) is another title for *The Dream of the Red Chamber*. In this outstanding translation, Hawkes does the first eighty chapters by Cao Qian and Minford the forty of the continuation, a rare mirroring in translation of the presumed double authorship of the original.

karmic causality until transcendent resolution after all those immense kalpas or until enlightenment. Given such deferral, completion does not sew up the strands of plot, and fulfillment does not require "the sense of an ending" or apocalypse. Something more is implied. There is always more to be told (and at extraordinary length in Sanskrit narratives). Continuing causality until long deferred enlightenment is the end, the telos from the beginning.

Moreover, as Murasaki Shikibu recognized, completion is also a matter of filling in the necessary details. The matter added after *m* need not be *n*; it may be theta or number 11. Repletion may satisfy as well as symmetry. A recipe is less important than a this-ness, a good plump quiddity. Easy progress (*festina lente*) may be happier than seizing the bell rope (*carpe diem*) to toll an end. There is no reason why the ending cannot be present in the beginning, as in *The Tale of the Heike* (*Heike Monogatari*), which opens with the slow majesty of a dead march, adapting the rhythm of poetic passages in *nō* to prose.

> At the Jetavana temple
> the bell gives voice
> to the impermanence of all
> as it reverberates;
> That the pairs of the teak trees
> in the hue of their flowers
> show the downfall of the splendid
> is a matter of reason;
> the magnificent ones as well
> will not long continue,
> only like a night in springtime
> when dreams are brief;
> the most stalwart ones as well
> are overthrown in the end;
> as those caught up by the tempest,
> they are blown away like dust.[6]

Indic temple bells (sounding the departure of the Buddha) reverberate in Japanese history and literary history. The beginning sounds the end. *The Tale of the Heike* goes on to treat of dozens of people involved in the downfall, described with surprising affection, of the haughty yet courtly Heike before the severer Genji forces. Those victors, too, like "the most

---

[6] Taken with some revisions from Miner-Odagiri-Morrell, 1985:163. Readers will recognize in this opening something akin to the declaration of epic argument in the western classical line—*Paradise Lost*, for example.

stalwart" Heike, like golden lads and girls, will take their turns to come to dust.

Not all narratives have their end in their beginning as this one does. Few are as symmetrical as Dante's *Comedy*, whether in large design or such touches as ending each part with the same word, "stars" (*stelle*). But a moving tendency or end, repletion or fulfillment, constitute hallmarks of narrative.[7]

The other hallmark considered here is the more complex moving, the continuum. Let us begin with a distant sighting. From the distance of the other two genres, we observe certain obvious things. Narrative shares in properties of drama and lyric, and they have in varying degree the tendency or entelechy of narrative, as also the continuity. Like music, all literature—including the one-liners in *The Greek Anthology* or *haiku*—has some continuity. But for narrative, moving continuance is so crucially important as to be a difference in degree that establishes the difference in kind. As Genji says of *monogatari*, "They have set down and preserved happenings from the age of the gods to our own."

We have seen in the preceding chapter how narrative could be incorporated in lyric, and we can quickly spot a narrative interval in drama. Sometimes it has less than full appeal, as in awkward exposition, too much reliance on messengers or chorus, or reading of documents aloud. But often it is very effective. A particularly good example occurs in *Othello* (1,3), where the noble Moor, accused of using charms or drugs to bewitch Desdemona to love him, defends himself before the Duke. The passage is too long to quote in full. Fortunately, it is a familiar one, and a few lines from the beginning, middle, and end ought to assuage the ghost of Aristotle.

> Her father lov'd me; oft invited me;
> Still [always] question'd me the story of my life
> From year to year, the battles, sieges, fortunes
> That I have pass'd. . . .
> These to hear
> Would Desdemona seriously incline;
> But still the house-affairs would draw her thence,
> Which ever as she could with haste dispatch,

[7] Here I must confess that although Boccaccio's formal design in the *Decameron* is obviously symmetrical, and although each story and even each day has a certain logic, I am baffled in my attempt to understand its thematic point or entelechy. Montaigne, Sterne— even Pascal, for all the uncertainties of the order of the *Pensées*—are as clear to me as the *Decameron* is mystifying. This confession should assist in giving some nuance to words like "fulfillment" and "end."

> She'd come again . . .
> She lov'd me for the dangers I had pass'd,
> And I lov'd her that she did pity them.
> This is the only witchcraft I have us'd.
> Here comes the lady; let her witness it.

With the last line we are back into the drama proper. The narrative continuum is over and gone.

One major effect of Othello's relation is to interrupt normal stage representation when this character turns narrator. We note the shift to the past tense and the return to the present in his last line. But why should we say we feel interruption? Othello's account is part of the same play, and indeed of the very *plot* of the play.

More than those two considerations are involved, however. This is drama, and it subjects the narrative to its dominance. Although it is true that just now we have been reading Othello's lines to ourselves, silently, they were meant to be spoken in the wooden O by an actor playing Othello, and not droning on in a monotone, but gesturing, moving, changing his tone of voice, making eye-contact with now this now that character, but chiefly the Duke. In a good production, this episode will carry *dramatic* impact. Yet it is narrative, as we recognize. For although Othello's account is indeed part of the play, it differs from ordinary stage action. It differs because Shakespeare finds it convenient to interrupt the dramatic *now* to deal with a *before*. That past continuity, telling of his courtship of Desdemona, can only be narrative.

Both the play and Othello's spech within it have plots, and in fact are constituents of the same larger plot. In other words, a first conclusion we must come to is that plot is not a *distinguishing* feature of narrative: it is not the basis for distinguishing Othello's relation from the rest of the play. At this stage it is necessary to assume that we know what plot is, since not all may be discussed at once. (Of course plot will claim later attention.)

If it is not plot that enables us to distinguish Othello's narrative, what does? Hitherto in the play, matters are known to us by their representation on the stage, by the fundamental estrangement and engagement, by the makeup of the theater discussed in the second chapter. With this speech by Othello, we pause. We shift to that long-continued past tense of narrative and history, that tense of narrative in the lyrics by Donne and Herbert. Since narrative can be told in the present tense, the past tense is also not necessary to narrative. It is, therefore, what the past tense contributes (and what may be contributed also by other means) that marks Othello's speech as a narrative moment in the play. The turn to the past goes to a point from which a continuum originates and sets forth to its fulfilled end. As Murasaki Shikibu recognized, these are the crucial features of narrative. It is they, within the past tense so to speak, that enable us to distinguish a sustained narrative speech in a play that includes this recollected plot.

We also observe that Othello's status—his role in a nondramatic sense—changes. His action does not cease (or it would be a dull moment in the play). From the situation before the Duke as judge, we may say that he is testifying, pleading a legal cause. Our term "narrative" of course derives from the Roman rhetoricians' *narratio*, which is the name for that part of an oration—in *Othello* judicial rather than deliberative or epideictic—in which someone relates what the facts of the case are, testifies to what has occurred.

Quintilian distinguished three kinds of narrative for the orator, for an oration. 1. *Historia*: "exposition of actual fact" ("in qua est gestae rei expositio"). 2. *Argumentum*: "Which, though not true, has yet a certain verisimilitude" ("falsum sed vero simile"). And 3. *Fabula*: "which is not merely not true but has little resemblance to the truth" ("non a veritate modo sed a forma veritatis remota").[8]

Wherever there is narration, it is of course necessary that some figure, identified or unidentified, some *persona narrationis*, relate. What, however, is it that that narrator does which is not done by the counterpart speaker of a lyric? Both may be said to have an implied responsibility. In testifying responsibly for a continuum rather than for an intense present, the narrator enters a truth claim for what is continued. That emerges very clearly from Othello's speech (of course within the fiction of the play), and it is an important reason why a *narratio* is so important a part of an oration. Command of the truth of what has happened confers great authority. Of course we know or can imagine situations both literary and forensic in which a narrator is but partly informed, mistaken, or unreliable. One of the reasons why Othello was so effective in speaking to Desdemona, and why he is so effective with the Duke, is that he can offer "ethical proof": he narrates what he can speak of from his own experience. In a double sense he is the subject of it. This is what is meant by saying that narrative has a point of view and, in the absence of contrary evidence (such as Iago will offer), that narration takes on a strong element of historical realism.

---

[8] The translations are those of H. E. Butler in the Loeb edition, Quintilian, 1953:1, 225, *Institutes* 2, 4 (see also 5, 10). Counterparts will be found in Cicero, *De Inventione* 1, 19 and in the pseudo-Ciceronian *Ad C. Herrenium* 1, 8. It is worth noting that Quintilian considers only *historia* to be nonfictional. The low Roman opinion of drama is clear in his association of *fabula* with tragedy.

As Murasaki Shikibu has her hero say, *monogatari* are basically a kind of reliable history.

SEQUENCE AND PLOT

We have seen one example why plot cannot be identified with narrative continuance. In pursuing this issue farther it will become increasingly necessary to define what is meant by certain simple terms, a necessity leaving one so red-handed that most people avoid it entirely. There are two crucial terms in this section.

If not all narrative continuances require *plot* as a *differentia*, we must concern ourselves with whatever invariant features of continuance we can discover.[9] One is *sequence*: succession in a given order. To change the order is to alter the sequence; it is not to destroy sequentiality, which is impossible in these matters, but to make another sequence, another continuum.

Sequentiality remains as long as there is a successive order within a whole. For there to be order, there must be intelligibility, which is not only a property of the sequence arranged by somebody but also a feature dependent on conventions and mental training to discern it. Beyond the first several numbers of a Fibonacci sequence, few but mathematicians would discern the order, find it intelligible.[10]

Order (and therefore sequence, therefore narrative continuum) also presumes units and wholeness. If units cannot be discerned, there may be wholeness but no succession. One thing does not constitute a succession. Without wholeness, the succession is zero, incomplete, or infinite. Units are cognizable entities: if they do not possess a knowable whatness, a something, there is no possibility of our recognizing them.

As a fulfilled continuum, narrative requires first of all these properties of sequentiality, which is not to say that we can identify narrative with sequentiality. Plot also requires sequentiality, but plot also cannot be identified with sequentiality.[11] Nor can sequentiality be identified with narrative or plot, although it is necessary to narrative continuum, as plot is not. On the other hand, a *plotted* sequentiality is a common if not nec-

[9] Features of the ensuing argument will be found to correspond with Ricoeur, 1984–85, vol. 1, whose two parts deal, respectively, with the traditional western concepts of temporality and with history and narrative. See also Ricoeur, 1984, especially "Study 7, Metaphor and Reference." Gadamer, 1982, The Second Part, stands behind Ricoeur's as well as my remarks. I prize these works, even if they must be adjusted for intercultural purposes, as we shall see in one instance shortly.

[10] The Fibonacci sequence or numbers (1, 1, 2, 3, 5, 8, 13, etc.) is one in which the successive number is the sum of the two preceding; the mathematical proportion involved—after the first three mentioned—is "the golden ratio."

[11] For another view of this set of issues, see Valdés, 1982:ch. 10.

essary version of narrative continuum. When we come on plot in a lyric (Donne's "Venus heard me sigh this song," etc.), we think the passage narrative rather than dramatic, although plays have plots.

If sequentiality is necessary to plot but not plot to sequence, then sequentiality is the logically prior principle. *Paradise Lost* is an epic so disordered from its natural chronology that the inferable "real" chronology does not fully begin until Book 9. The plot remains the same, whatever its sequence in the narrated version.[12] Of course each possible ordering would have sequentiality, but the sequences would differ. By definition, one cannot change the sequence of a sequence without changing it, whereas one can change the sequence of a plot without altering the plot.

A second example with proof is furnished by the Chinese fictional-historical prose narrative, *The Romance of the Three Kingdoms* (*Sanguo Zhiyanyi*; the *zhi* is commonly omitted).[13] This narrative is dazzling in the clarity of its handling of three plots: affairs in the three rival kingdoms of Shu, Wu, and Wei. Two (or more) events not only can but do occur concurrently, simultaneously. All that is logically required is that different events happening at the same time happen to different people in different places, as in Wu and Wei. But narrative cannot relate two or more simultaneous events simultaneously. One must be told before the other(s). Or their parts may be interwoven (another way of saying the same thing), which is the problem so superbly dealt with in *The Three Kingdoms*. The plot would remain the same no matter what the sequence of interweaving, but any change in sequence is just that.

This logical priority of sequentiality to plot makes sequence rather than plot the radical of narrative continuance. Obviously every author of narrative will seek out the most effective sequence in which to relate the plot. By a counterpart principle, readers will find one sequential order more satisfying than another.

Western novelists have been known to fret over plot conventions, particularly the final marrying off and otherwise disposing of characters. And in the great efflorescence of study of narrative in recent years, plot has been slighted as something apparently too old-fashioned to deserve prolonged attention. One exception is Seymour Chatman who says, as clearly as one could wish, "A narrative without a plot is a logical impossibility" (Chatman, 1983:47). Although I obviously disagree with that

---

[12] See Chatman, 1983:19–20, for the Russian Formalists' distinction between "the sum total of events to be related in the narrative" (*fabula*) and "the 'order of the appearance (of the events) in the work itself' " (*sjuzet*).

[13] See *Three Kingdoms*, 1959. It is a somewhat fictionalized version of the history, *Sanguo Zhi*, and the traditional thing to say of it is that it is 70 percent history and 30 percent ficiton. The premises behind that saying challenge usual western assumptions about an either/or fact/fiction distinction.

idea, it can only promote intellectual health to have somebody say what most (western) people think, even if they find discussion of mere plot an irritation. As someone who finds great satisfaction in plotted narratives, I think it has been slighted in discussions of narrative. But I cannot persuade myself that plot is necessary to narrative.

That will require some discussion, but to clarify my emphasis, I shall enter an analogy. Just as fictionality is the common basis for *literary* (not nonverbal artistic) expression—at least in western practice; and just as fictionality is not necessary to, or identical with, what I have termed the virtual: so for plot and narrative. Plot is typically a feature of literary narrative, but it is not necessary to, or identical with, narrative, but it is not necessary to, or identical with, narrative. Of course a controverted issue cannot be decided without further definition of terms.

For reasons by no means clear, there have been few descriptions of plot. No doubt something could be learned about the range of meaning the word possesses by comparing the associated meanings of the words used for English "plot" in other languages. But we may as well face the issue as directly as possible. Apparently, Aristotle's *mythos* is of no help to us, since it had a technical meaning in Athenian dramaturgy (Else, 1967:243–44). Let us seek a minimal description. At a minimum, plot is the continuation of a group of people in places and times. By "people" is meant narrative or dramatic characters, not all of whom need be present at the outset and not all of whom need continue to the close.[14] Places and times would seem to need no defining.[15]

For a bit less minimal description of plot, it is a continuation in sequence of a sustained group of people in places and times with use of development, causality, and contingency. Some of these elements are obvious enough, but pursuit of a few may tell us some things.

Time and times, along with place and space, may need no defining, but they require discussion. (For the most distinguished contemporary discussion of time in relation to narrative see Ricoeur, 1984–85:3 vols. For cogent brevity, see Valdés, 1982:167.) Late in the last chapter it was remarked how important time has been in discussions of narrative. One of the classic moments in western thought is Augustine's discussion of time in his *Confessions* (11 and 12). That moment has its counterpart in the Buddhist concept of the "three worlds": the past, or that which has passed on; the present, or that which has begun to be; and the future, or that not

---

[14] For a number of studies of issues concerning character, see Alsina, 1985. For sustained treatment, see Hochman, 1985. Both books are important, both Eurocentric.

[15] Actually, something will be said of both, and it is worth remarking that I have deliberately chosen place(s) over space, since spatiality leads us all too readily into metaphors that are then hypostatized.

yet come. The point is that these are but convenient terms to speak of transience, whereas time has no real existence (Nakamura, 1962:207, under "sanze").

Mere convenience perhaps, but it seems we cannot put the matter from our minds, even after deciding that only the present is real or that the distinctions are illusory. "It is time, ladies and gentlemen, time." In the public catalogue of the Princeton University Library one will find many subject entries for time but none for place. There is a Time Museum in Illinois, and there are collections of chronometers in principal museums. There are highly esteemed modern studies of time: for example, Harald Weinrich on tense and time in *Tempus*, Paul Ricoeur on *Time and Narrative*, and that highly schematic study by Emil Staiger, *Die Zeit als Einbildungskraft des Dichters*. With so much critical space devoted to time, it is time to concern ourselves with space.

There is a sense in which time and space are reciprocal. A given star is so many light-years' distance from the earth. But to put matters so conceals the requisite velocity of light across tracts of space. Time is but one of three factors involved. Such is the solvent subjectivity of time that it occupies the minds of students of narrative at the expense of other radical features of narrative. Of course space in designated kind, place, may also be conceived of subjectively. There are Greek "nostos," German "Heimat," Japanese "furuzato."

It is strange how little attention place has received. It is all the stranger, because its logical priority to time in literature can be demonstrated easily enough.

For the sake of clarity, let us begin by considering the issue in terms of narrative with a plot. To say it again, the three essential (but not sufficient) elements for a narrative are, in order of increasing importance, time, place, and characters (versions of people). The time may be changed without change in place, characters, or plot line. In fact, that is precisely the invisible process of narrative continuance at its simplest: a group of characters live in a given place as time passes in succession. A change in place has much greater effect, requiring a change in either time or characters, who cannot logically be in different places at the same time. In fact a change of place is a common way to change the plot-line, as making wholly natural a switch to another group of characters. That is to say that characters are the most important of all, since to change them utterly requires a change in plot-line. And not just that. It is also necessary to have a change in place and time, unless one group of characters is made to exit the place as others occupy it, or unless the narrator gives us some equivalent of "And at that very time. . . ." These considerations are entirely evident. Moreover, reflection shows that they hold even in an unplotted lyric. It is one thing if Petrarch writes about how long it seems since he has seen Laura. It is more important if he can be in her presence. And it is most important if he turns from her to love of Christ. Perhaps our concern with time *as a subject* since Proust has blinded us to the greater importance of place and characters as *narrative elements*.

Since these are logical matters, they are true of any culture we can conceive of. Yet handling of them may differ from one age or culture to another, and a comparative aim may be served by considering primarily space rather than time or characters. To enable such comparison, one must designate useful topics. In what follows, designated space (i.e., place) will be the concern. Three kinds of place will be considered after the fashion of grammarians distinguishing nouns. That is, there is common place, an unnamed, unidentified location. There is also proper place, that which is named and is taken to exist. Improper place is of two chief kinds: that which is taken not really to exist, like Shakespeare's seacoast of Bohemia (*The Winter's Tale*, 3, 3, 1–2); and that which was once thought proper and existent but is now either disbelieved or used metaphorically. As illustration, here is a familiar passage from *Twelfth Night* (1, 2, 1–4):

> VIOLA. What country, friends, is this?
> CAPTAIN. This is Illyria, lady.
> VIOLA. And what should I do in Illyria?
>   My brother he is in Elyzium.   (Shakespeare, 1972:881)

The space of the implied sea voyage is common place. Illyria is a proper place, a "region bordering the east coast of the Adriatic" (ibid., note). Elyzium is, however, improper place since although it may once have been thought proper and existing, it is now either disbelieved or used metaphorically for the Christian heaven.

Common place is the basic feature of literary spatiality in any extended work. Sometimes no place is specified, as is true of many western lyrics, or it is specified in proper terms (Paris) and then later becomes common by the lack of any further need to specify. This can happen even when there is a change of place. In *Mansfield Park*, many of the residents of Mansfield Park make an expedition to the Rushworths', whose eldest son, Tom, is engaged to Maria Bertram. Chapter 9 begins, "Mr. Rushworth was at the door to receive his fair lady" (Austen, 1926:3, 84). The journey closing the preceding chapter has implied change of place, and the introduction of a nontraveling character, "Mr. Rushworth," completes the implicit shift in place. It will be observed that time need not be mentioned, because logically prior place here can imply the time, and that the decisive factor making sense of place as well as time is a character, a proper name.

The movement basic to narrative is often of this kind, involving common place and regularly successive time. Literary critics prefer to talk about temporal complications and change rather than place and the ordinary inertial versions of persons, place, and time. Uniformity, sameness, wholly regular succession are ignored, although they alone enable us to make sense. Much the same is true of histories. One authority may begin, "The history of imperial Rome consists of recurrent crisis." Another: "The history of imperial Rome consists of fundamental continuities." It is not difficult to guess which would be the choice of most critics today. But the choice of crisis over continuity masks a radical dependence on inertial place for the presumed identity, "imperial Rome." It is significant that the novels of Samuel Beckett are often not very clear as to time. They are clearer as to place and clearest as to characters. Some substantial narrative sum is required of Beckett if his reader is going to sustain interest in the art of subtraction.

Since much of what is being talked about goes against the grain, it will not be amiss to consider the more familiar. Here is Paul Ricoeur in a passage from *Time and Narrative*:

> We are in debt to Käte Hamburger for the clear distinction she makes between the grammatical form of verb tenses, in particular the past tenses, and their temporal significance in the realm of fiction. No one has stressed more than she has that break that literary fiction introduces into the functioning of discourse. . . . It results entirely from the fact that fiction replaces the I-Origo of assertive discourse, an origin that itself is real, with the I-Origines belonging to the characters in fiction. . . . We could not be closer to Aristotle, for whom fiction is a mimesis of active characters. (1984–85:2)[16]

The attention devoted to time as a feature of narrative is to be expected in a book with Ricoeur's title (originally *Temps et récit*). Yet neither "place" nor "space" is mentioned in the index. "Character" and "characters" are, but far less prominently than time.

The banners flown are familiar ones. Literature is fictional. That status is determined by fictional rather than real first-persons, whose fictionality is established by verb tense, particularly "past tenses." One banner is missing—"representation."

These charmingly familiar ideas are parochial. Intercultural evidence

---

[16] My ellipses give a somewhat distorted sense of the references of pronouns, but the version given is faithful to the spirit of the original.

shows that literature may be factual rather than fictional. Moreover, to emphasize a related matter again, totally fictional writing could not be understood. More than that, however, the very idea of fictionality presumes that which is not feigned, fact. General Foods, Inc., is fictionally "incorporated," embodied, as a "person at law" in order to receive and pay money, to sue and be sued (among other things) *as if it were* a real, factual person. And without the conception of factual, real people, the idea of *fictio* would not have emerged in Roman law.

It is worth staying with the logical contrast of fact and fiction rather than introducing history, because of the ambiguous meaning of "history" both as actual event or fact and as account of the events. For the latter, in the west sooner or later the issue arises—at least for versions at all well written—of the degree to which they are themselves entoiled in fiction.[17] The fact/fiction distinction in itself is basically more realist, and to the extent that we think of fiction mimetically as a representation of reality, many critics and most writers have assumed that fiction may be true, just as truth may be stranger than fiction. As we have seen, affective-expressive poetics are realist in nature on other grounds, and it is no wonder that in such poetics there tends to be an assumption (apart from drama) that literature is factual in the absence of evidence to the contrary.

Persons, places, and times may all be factual, and narrative (what is at issue here) is feasible in languages without tense. Again: Chinese is not only without tense but also without the aspectual, modal, and assertive inflections of tenseless Japanese.

The parochial nature of those assumptions can be suggested by a plain passage from the work esteemed as Matsuo Bashō's narrative masterpiece, *The Narrow Road Through the Provinces* (*Oku no Hosomichi*).[18]

> The Mogami River begins in Michinoku Province, and its upper reaches mark the boundary of Yamagata. In the middle of its course there are such hazardous places as Goten and Hayabusa. Thereafter it flows along the northern side of Mount Itajiki and empties into the sea at Sakata. Along both banks the mountains rise upon us as if to close over the river, and the vegetation shows wildly luxuriant. Yet through such passage boats drop downstream toward the sea. Is it not because they do carry rice that they have been called rice boats in older poetry? (Miner, 1976:180 slightly revised)

---

[17] This will be evident from the deeply moving third volume of Ricoeur, 1984–85. See especially the second and far longer of its two parts: "Poetics of Narrative: History, Fiction, Time," pp. 99–274 (and notes). A very different meditation would have followed "History, Fact, Time."

[18] More information is given about this work below, at a less distracting point.

The factuality of the passage can be demonstrated: the people implied or mentioned in neighboring passages are historically real. The places are proper and factual. There is confirmation in the nonliterary diary kept by Bashō's traveling companion, Iwanami Sora. Time, which is the subject of two notable prose poems in the work, scarcely exists *as a subject* until the close of the passage. In the original, tense and time are missing as elements of the relation. Fictionality and mimesis do not exist. There is no plot in the passage, yet there is narrative movement in following the course of the Mogami from origin to the sea and then fulfillment in the last three sentences. Moreover, the passage shows to perfection that the nonmimetic nature of affective-expressive writing differs from recent antimimetic writing in the west. The places mentioned are taken to be real and, as the last sentence shows, certain well-known poems about the boats are also accorded factual status.

Of course fictional writing does exist outside Europe, as in these stanzas by the principal *renga* poet, Sōgi.

11	Me ni kakaru	With utter clarity
	kumo no naki made	and not a cloud to arrest the eye
	tsuki sumite	the moon shines on
12	Kiyomigasekido	and the Kiyomi Barrier gate
	nami zo akeyuku	opens as waves move with the dawn
		(Miner, 1979c:239, slightly revised)

In Japanese, night opens rather than dawn breaks, and here the temporal opening should suggest the opening of the barrier gate just at the time the waves move. Since "Kiyomi" means "Pure View" or "Pure Seeing," the twelfth stanza associates with the moon in the cloudless sky of stanza 11. Sōgi is writing about a historically real (i.e., proper) place but in a fiction. He seems to have composed these stanzas in late spring or early summer, whereas by conventions of the *renga* code, this is an autumn moon. Moreover, the Kiyomi Barrier no longer existed in Sōgi's lifetime. The temporal implication of allusion to what exists no more has the effect of heightening the affective intensity of place. Somewhat similarly a "first-person point of view" is implied by the "eye" ("me") of the eleventh stanza, but this subjectivity also heightens the sense of place, as we shall have grounds for understanding later in a consideration of points of view and attention.

Western poetry includes the topographical from ancient to present times. Classical western examples will be found in the *Greek Anthology*. Horace favored a Bandusian fountain, Martial houses, and Ausonius a river.[19] There is no need to follow through country-house poems and Romantic use of place to prove that western poets have chosen place as a subject of poetry. But it is worth notice that western authors use factual place in the imagined times of fictions, as we can see in Shakespeare's comedies and the novel from La Fayette and Defoe.

To every people, some places take on value for what they evoke, whether for beauty, religion, or battle. Jerusalem is exceptional in being a holy city to three religions. Red Cliff probably means nothing today to all but a few non-Chinese. People have heard about Mount Fuji but not about the codification of place names for Japanese poetry. Lists were drawn up as early as the eleventh century, extended in the twelfth, and perfected by none other than Sōgi in the fifteenth (Miner-Odagiri-Morrell, 1985:433–41). To qualify, a place had to have some distinguishing property celebrated by a famous poet. Without those qualifications, a place was absorbed into common place, no matter how real it was or how precious to those who lived in or near it. Japanese are as aware of time as any people. But one does not need to *look* for Japanese poems on place.[20]

Moreover, place matters more than time even in those instances when it does not appear to. Here is Bashō in a letter to an old friend: "I shall never forget you among thoughts of life and death, the subservience of the weak to the powerful, mutability, and swift time" (Miner, 1979c:115). The vision of human suffering in time assumes the greater importance of place and people. The letter writer mentions the death of the young warrior Atsumori at Suma. Bashō has arrived at Suma on one of his foot-journeys, and the place leads him to think of suffering people there: Atsumori, also historical Ariwara Yukihira in exile there, and fictional Genji in exile. The Arima hot springs nearby would not have aroused such thoughts in the traveling old poet.

Let us study time and literature. Let us recognize that it comes in two dominant versions, common and improper (there are also proper kinds such as Christmas and Bastille Day). Time is, in fact, a fascinating literary topic. But we must recognize that in literature common, proper, and improper place holds priority over time. To be sure, in a given poem time may be the more important *subject*, but as we consider the *moving* continuum of narrative, we cannot escape the greater importance of place over time.

[19] *Greek Anthology*, 8:170–254, especially 177; 15:21, 22, 24–27; Horace, *Odes*, 3:13; Martial, 3:58, 4:44, 7:17, 10:30; Ausonius, *Mosella*. There are of course numerous other examples.

[20] In 1104 sixteen poets contributed hundred-poem sequences for what has come to be known as *The Hundred-Poem Sequences in the Reign of Horikawa* (*Horikawa Hyakushu*). Nearly 28 percent of the five-line poems feature a place name, often with two of the five lines devoted to it and its embellishments. See Takeshita, 1988.

The hierarchy from characters to place to time is true of all narrative, but characters are especially crucial to unplotted narrative.[21] To understand the reasons for that, we must examine their great importance to plotted narrative and consider certain features of plot.

Places and times may be changed in a narrative without changing the people, without making a new plot. To change the people, on the other hand, is to change the plot. When we switch from Telemachus to Odysseus in the *Odyssey*, we move from the subordinate to the main plot; it will be many books before Telemachus again casts his shadow on the narrative field. When people are present but altered from what we consider normal, the effect is to shake our sense of reality. Some authors do so for just that end. Rabelais is much given to it, as for example in Erich Auerbach's beloved passage, the world in Pantagruel's mouth (Auerbach, 1971:ch. 12). All four of Gulliver's voyages illustrate the principle admirably, and Carroll's *Through the Looking-Glass* offers a wonderfully significant reflection of the mimetic mirror in an inversion. It is easy to understand why, in his antimimetic crusade against the doctrine of the real, Beckett should make strange central characters narrate their own stories, why those narrators grow steadily odder, and why characters other than the "first-person" narrator grow scarcer from one novel of his trilogy to the next.

We also look to a plot for development, a movement rich in possibilities of fulfillment. Causality is of crucial importance to plots, not just for what everyone knows—that it relates episodes to each other—as for its relating of character to action and to other characters. Character motivation and other features of personality are the chief explanatory causes in plots. Aristotle was concerned with the matter for dramatic plots, taking morality to be the grounds of distinction. Goodness and badness do hold far greater affective importance than we are often willing to acknowledge. (Surely, we think, there *must* be fancier matters than that.) The qualities also enable us to identify characters and the issues they raise, whether by themselves or in relation to others. But it is very easy to go wrong in moral matters, particularly when important ideological factors are involved. Aristotle himself offers a glaring example of a powerful mind erring, as in this infrequently quoted passage of a moral nature.

> In connection with the [chief tragic] characters, there are four things one should aim at. First, and most important, that they be good. Now they will have character if in the way mentioned their speech or their action clearly reveals a moral choice (whatever it may be), and good

---

[21] For a discussion of literary characters in more detail than is suitable here, see the works cited in n. 14.

character if a good choice. But goodness exists in each class of people: there is in fact such a thing as a good woman and such a thing as a good slave, although one of these classes is inferior and the other, as a class, is worthless.[22]

Our sense of moral causation does not move in lock-step with Greek hoplites. Our very revulsion over the morality of that passage is, however, moral itself.

Causation by character motive and personality offers a wider spectrum than the moral alone. In *Dombey and Son* the but dimly perceptive yet generous-hearted Mr. Toots offers reason for laughter, and his dog, Diogenes, seems wonderfully misnamed. Another Dickensian character or two of even lesser powers of mind—Barnaby Rudge and his crow—show that characters of even the poorest capacities for reason and moral choice may yet have motivated personalities that propel the plot. What is true of such lesser characters is of course even truer of intelligent, complex ones.

Cause and effect are important in a plot, because they help us make sense of it. We smell authorial convenience rather than logic in effects without causes. Of course the effect may be shown before the cause. Not only detective stories, although certainly they, require that the effect be known before the cause is revealed. To establish the cause, we need not only the fingerprints on the gun but also a set of motives. Of course the reversal of logical sequence by narrative sequence will be rejected if it is suggested that the effect actually preceded its cause. The murdered heiress may not be killed until the lethal gun is fired.

Contingency is only less important than development and causality. The accidents and ifs of narrative may prove momentous. Yeats writes somewhere, deeply impressed, about an Arabian story in which a man casually drops to the ground the stone of a date he has eaten. Whereat a genie materializes from invisibility threatening to take the man's life for blinding his also invisible son in one eye with the date stone. Of course too much coincidence stretches our sense of authorial fair-dealing. Yet contingencies like that date stone may assist in sending the plot ahead suddenly or in taking it toward fulfillment. Closely examined, development and causality are very often cosseted exercises of contingency. It is no accident that the contingent was once included among "the contrivances of Providence."

Plot is one of the pleasures of narrative and drama, and a well-made plot makes good pleasure. Yet, having offered such incense on the altar of plot, it is now time for me to join other students of narrative and to rec-

---

[22] Else, 1967:455 (ch. 15). The Bywater translation used by McKeon (1947:643) tries to pretty this up.

ognize it as a lesser divinity. Is it not the diligent but maimed Vulcan of the literary pantheon?

We may begin our next search with a question or two about a conspicuously well made plot, that of *The Romance of the Three Kingdoms*. In recounting the struggle for supremacy among Shu, Wei, and Wu, the author switches from one to the other with astonishing naturalness and lack of strain. The people of the rival kingdoms do meet when alliances are temporarily formed, when embassies visit, or when battle is joined. But we always have a sense of difference, with as it were a separate history occurring in Shu, Wei, and Wu. By some miracle, after a switch to a different kingdom, the author does not make us feel that we need an account of events during the two years since we last considered the kingdom switched to.

If, however, we arrest the narrative continuum, resolving not to be moved by the author's skill, we may raise some questions. It is surely true that we have three interrelated plots, and that at one time we usually have only one functioning. How then shall we account—as in *The Three Kingdoms*—for the present existence of a presently nonexisting plot? In this beautifully plotted story, two-thirds of the plot is absent, deplotted, most of the time. Many of the chapters in *Tom Jones* and *Moby-Dick* are so far unplotted that they interrupt the plot. What is the importance of a given plot if it can be absent two-thirds of the time? How does plot contribute to the necessary continuum of narrative when it is so frequently interruptible?

Or again, sometimes what seems the opposite occurs. In *The Odyssey* (9–12) there is that lengthy section in Phaeacia where Odysseus relates the story of some of his prior experiences—the first we hear of them. Do the two plots run simultaneously: Odysseus being at once in Phaeacia and in the toils of travel? If so, Homer did things with place that Ionesco and Beckett failed to manage, and we must think of plot as something separable from the total narrative. One of three may be on and two off. Or there may be but one switch, and that off.

There is, then, *no total plot* singular in *The Odyssey*, in *The Romance of the Three Kingdoms*, in *Tom Jones*, or in *Moby-Dick*. There certainly is a *total narrative*, with plots plural used intermittently or overlappingly.

We may further question the importance of plot, using as example Fu Shen's *Six Records of a Floating Life*. Only four "records" have survived, but the existence of spurious chapters testifies to the interest the story has had for all its readers. The author was one of those Chinese aspirants who failed the major examinations that would have been the means to privileged life as a literatus-official (*wenren*). Not having so much of the world to write about, he chose to write about himself, his infrequent ups and his usual downs. One thing he does have, love of his wife, Yun, something extraordinary for traditional Chinese literature. The book does not have a well-made plot; sometimes there is no plot at all.

Fu Shen is digressive, essayistic. The death of Yun, and his grief, are related in the third chapter or record. But she reappears in the fourth. There is no reason why he should not think of her after her death and recall something she did. Once again, we discover that for all the importance that plot holds, the sequence of the relating holds greater importance—otherwise a different sequence would have been found desirable and have been used.

Fu Shen does not follow one method. He may use plot, or he may drop it for a disquisition on growing flowers—much like Melville's on whales or whaling. Now, where is the narrative when the plot stops? It is not in the plot. Where is the plot? It is not in the narrative. The writing continues. The narrative moves in its continuum toward fulfillment.

A couple of examples from *Six Records* will focus the issues. At one point, Fu Shen reports to Yun what a fine local festival he has seen.

> "What a shame that I cannot go just because I am not a man," said Yun.
> "If you wore one of my hats and some of my clothes, you could look like a man."

The disguise proves successful. There is one little incident.

> At the last place we came to, young women and girls were sitting behind the throne that had been erected there. They were the family of a Mr. Yang, one of the organizers of the festival. Without thinking, Yun walked over and began to chat with them as a woman quite naturally might, and as she bent over to do so she inadvertently laid her hand on the shoulder of one of the young ladies.
> One of the maids angrily jumped up and shouted, "What kind of rogue are you, to behave like that!" I went over to try to explain, but Yun, seeing how embarrassing the situation could become, quickly took off her hat and kicked up her foot, saying, "See, I am a woman too!"
> At first they all stared at Yun in surprise, but then their anger turned to laughter. We stayed to have some tea and refreshments with them, and then called sedan chairs and went home.[23]

---

[23] Fu, 1983:44–45. The punctuation has been slightly altered. The translators give the surname, Fu, second, and their title adds to the proper Chinese one, *Fu Shen Liuji* (*Fu Shen's Six Records*). The translation is lively, however, and well annotated.

The plot is revealing. Yun wishes to see the festival, and in his love for her (they agree that they would like to be born of exchanged sexes and marry again in another life) Fu Shen persuades her to go in disguise. We see from this that, although poor, the couple has a high enough social standing for the woman to be thought to disgrace herself by showing up in public. Presumably the women she chats with are there, either because they are of lower status, or more likely because they have an official capacity at the temple. Yun's demonstration of her femaleness involves showing her long hair and her woman's bound foot. Plot also assists in articulating this small but agreeable episode.

Much of the second record, however, is taken up with essayistic fact, and plot is very fitful. The following paragraph offers a microcosm of the whole.

> Poor scholars who live in small crowded houses should rearrange their rooms in imitation of the sterns of the Taiping boats of my home country, the steps of which can be made into three beds by extending them at front and back. Each bed is then separated from its neighbour by a board covered with paper. Looking at them when they are laid out is like walking a long road—you do not have a confined feeling at all. When Yun and I were living in Yangchou we arranged our house in this fashion. Though the house had only two spans [architectural modules], we divided it into two bedrooms, a kitchen, and a living room, and still had plenty of space left over. Yun had laughed about our handiwork, saying, "The layout is fine, but it still does not quite have the feel of a rich home." I had . . . to admit she was right! (Fu, 1983:61)

Anyone can see that plot enters at "When Yun and I were living in Yang-chou. . . ." Specified people, a specified place, and a time admittedly requiring specification from other evidence, but acceptable.[24] By what law other than "All narratives shall have plot" is the part preceding the entry of plot not narrative? In fact, it is only on a plot hunt that one notices at all that plot comes and goes in the continuous narrative movement of a lengthy example and many briefer ones (as we have also seen from Bashō on the Mogami River). Yet: "A narrative without a plot is a logical impossibility" (Chatman, 1983:47). If that is true, the first half of the last paragraph quoted is not narrative, and we have the risible spectacle of a narrative beginning three-quarters on in a paragraph.

[24] This illustrates well the general importance of each of the three constituents of plot. In Eldershaw, 1984, which is set in Australia four centuries hence, the novelist or historian Knarf says the following about time: "I've manipulated time. I've pressed events closer together than they actually were. Something had to go, and time was the expendable. . . . To spin out time which contains no new element is not to increase but decrease verisimilitude" (p. 205).

Of course all unplotted writing is not narrative. The pragmatics of the issue are about as important as its definition. In other words, is a given nonplotted example sufficient in movement and fulfillment for us usefully to call it narrative? I shall say again that I think any reader would consider the passage from Fu Shen to be narrative, although the doctrinaire might renege upon its being pointed out that plot makes a tardy entrance. But is the situation somehow different only when pointed out? Because the author is Chinese? We have a generous amount of western evidence to choose from.

There is the general evidence. It is a fact that there are more versions of nonliterary narrative than there are of nonliterary drama and nonliterary lyric. That is, there are more versions in writing. In speech and action, narrative perhaps cannot be claimed to be foremost. Literature proper has long since been a written art, even for play scripts and song lyrics. To say that the scripts and the lyrics do not fully constitute a play or a song reminds us that narrative is sufficient in writing to a degree that drama is necessarily not and to a degree that a given lyric may not be.

These reflections suggest the importance of considering a kind of writing that is at once nonliterary and yet narrative. One kind offering many examples is history. For although not all histories are written in narrative, many are. The first attempt in English to sort out these matters seems to have been Dryden's in his "Life of Plutarch." "History is principally divided," he writes, "into these three species: *commentaries* or *annals*; *history* properly so called; and *biographia*."[25] He then goes on to characterize each kind, and it is his versions of the first and second that concern us. "Commentaries or annals are (as I may so call them) naked history; or the plain relation of fact, according to the succession of time, divested of all the other ornaments. . . . [I]n few words, a bare narration is its business" (p. 5). As examples he gives "the *Commentaries* of Caesar" and "the *Annals* of Tacitus," and even much of Thucydides, because although the Greek historian used many of the ornaments of history proper, he related "the particular occurrences of the time, in the order as they happened, and his eighth book is wholly written after the way of annals" (p. 5). Yet the world thinks that the histories by Caesar, Tacitus, and Thucydides are narrative.

Then there is history proper.

History, properly so called, may be described by the addition of those parts which are not required to annals: and therefore there is little

---

[25] Watson, 1962:2, 5. Further page references will be entered in the main discussion and refer to the second volume of this edition. Dryden later speaks of "biography" (p. 8), the first usage given in the *Oxford English Dictionary*.

farther to be said of it: only that the dignity and gravity of style is here necessary. That the guesses of secret causes inducing to the actions be drawn at least from the most probable circumstances. . . . That nothing of concernment be omitted, but things of trivial moment are still [always] to be neglected. . . . (p. 6)

We may ignore what Dryden enters in the way of rhetorical and moral dimensions, not that they may not be crucial to our judgment of a given history, but that they are separate from the issue of what narrative is. Caesar and Tacitus offer "bare narrative." The immediate issue is whether they offer plot. Dryden uses "narrative" and "relation" more or less interchangeably. (See Watson, 1962:2, 301 for "narrative" and 302 for "relation.") He also uses the terms "plot" (302), "fable" (298), and "episode" (ibid.). He does not identify narrative or relation with plot, fable, or episode. On his grounds, there may be narrative without plot. Does Dryden nod?

The immediate issue is whether narrative histories may lack plots. It is not presumed that all narrative histories lack plots, and literary narratives are not presently under discussion. There are so many narrative histories that we do not want for examples. The problem, if any exists, is rather knowing what plot means. To repeat, my conception is that of continuance of connected people in place(s) and time(s) to some end, with whatever necessary qualifications as specified. If someone else has a different definition, that may be used as we now turn to an example of narrative history.

George Saintsbury wrote a number of histories that are narrative. Among them is one reprinted within memory, *A History of [English] Prose Rhythm*. One can pick representative passages with ease, since the same method is employed throughout his account. What follows is a portion of what a marginal note terms "The plainest styles, vulgar and not vulgar" at the end of the seventeenth century. (This initiates a series of lengthy quotations: the movement of narrative is not a brief one.)

The Photian nemesis did not take long to show itself. Your "naked natural way" does not easily escape the fate of being also, as *Hobbes*, who lived nearly long enough to see the whole transformation scene, had already translated it in his disillusionising fashion, "poor and brutish." In the very group itself which we have been discussing, *Locke* showed a great part of the danger, and was only saved from showing the whole of it by the gravity of his subjects, and by the fortunate fact that he had no propensity to joking. But the general tendency of the age was different; and in the last quarter of the century the vulgarising of English style and English rhythm—for rhythm is like some delicate meats, it taints at once in corrupt company—is flagrant. It is not quite fair, though it has been done, to charge this on *L'Estrange*; and (though the eighteenth century would have done this) nobody is now likely to charge it on *Bunyan*. I do not think that whatever *Tom Brown's* delinquencies (and they are not inconsiderable) it is fair to charge it on *Tom*—who was saved in form by a little scholarship, as *Bentley* was not by much. The editor of the *Observator*, and the author of the *Letters from the Dead to the Living*, use slang and neologism without the slightest compunction, and though *Tom* at least was by no means without a vein of poetry, their subjects did not invite "high strains" of any kind. But though both, and especially *Tom*, can be horribly coarse in substance and diction, their rhythm is never vulgar: it is purely conversational, but of a not very polished type.

As for *Bunyan*, here as everywhere, he stands quite by himself. . . . (Saintsbury, 1967:238–39; stress added)

By the criteria used here, and probably by other criteria as well, this is narrative without a plot. It is narrative because it has fulfillment in its movement from medieval beginnings across what Saintsbury might term (although heaven knows there is no need to put words in his mouth) an extensive plain, now arid, now irriguous, to its fulfillment in a certain modern historian of prose rhythm whom one could mention. And it is narrative because of the continuum of the centuries, with occasional backward and forward considerations. It is not plotted narrative because of the handling of the three elements of narrative continuance. The least crucial, although still important, time, is intermittently signaled, whether by dates, by marginal references, or by names and other designations of people whose dates we are expected more or less to know. The rather more crucial element, place, is generalized, England. A *literary* narrative would need to be more specific, situating most of these writers in London and Bunyan in Bedford, possibly in Bedford jail. But the really crucial matter is the people, the *narrationis personae*. There is no core group added to and subtracted from. The waggish Tom Brown gets several glances, and Bunyan two. Locke and Bentley are mentioned once. Two or three pages later there may be another reference to a Locke, but an essentially different group of people is considered. None of these "characters" interacts with another, and by the next chapter there is total replacement. Well before Samuel Johnson appears, the writers mentioned in this passage are forgot in favor of writers discussed and then forgot—*insofar as narrative is concerned*. As Dryden assumed, historical writing is often narrative in nature. As Saintsbury shows, historical narrative need not be plotted narrative.

Unplotted narrative can be found without difficulty. But finding it in historical narrative does not, perhaps, show that unplotted *literary* narrative exists. We owe it to Fu Shen to keep in mind that second passage quoted from his *Six Records*. But to stay with what is more familiar to most readers, the most highly esteemed narrative in western literature, the *Iliad*, will provide an example of what we seek. There is no way of claiming there is a plot in most of the Catalogue of the Ships (Book 2).

There may be yet another issue: must plotless *literary* narrative be fictional? Some people may well believe that the account in the *Iliad* is fictional. Let us suppose that it is. Then the issue turns on whether factual literary narrative exists. The answer is clearly yes. In the spring of 1689 Matsuo Bashō and that younger friend, Iwanami Sora, set out on foot upon that journey that took them in due course to the Mogami River. The journey would occupy Bashō for two and a half years. He wrote up the first half year in *The Narrow Road Through the Provinces* (*Oku no Hosomichi*) from a diary he kept on the road. From various kinds of evidence—geography, history, and above all Sora's nonliterary diary—we know that Bashō's account is factual.[26] Going beyond Sendai and that famous beauty spot, Matsushima, the travelers went inland to Hiraizumi. It had been the site of a dissident court five centuries before. Minamoto Yoshitsune had fled there when his brother, Yoritomo, wished to do away with him as a possible rival. Yoshitsune was assisted by a small band including a warrior popularly known as Izumi Saburō, but was betrayed by a member of that court's family, Fujiwara Yasuhira. Here is Bashō's description of the scene.

The splendors of the three generations of Hiraizumi now make the briefest of dreams, and of the grand facade there are only faint remains stretching out for two and a half miles. Hidehira's castle is now levelled to overgrown fields and, of all the splendors of the past, only Mount Kinkei retains its form. Climbing up to the high ramparts of what had been Yoshitsune's stronghold, one can see down below the Kitakami River flowing in a wide stream from the south. The Koromo River pours past the site of loyal Izumi Saburō's castle, then beneath these ramparts, and at last into the Kitakami. The old relics of others like Yasuhira are to be found separated to the west at Koromo Barrier, which controlled the southern approach against the incursions by the

---

[26] There are incidental contrafactual matters and one major one. There is a passage (Miner, 1976:187–88) describing an affecting incident involving prostitutes. This is made up out of whole cloth, is fictional. The reason is that Bashō conceived the order of the journey on the three-part pattern of *haikai* linked poetry, and at that point he wanted some equivalent of stanzas on love, which in *haikai* is often skewed as here. It was a great shock to Japanese to discover the fictionality of that passage.

northern tribesmen. Yoshitsune and his brave adherents took refuge in this citadel, but the most famous names claim the world only a little while, and now the level grass covers their traces. What Du Fu wrote came to my mind—

The country crumbles, but mountains and rivers endure;
A late spring visits the castle, replacing it with fresh grasses . . .

and sitting down on my pilgrim's hat I wept over the ruins of time.

The summer plants:
the efforts of those men of war
yield traces of dream. (Miner, 1976:176–77; revised)

Whatever may be the deficiencies of the translation, the prose of the original is of a style that can only be termed literary, as the harmonious presence of two poetic passages confirms. The matter related is doubly factual: the facts of history are recalled, and so also the facts of the visit to the site. Moreover the couplet by Du Fu and the *hokku* by Bashō are taken on the same terms. Neither is fictional.

Perhaps a further issue remains. Granted that literary narrative may be factual, can it—like historical narrative—exist without plot? Once again *Iliad* 2 might be mentioned, and for a prose example we might turn to Dryden's "honest Montaigne." But we may look instead at the memorable conclusion (less its heavy italics) to Izaak Walton's "Life of Dr. John Donne."

> He did much contemplate (especially after he entered into his Sacred Calling) the mercies of Almighty God, the immortality of the Soul, and the joyes of Heaven; and would often say in a kind of sacred extasie—Blessed be God that he is God only, and divinely like himself.
>
> He was by nature highly passionate, but more apt to reluct at the excesses of it. A great lover of the offices [duties] of humanity, and of so merciful a spirit, that he never beheld the miseries of Mankind without pity and relief.
>
> He was earnest and unwearied in the search of knowledge; with which, his vigorous soul is now satisfied, and employed in a continual praise of that God that first breathed it into his active body; that body which once was a Temple of the Holy Ghost, and is now become a small quantity of Christian dust:
>
> But I shall see it reanimated. (Walton, 1962:84)

Many of the earlier portions of this biography (and through the first paragraph here) do have plot. If it stops at the end, it does so for an old narrative reason, to introduce description. In epic, a *descriptio* may present the shield of Achilles (Aeneas, Rinaldo, Satan, etc.). It may introduce a hero or describe the natural scenery that a Spenserian hero must "read" correctly. Or it may be a set piece like Virgil's of night: *nox erat . . .*, *nox ruit . . .*, and so on. It may be a vision, as when Spenser's Calidore sees the Graces dancing, or as when Walton contemplates a handful of Christian dust at the Day of Judgment. Description abates plot, as lyric does, and it is no accident that descriptions are often taken to be lyric. In any event, as should now be clear, narrative does not require plot.

The point might have been made by going to Lucretius, but for some reason discussions of narrative seem to turn on prose. Before moving to problems that verse narrative may illustrate, however, let us consider a matter left in suspense (this chapter does concern narrative, after all) and otherwise retrace our steps. It was observed earlier that although characters, versions of people, are more important as narrative elements than are place and time in plotted narratives, characters may be yet more important in unplotted narrative. That is, it becomes more necessary to specify them. In a plotted narrative such as a Jamesian or Woolfian novel, we often linger for lengthy periods in the thoughts of a single character musing on one other character or no other character at all. The musing character thus becomes central to us in mind and personality. That sustained subjectivity is difficult to manage and rarely needed in unplotted narrative. Instead, we are apt to encounter numerous characters seen, as it were, from their outside and unconnected, unplotted, as in Saintsbury's history. If, for some reason, as in the isolation of Bashō and Sora in remote provinces, people are scarce or unimportant, then place becomes crucial, as in the account of the Mogami River. The celebration of Hiraizumi shows a balance more nearly like plotted narrative, and with time an important *subject*, along with place and characters.

In seeking to describe narrative continuum, we have considered a number of elements and have come up with certain propositions. Plot is a very common constituent of narrative, because it offers with one mighty stroke the movement necessary. Yet what is common in literary narrative is not therefore necessary. Movement and fulfillment can be supplied by other means. As we have also seen, literary narrative may be factual rather than fictional, although in the west the mimetic legacy makes that less frequent than in east Asia.

Narrative Bounds

Those points established as at least the thesis here, it is now useful (as it would not have been earlier) to raise questions about the bounds of narrative. By moving to verse, one step has been taken toward a boundary: witness the absence of theoretical discussions of verse narrative. A passage from Whitman's *Song of Myself* (sect. 15) will serve; it includes the opening (11.264–70) and close (324–29) of the section.

> The pure contralto sings in the organ loft,
> The carpenter dresses his plank, the tongue of his foreplane
>   whistles its wild ascending lisp,
> The married and unmarried children ride home to their
>   Thanksgiving dinner,
> The pilot seizes the king-pin, he heaves down with a strong arm,
> The mate stands braced in the whale-boat, lance and harpoon are
>   ready,
> The duck-shooter walks by silent and curious stretches,
> The deacons are ordain'd with cross'd hands at the altar, . . .
> The city sleeps and the country sleeps,
> The living sleep for their time, the dead sleep for their time,
> The old husband sleeps by his wife and the young husband sleeps
>   by his wife;
> And these tend inward to me, and I tend outward to them,
> And such as it is to be of these more or less I am,
> And of these one and all I weave the song of myself.
>
> (Whitman, 1973:41, 44)

One of the longest sections in the poem, this one displays dozens of people doing things. Each is immersed in a personal plot, so preventing the existence of a large, general, continuous, and in a word genuine plot. Whether this section is fictional or not is a difficult question. If Whitman had to see all this for it to be fact, then it is fiction. If one can presume facts from experience, it is factual. And is it plotless narrative? Since it has continuousness and reaches fulfillment at its close, it is narrative by the standards used here. Nor need we necessarily make lyric of a *song* of himself: "Arms and the man I sing. . . ." Some sections are, however, more lyrical, and the whole is collective rather than single. In short, the most concise description of the whole of *Song of Myself* is of plotless narrative with lyric intervals and plotted passages. Even if one were to hold that the sections of the poem are lyrics, in their collectedness they offer us plotless narrative.

No other distinguished literary practice illustrates the issue as well as Japanese linked poetry.[27] In early spring of 1488, three *renga* poets sat to-

---

[27] There are two kinds. *Renga*, the earlier to emerge, used a diction like that of court poetry and retained elevated subject matter. *Haikai* (*haikai renga*) later introduced Sinified words and quotidian matters, including humor, that gave it a lower decorum. The canons of what may be termed the *renga* code were largely the same.

ward evening to compose a sequence of one hundred stanzas in honor of
Gotoba (r. 1183–98), who had had a palace at Minase, and at whose shrine
as a kind of god of poetry they would offer a fair copy of their sequence.
Before entering into further explanation, it seems desirable to give as a
sample the first eight stanzas of the most famous sequence, *One Hundred
Stanzas by Three Poets at Minase* (*Minase Sangin Hyakuin*).

1	Yuki nagara	Despite some snow
	yamamoto kasumu	the base of hills spreads with haze
	yūbe kana	the twilight scene
	Sōgi	

	Yuki nagara	Despite some snow
	yamamoto kasumu	the base of hills spreads with haze
	yūbe kana	the twilight scene
2	yuku mizu tōku	where the waters flow afar
	ume niou sato	the village glows sweet with plums
	Shōhaku	

	Yuku mizu tōku	Where the waters flow afar
	ume niou sato	the village glows sweet with plums
3	kawakaze ni	in the river wind
	hitomura yanagi	a single stand of willow trees
	haru miete	shows spring color
	Sōchō	

	Kawakaze ni	In the river wind
	hitomura yanagi	a single stand of willow trees
	haru miete	shows spring color
4	fune sasu oto mo	daybreak comes on distinctly
	shiruki akegata	with sounds of a punted boat
	Sōgi	

	Fune sasu oto mo	Daybreak comes on distinctly
	shiruki akegata	with sounds of a punted boat
5	tsuki ya nao	does not the moon
	kiriwataru yo ni	of a fog-enveloped night
	nokoru ran	stay yet in the sky
	Shōhaku	

	Tsuki ya nao	Does not the moon
	kiriwataru yo ni	of a fog-enveloped night
	nokoru ran	stay yet in the sky

6 Shimo oku nohara   as wide fields settle with frost
   aki wa kurekeri   autumn has approached its end
   Sōchō

   Shimo oku nohara   As wide fields settle with frost
   aki wa kurekeri   autumn has approached its end
7   naku mushi no   the insects cry out
   kokoro to mo naku   but without regard for such desires
      kusa karete   the grasses wither
   Sōgi

      Naku mushi no   The insects cry out
   kokoro to mo naku   but without regard for such desires
      kusa karete   the grasses wither
8 kakine o toeba   as I come to the fence in visit
   arawanaru michi   the once covered path is clear
   Shōhaku   (Miner, 1979C:185–87; revised)

As we expect, the first stanza is factual: a description of the early spring scene before the poets. All ninety-nine following are fictional. This writing is termed linked, because each stanza is related semantically to its predecessor and therefore to its successor, but to no other stanza. There are no recollections, no repetitions of motif or idea. This feature, with joint composition on the spot (a stanza about every two minutes) and with lyric units, makes it impossible for linked poetry to have a plot, at least by my definition. (If, however, plot be attributed—mistakenly in my view—to the passage from Saintsbury, then the selections from Whitman and linked poetry have plots.) Many people find it difficult or impossible to think of linked poetry as lyric stanzas formed into plotless narrative. I believe it is.[28]

The difficulties posed by linked poetry are numerous and profound. It will serve larger purposes to defamiliarize that poetry by offering a brief, simplified version of the *renga* code—its elaborate canons. (It has been said that they took twenty years to master, and only after that could it be ascertained whether one had talent.)

---

[28] Konishi makes the matter unusually complex. He begins with a neologism, *sakushū*, which may perhaps be rendered as "expressive agent," that is, a subjectivity sharing in authorship and narratorship. He then says that the expressive agent has free rein to think, feel, and observe only in the opening stanza. "In a sense, the expressive agent is without existence in those [succeeding] ninety-nine stanzas. In its denial of the vantagepoint for the expressive agent to think, feel, and observe, *renga* cannot be the same thing as lyric or narrative poetry in the western sense" (Konishi, 1971:78). He goes on to liken *renga* to music, except that this poetry is a flow of words rather than of sounds (79). He seems to argue that *renga* is *sui generis*, or that it is a kind of narrative or lyric unlike those "in the western sense." Either may be true but not, I think, in the radical senses he presumes.

One hundred stanzas were written on the fronts and backs of four sheets of paper. Eight were written on the front of the first sheet, and eight on the back of the fourth. All other sides had fourteen. The first front was considered a stately introduction (*jo*), and the fourth back a fast close (*kyū*). All the rest was the development or breakage section (*ha*), with fluctuation, agitation. (*Nō* took over this *jo-ha-kyū* rhythm from *renga*.)

Three Poets begins with three stanzas on the topic of spring and, after a miscellaneous stanza (on no season), has three stanzas on autumn followed by another miscellaneous stanza. Three was the minimum run for those seasons, whereas two were enough for summer and winter. A moon stanza was required on each side of a sheet (except for the back of the fourth) and a flower stanza on each sheet, four in all. There were formal positions for each: a moon was expected in stanza seven (the penultimate) on the first sheet (Shōhaku introduces it two stanzas early). On the other three front sides, the moon's formal position is likewise penultimate. On the backs, the flower stanzas displace the moons and take penultimate place, with the moon's formal position moving to three stanzas earlier. One pleasure comes from observing the accord or discord between the formal code and practice.

All stanzas after the first are thought of as joined stanzas. They are, however, considered on their own for topics, subtopics (love, travel, etc.), motifs (dwellings, peaks, waters, etc.), and impressiveness. Four degrees of impressiveness were distinguished, ascending from ground to ground-design, to design-ground, and to design. But skill came to be thought to rest in the art of joining stanzas, and four degrees of closeness were distinguished: close, close-distant, distant-close, and distant. With the practice of Sōgi, the senior poet there at Minase, the sequence took precedence over striking individual stanzas, and variation in impressiveness was as important as in other matters.

Some canons were inviolable rules. For example, many words could not be repeated in a set number of stanzas. The general word for insects (as opposed to a named cricket) might appear only once in a hundred stanzas. Sōgi's use of "mushi" in the seventh stanza therefore precludes further use in the sequence.

These matters can be illustrated by a look at a few joinings of stanzas, beginning with the fourth by Sōgi as followed up by Shōhaku. Sōgi's daybreak stanza is ground-design, miscellaneous; it has the motifs of waters (from the boat) and night (as we have seen, our daybreak is Japanese nightopening). Shōhaku adds a ground-design autumn stanza. Its motifs are radiance (moon), night (the word and the moon), and rising things (fog). The relation is close-distant. The closeness derives from his contrastive transformance of Sōgi's distinct into an occluded scene, and his splendid stroke of taking the sound of boat polling to reveal quiet—otherwise so soft a sound could not be heard distinctly—as the moon cannot really be seen as anything more than a faint glow. The distance derives from shift to a seasonal topic and a temporal leap from the end of one night to the end of the next—or some much later one.

Sōchō follows, adding to Shōhaku's stanza. It is a ground stanza necessarily continuing the autumn topic, with the motif of "falling things" (dew) set against the preceding "rising" fog. These closing days of autumn make the moon of the preceding stanza more precious. This is also close-distant, moving from Shōhaku's unspecified moment of night sky to earth and through most of autumn. Although a ground stanza, it does its work perfectly: whether Sōchō understood it or not, Sōgi did, and saw that the moment had come for his design stanza that follows.

This is not from an Oxford Book of Narrative Verse. It is poetry seemingly random in alternating composition and yet governed by an extraordinarily complex code, of which only a few basic features have been mentioned. Some things are clear. Plot is out of the question, or at least it can continue no longer than five lines—the immediate integer of poetic sense. In fact from one stanza to the next, the most important constituent of narrative, people, may suddenly appear or vanish. Even in a given stanza, as another is added to it, the people may change in condition of being: from young to old, from lay to clerical, from male to female, from resident to traveler. Similar things go on with places and times, as we have just seen.

In the terms employed here, the issue is whether there is a continuum fulfilled. The manner of composition seems to me to guarantee continuing sequence, and the renga canons to guarantee fulfillment. I therefore judge this to be a kind of unplotted but fictional narrative (fictional, that is, after the first stanza).

Especially with marginal cases, it is useful to inquire what we gain by a decision. To hold that linked poetry is lyric affords us the luxury of reading the 250 lines (or 495, counting repetition of all but the first and last stanzas) as a mighty lyric, a sustained and intensified presence created by three poets composing in turn. To hold that linked poetry is narrative allows us to discover fulfilled continuity in sequentiality rather than plot. The narrative line is purer, the continuance finer. The awkwardness of taking linked poetry as narrative is that the units are lyric.

There are other awkwardnesses in taking sequences to be lyric. One such relates to our definition of lyric as intensified presence. In linked poetry the degree of intensity is deliberately varied. Another awkwardness of taking it as a lyric is that there are thousand and ten-thousand stanza sequences. Is there really such a thing as a 2,500 or 25,000-line lyric?[29]

If not all questions have been answered, certainly many issues have been better defined for study of sequences and collections in recent years. Until most recently, our understanding was hampered by the fact that study was done in such diverse subjects as the Roman poetry roll, Japanese court poetry, sonnet sequences, and modern poetry—with students in one field little aware of what was going on in others. It will not be amiss to approach the subject with a little unplotted narration.

A major discussion appeared in an article, now a classic, by Konishi Jin'ichi on principles of integration in anthologies and sequences of Japanese court poetry.[30] He showed that patterns of temporal progression in the books devoted to the seasons and love in royal collections led the way to devising progressions for books on other topics (e.g., travel, lament) and to ways of adding association—verbal, conventional, and conceptual—to progression. This integration was made possible by the practice of compiling by topic. Poems by a given poet are scattered throughout a collection, and the whole is given its order by a compiler or compilers royally commissioned to combine poetry of the past and present, by other poets and the compiler(s) as well. It does not seem an accident that this practice was perfected in the twelfth century, when *renga* had emerged as a pastime, nor any accident that *renga* emerged at that time and not before.

Sometime after Konishi, western classicists were discovering that the length of the Roman poetry roll (the western codex was not invented until late antiquity) encouraged ordering of groups of poems fitting into a roll. Virgil's *Eclogues* and Horace's *Odes* are conspicuous examples (Miner, 1985B). More recently full-length studies have appeared. Those include one of developments in western lyric sequences from Petrarch to Neruda, concentrating on such matters as character, time, and figuration; if Petrarch established character as the center of a lyric sequence, by Yeats the lyric character had become less secure, split into multiple perspectives (Greene, 1985). Another devotes attention to a single writer, D. H. Law-

---

[29] Sōgi composed his solo *Thousand Stanzas at Mishima* (*Mishima Senku*) in three days, presumably three hundred on two days and four hundred on one. The royal collections are integrated in ways adapted by *renga*. Chinese also have linked poems and collections, but they lack the *renga* or royal collection code. I judge the Chinese kinds to be lyrics and non-narrative collections of lyrics.

[30] Konishi, 1958. Versions of this account were incorporated by Brower-Miner, 1961 and by Miner, 1968. In a separate investigation, Louis L. Martz had discussed the unity of George Herbert's lyric collection, *The Temple* (Martz, 1954). No doubt inspired by both Konishi and Martz, I discussed Dryden's *Fables* (twice as long as *Paradise Lost*) as a unified collection (Miner, 1967, followed up by others as well as myself).

rence as a poet, exploring the issue of the integer in these autobiographical writings, concluding that it is not the "bits" of poems but a given ordered sequence. Moreover, the same "bits" could be recombined into a new sequence. Whatever its "bits," each sequence is held to be an autobiographical story and *apologia* of the writer.[31]

These studies relate to our issue of the bounds of narrative. It is clear (to me) that some sequences and collections are justly termed narrative and others not. There will also be examples whose status may be disputed. Spenser's *Amoretti* is a clear example of a narrative sequence in its telling of the story of his wooing the woman whose marriage with him is celebrated in the attached *Epithalamion*. On the other hand, poems may be ordered in a collection without their being narrative. One might arrange them in chronological order of composition, as is frequently done. That is an order not productive of narrative. Other ordering principles could be imagined, whether worth using or not: length of poem from shortest to longest (or the reverse), alphabetically, using the initial letters of a poem or titles, and so on. For the purposes of narrative, ordering is not enough—a kind of integration affording fulfilled continuum is necessary.

Dryden's *Fables* offers a test case. Most of the individual "fables" are clearly stories, narratives. But the issue is whether or not there is a narrative in the whole collection. The links between stories establish (purely as linkings) more a presumption of purpose than actual integration. That will be found, most of us now think, in the recurrent treatments of issues and situations, in Dryden's use of Christian poems at particular junctures, in his manipulation of Ovid's narrative in the second half of the *Metamorphoses*, and in his arrival at a chastened view of the human condition in the final, officially happy but bleak poem, *Cymon and Iphigenia*. That is, these matters impart the continuum and fulfillment necessary to narrative.

The major theoretical difference between *Fables* and *renga* is that the former is made up of lengthy units mostly narrative in nature, whereas the latter is made up of shorter units lyric in nature. There is multiple authorship in both cases, since *Fables* consists largely of translations. But the continuum of *renga* is more obvious in authorship, since *Three Poets at Minase* was composed precisely by those three we have noted, each of whom could expect that a few hours later the last stanza would be finished after darkness had fallen. And in the *renga* code there was provided both the means of integration and the basis of fulfillment—concluding

[31] Laird, 1988. For further discussion, see the chapters by various hands in Fraistat, 1986 and the massive study of sonnet sequences in Roche, 1989.

with the "fast close" and in fact with religious affirmation. If in spite of these things, linked poetry be excluded from narrative, it will have to be excluded (as Konishi argued) from lyric as well and established as a fourth genre (Konishi, 1971:56, 78).

NARRATIVE IN VERSE AND PROSE

What are the differences? There are a number of important issues, both conceptual and practical. The first has been alluded to, the paucity of theoretical study of verse narrative as narrative. To be narrative, it must have the same essential properties as prose narrative. Yet there must be some difference, both as our experience leads us to assume and as the absence of treatment of it may perhaps also imply. The western answer would probably be that traditional verse narrative, perhaps verse narrative *tout court*, is more elevated, that the attitude of prose narrative is of lesser awe, "lower." Certainly it has been the genius of the western novel to explore an extraordinary range of experience, especially of certain psychological or subjective states, that the heroic did not. Marxists and others have treated the novel as an expression of the growth in "reflection" (with or without Marxian "contradictions") in bourgeois experience.[32] There is a seeming confirmation of this view in the early western conceptions of the three genres. They emerged during the Italian Renaissance and found first English expression by Milton. In his *Reason of Church-Government* he speaks of "that Epick form," "those Dramatick constitutions," and "those magnifick Odes and Hymns" (Patterson, 1931–38:vol. 3, pt. 1, 813–15). Dryden followed and clarified somewhat in the preface "To the Reader" prefixed to his *Essay of Dramatic Poesy*, speaking of "this [i.e., dramatic], the epic, or the lyric way" (Watson, 1962:1, 17). Dryden could treat the lyric in descriptive terms, freeing it from Milton's normative description, but he no more than Milton could avoid a normative view of narrative, that it was epic. (He had not yet written about history.) Of course neither envisioned the novel, which was then in gestation. Narrative was heroic. We may ask what happened to their memories of Apuleius, Lucian, Rabelais, Boccaccio, Cervantes, and others? The answer would be that they are low. Lucretius and Ovid were epic and therefore counted. In short, the Miltons and Drydens exhibit the opposite failing from that usual today, when narrative is mostly defined on the basis of the (western) novel.

Of course none of this takes into account the prose narratives of east

---

[32] Two very attractive accounts, mostly of English prose narrative, will be found in Damrosch, 1985 and M. McKeon, 1987. Damrosch stresses philosophical, religious, and psychological issues. McKeon elaborates, from a mildly Marxian perspective, upon issues of "virtue" and "truth."

Asia, beginning in Japan and followed up in China. I know of no qualities (e.g., the awesome or heroic, foundation stories, etc.) associated in the west with verse narrative that cannot be found in the prose narrative of Japan and China. Table erased, we are at degree zero. We have only a few suggestions here and there to tell us of the difference between verse and prose narrative, although as always there is some value in clearing the critical counter of useless Eurocentric goods. What follows will go no great distance. But something must be suggested in an effort to serve, if only as the Horatian whetstone, the sharpening of others' wits.

The simplest fact is that verse is of more regular rhythm than prose. That attention to the simple leads us, however, to the further reflection that verse narrative is verbally, linguistically richer than prose narrative, whereas its narrative procedures are simpler. The *Iliad* is beautifully organized, a model of unity of relation and of effect. But we need only compare it with the more episodic *Odyssey* to see how simple in large-scale relation the *Iliad* is. The *Odyssey* introduces doubled narration of two kinds, the first in a beginning with a Telemachus plot-line followed by an Odysseus plot-line. The second doubled narration is achieved in delivery during that sustained episode of Odysseus relating his story to the Phaeacians. Both innovations, simple as they may be, produce a very great rise in subjectivity. The change is no doubt altogether suitable to a hero of many devices, especially one with his particular Olympian advisor. Subsequent writers of verse narrative built on the *Odyssey* model, seemingly on the principle that the technically more complex is the point of departure. (We are considering heroic poetry in the classical, not the Germanic and other medieval kinds. The differences in account would be more historical than theoretical, however.)

So let us summon our Wissenschaft and invoke Memory rather than her daughters. Virgil was a man of queasy stomach (Horace, *Journey to Brundisium*) and naturally felt he must incorporate both homeric poems in his *Aeneid*. It is no secret that the former, odyssean half is the more highly esteemed, or that if Helen's face launched a thousand ships, as a character Dido is kilohelen. Because completed long narratives are rare— besides the architectonics involved, the verbal requirement itself is so onerous—writers of verse narrative tend to build more on their predecessors and therefore find that they must distinguish their work in some respect.

Dante of the big hooked nose diminishes Virgil into a character inferior to his Christian self (also treating Virgil mostly as a lyric poet, according to *dantisti* recently), and it is the Dante figure who completes the journey through the *Purgatorio* and who arrives triumphantly in the *Paradiso*.

Ovid used means that are stronger in some ways, since whether Dante owned it or not, he owed Virgil the conception of a teleological poem.

Ovid looked on Virgil's foundation myth, fatal metaphysics, and adaptation of Homer. He seems to have liked too well what he saw so readily. So he responded with an amusement bordering on fear and the declaration that he will tell a teleological story, running from the beginning of the world (*ab origine mundi*) to his own times (*ad mea . . . tempora*) and in unbroken song (*perpetuum . . . carmen*)—essentially a version of the basic conception of narrative being used here. But most of his poem, which has been the secret favorite in Latin literature of poets for centuries, rattles from episode to episode, sometimes with brilliant transitions, sometimes with logical joining, and frequently with airy carelessness.

Poor Lucan set out to create an epic whose claim was historical accuracy, died before reaching an end, and finally suffered the double indignity of being called a historical instead of epic poet and having the *Pharsalia* completed in Latin by Tom May. In his *Teseida* Boccaccio essayed the neoclassic or humanist epic, but his greatest success came with a desertion of verse narrative for the prose of the *Decameron*. Ariosto saw deeply into the process or problem of the growing complexity of narration and subjectivity. In *Orlando Furioso* it seems, sometimes, as if every heroic cliche is in the poet's windmill. He is a narrative dictator, demonstrating his power over the poem and the reader. Almost every canto begins with some stanzas in which he appears *in propria persona ariostonis*, which is to say strongly and deviously. More than that, he refuses to allow his reader any rest, and in each canto violently switches from one plot to another of his labyrinthine story, and that he keeps his astonishing song interesting is the best geste of all.

After that mad poem by a sane poet, the sometimes mad Tasso wrote a poem he determined to be sane by subjecting it to allegoretic interpretation, especially of the "marvels" of *Jerusalem Delivered*, even while he worked at revising and perfecting it. Milton harkened to earlier poets from Homer forward, writing "Things unattempted yet in Prose or Rhime" (*Paradise Lost* 1, 16), an accurate attempt at Englishing Ariosto's "Cosa non detta in prosa mai, né in rima" (1, 2). He praised Spenser and dismissed systematic allegory in favor of Protestant literalness. He praised Cowley's *Davideis* and put it from his mind. He did not mention *Hudibras*, but he learned about dissimiles there. He out-odysseyed the *Odyssey* in layered narrative, contemptuously dismissed war as a subject and spent two books on it. He did this while fashioning a syntactic and verbal style that has defeated all who tried to emulate it.

It is small wonder that the awestruck Dryden, admiring *Paradise Lost* with resignation ("It cuts us all out, and the ancients, too"), should turn to an episodic, collective work for his grandest enterprise, *Fables Ancient and Modern*. His models were the looser ones of Chaucer, Boccaccio (transversed), and especially Ovid Christianized.

This travesty of the history of the epic in its classical western line is intended to stress two things. One is a repetition of a point made earlier: the Homer-to-Dryden account is a narrative, one without a plot. For if there can be plotless narrative about literature, it is impossible to understand why there cannot be the same in literature. The second matter takes us to a characteristic of verse narrative as opposed to prose narrative. The difficulties of writing successful long poetic narratives make each practitioner far more attentive to predecessors and contemporaries than is normal for writers of prose narrative. It is significant that Harold Bloom's theories about the anxiety of influence involve writers of verse rather than prose—"Strong poets," not "strong authors" (Bloom, 1973, 1975, 1982). For example, the succession from Ariosto to Tasso is a very great simplification. For any adequate account we should need to take consider not only their predecessor Boiardo along with Torquato Tasso's father but a number of other aspirants to heroic poetry.

There are differences, then, between narrative in verse and narrative in prose, difficult as they are to specify. The rhythm of verse is far more complex and recurrent than that of prose, so that style matters crucially. Should an English writer of heroic narrative follow the Italians, as Spenser and Davenant did (also Fairfax in translating Tasso) by using stanzas? Or should the poet use unrhymed verse, as Milton held, following the practice of his pristine models (even if English verse is accentual rather than quantitative)? Or is Dryden's heroic couplet the medium for that historically briefest of periods, the modern? The two brief generations of Romantic productivity in England could not reach a decision on the kinds of verse to use for narrative, except that the imitation of Milton was disastrous.

In verse there is also a more clearly drawn contrariety between authorial efforts to intrude or otherwise display control as against authorial efforts to let the story seem to tell itself. The focus of complexity and of interesting problems in verse narrative are the more immediate ones of verbal command and the remoter ones of authorial self-demonstration or withdrawal. It is typical of Milton that after writing, in *Paradise Lost*, the most complex narrative since Dante's, in a style never heard before or since, with wholesale disruption of natural plot-line and chronology, and with frequent authorial intrusions, he should then and still blind write *Paradise Regained*, using a far simpler style, more straightforward chronology, and a minimum of self-attention.

Of course early Indian narrative has been left out of this account. Its practice seems to confirm what has just been said of later, western verse narratives. Here is an excerpt from an account of "Legends of Authorship and Implicit Poetics in Sanskrit Literature":

> Early Indian literature employs two variant ways of representing authorship. An author may literally exist as a character within the text attributed to him (making explicit the author implied by the work) or he may be the hero of a legend that is attached to the text. In many cases, the legends surrounding the verses are mythical contexts for the poetry. A literary legend dramatizes the poetic personality in the text. It may also point to the work's dominant poetic structures, in much the same way that the prologue of a Sanskrit drama announces its dramatic structures. They explain the poetry by means that are different from academic analyses of Sanskrit poetics, which characteristically focus on formal elements of individual stanzas. [33]

Here also, if in another guise, we see on the one hand attention to simple large matters such as authors and "poetic structures," and on the other hand attention to matters of verbal and syntactic style, with their effects.

Even at this rudimentary state of the art, we can go some distance further in comparing verse with prose narrative. The grander if simpler features of verse narrative relate to dramatic possibilities. Because "dramatic" is used so loosely, I must refer to the sense posited in the second chapter. The largeness of verse narrative's general effects is estranging and then engaging, once we adjust.

There is the related matter of epic speech, of *logos*. Well before drama existed in Greece, the first book of the *Iliad* showed, *in narrative*, how well the *logos* could do two things. One was to represent *mythos*, fable, and history—the last with associations of prose writing also feasible. The second is the strong implication of speech and oration. [34] Milton's presumed "dramatic" first two books of *Paradise Lost* are founded on the Homeric *logos*, as the divine council of his third book is indebted positively to the theodicy-*logos* of *Odyssey* 1, 26–43 (Blessington, 1979:47–49) and negatively to the bickering *logoi* of the Olympian deities at the end of *Iliad* 1.

In rejecting the reflex impulse to term anything interesting "dramatic," and in emphasizing the narrative genealogy just now, I wish to say that it is in these simpler large matters that narrative has strong affinities with drama. Lyric is not only more intense but finer, so that to judge narrative or drama by lyric canons is to invite Deconstructive "reading." It is not altogether an accident that Milton first envisioned what was to be *Paradise Lost* as a tragedy, *Adam Unparadised*, or that Dryden started to make a

---

[33] B. S. Miller, 1987. The last sentence relates to the point made about Indian poetics in the first chapter.

[34] See Liddell-Scott, 1951:under *logos*, IV–VII.

dramatic version, *The State of Innocence*. Of course it is even less of an accident that both gave over, but the instincts of two such "strong poets" testifies to elements shared by verse narrative and drama. These are usually unnoticed by us, probably because they are simple and obvious. In that, they differ from prose narrative, which complicates what is simple and renders the remote into what is promoted.

The attention authors of verse narrative pay to style works in a different direction. By comparison with prose narrative, verse has an intensified presence that associates it with lyricism. This is shown by various things in differing traditions of verse narrative. Within the western classical epic tradition, lyric is incorporated into epic by a variety of means. Songs and hymns may be included. Similes are a traditional feature, as are the kinds of narrative *descriptio* mentioned earlier. Various other lyric lingerings and interruptions show as much. The readiest evidence for this (although evidence abounds elsewhere) is to be found in those epic poets who were also writers of distinguished lyrics. Although many might be named, two obvious ones are Tasso and Milton.[35]

East Asian narrative is dominantly, although not only, in prose. Given the lyric (and historical) base of east Asian poetics, it is not surprising that a narrative with the historical touches of *The Tale of Genji* should include almost eight hundred lyric poems as if written or spoken by the characters, not to mention others quoted in part. Because the contexts of these lyrics are prose rather than verse, and because the lyrics are genuine lyrics made for fictional occasions like those of lyrics then written for real occasions, these lyrics stand out much more prominently than does a lyric passage in Virgil or Spenser.

It is worth reflecting on the nature of the changes in literary presumptions and style that would be necessary to make *Madame Bovary* or *The Magic Mountain* fit with so much lyric poetry. In east Asian literatures, the narrative affiliations with lyric and drama are not to be sought in verse narrative but in drama. Both *nō* and the so-called Peking opera show that. In their dramatic context, various uses of narrative fit with energies of presenting in operatic passages and song. Frequently, however, there is a difficulty in separating narrative from lyric in these kinds of drama: yet another testimony to the founding of their originative poetics on lyric buttressed by certain kinds of history. There are, then, identifiable rea-

---

[35] On Tasso, see Getto, 1951: "Struttura e Poesia Nella " 'Gerusalemme Liberata,' " pp. 379–417, on lyric elements in that epic; and for his remarks on Tasso as a lyric poet, "Esperienze Liriche," pp. 251–97. On *Paradise Lost* as an example of *genera mista*, see Lewalski, 1985. For a study of *Paradise Lost*—along with the *Iliad* and *Aeneid*—in terms of narrative, drama, and lyric, see Bayly, 1789.

sons for distinguishing verse from prose narrative, reasons showing how much more the distinction needs to be investigated.

NARRATIVE UNITS

Another all but equally ignored matter, at least in theoretical terms, is the subject of narrative units. Simple logic shows that (with the addition of textual lacunae) there are only four possible kinds of units. The first is the whole. After all has been said about circular design, "spatial form," intertextuality, and "open endings," the prime integer is the whole. Before it begins to continue, there is nothing; after it last discontinues, there is no more: *incipit . . . explicit*. The second possible unit is that of division into chapters or other parts, such as the fifty-four of *The Tale of Genji*. A third possible unit is a larger grouping of chapters or parts. It is a commonplace of criticism of *The Tale of Genji* that its chapters group into three divisions: 1–33, 34–41, and 42–54. The fourth possible unit is that which is briefer than a chapter. Of these four kinds, the first two—the whole and the parts labeled as chapters—are given by the author (unless the text is in jeopardy), and as such are not open to debate as to their being units. The second pair—units grouping chapters or parts, and units smaller than chapters—are units distinguished by readers. They are matters of interpretation and so are open to debate.

The Romance of the Three Kingdoms will illustrate these distinctions. The whole and the usual number of 120 chapters in these "classical" Chinese narratives provide the two authorial units. Grouping of *multiple* chapters is clear in the run of them about three-quarters on when Kungming leads forces south to gain control of the Man peoples and their territory. I can imagine disagreement as to where that grouping ends, but any reader recognizes that some such combination of chapters exists.

The readiest example of *subchapter* units is provided by Chapter 90, describing the last sequence of battles between Kungming and the Man chieftain, Menghou. Seven times Kungming succeeds against odds in capturing Menghou, and each time but the last he lets him go, because until then the chieftain does not submit voluntarily. The repeated trials of Sir Gawain with the Green Knight are similar. Yet each trial is different. Each advances the story, somewhat like Dante's series of conversations with those condemned in the *Inferno*.

The move from these quite apparent but little explored matters to other issues is like that from peace to battle. We can all agree that different narratives or different purposes with the same work make a number of schemes of subchapter units fruitful—at least to the individual fruit-gatherer. One kind will be discussed at the close of this chapter in connection with narrative point of view. Another, now to be considered, employs attention to beginnings and/or endings.

For centuries editors of *The Tale of Genji* have been supplying subtitles or brief summaries of episodes within the fifty-four chapters. They do not show much agreement, and for that matter the distinguishing of sentences, punctuation, and persons referred to is editorial textual imposition. Consulting a diplomatic facsimile (in modern printed characters) of the oldest texts shows why the editors have intervened. There is absolutely no punctuation. The only indentations in the upper margin do not indicate sentences, paragraphs, or even sections but the appearance of a poem.

In such extremity, every reader has a try, and this one has a thesis that the beginnings of narrative units in *The Tale of Genji* can be distinguished by specification of one of the three elements fundamental to plot: a person, place, or time—with also something else (usually narratorial intervention). Certainly there are patterns to the beginnings (and for that matter, the endings) of chapters, and they are those just named for subchapter units. For example, "Writing Practice" ("Tenarai") opens with all three major specifications, going in ascending order from time, to place, to person:

"Sono koro" (indicating new matter)	"At that time" *Time*
"Yokawa ni"	"in Yokawa" *Place*
"nanigashi sōzu to ka iite"	"a bishop of some name" *Person*

Since the tools used are the chief elements of narrative, it is not surprising that they may be used to distinguish the beginnings of chapter and subchapter-units. Of course this is a simplified version.[36]

That simplification has a benefit in its fourth category of beginning: it tells us that we must add the self-stylized author and narrator to people, places, and times as constituents of narratives. Although that supposition may be anathema to many recent critics—who prefer to say (I am not sure what they think) that texts tell themselves and do other things involving

[36] For the material simplified here, see Miner, 1982:231–57. The scheme proposed there and outlined here is less the issue than is finding grounds—answering to theory, history, and practice—for distinguishing cognoscible units. In *The Tale of Genji* that is a fundamental problem. One either submits expediently to the decisions of a given editor or devises one's own principles.

human agency, it accords with what Barbara Miller has observed of Sanskrit narrative (quoted above).

POINTS OF VIEW AND ATTENTION

From verse narrative and narrative units, we are prepared for the final promised topic, a review of the concept of narrative points of view. "Point of view" is a metaphor for narratorship, both as a fact and as a specific variety (e.g., "first-person"). Since an unnarrated narrative is a contradiction, narratorship extends from beginning to end, affording one of the principal features of continuities and sometimes of fulfillment as well. The plural, continuities, is required, both because a wide range of effects is involved and because point of view may be shifted.

In that there is another basis for distinguishing narrative units. Since narrators are versions of people, there is renewed testimony to the importance of people over places and times in narrative. The concept, the fact, is not only important but also fraught with a number of uncertainties, matters that we are only beginning to understand.[37]

Western consideration of points of view dates from the Greek Academy's distinction between mimesis and diegesis, but the idea has received sustained attention only since Henry James. It was traditionally assumed that the narrator of verse narrative was more or less identifiable with the poet, so that until the novel came into being there seemed to be little reason to air the issue. The narrator was identified with the author, a first-person was implied. Even Samuel Butler and Sterne, for all their strong measures, became what they wrote, Hudibras and Shandyean.

James made effective use of shifts of point of view among his characters, whether major ones or those lesser ones he termed "reflectors." Like every other concept of consequence, however, that of points of view means different things to different people, and it will be useful to review what seems to be widely thought on the subject. Here is a set of distinctions commonly made.

> *Omniscient.* In principle, the narrator has access to the complete lives and thoughts of the characters. (See third-person.) But the term is also used for lesser command.
>
> *First-person.* The narrator's own story is told, with access to the inner lives of none of the other characters. Much of the effect depends on whether the narrator is the principal or a subsidiary character.

---

[37] Booth, 1983, provides a bibliography and a discussion: see index under "point of view." Lanser, 1981, is centrally concerned with point of view (for example, with its ideological implications). Her first chapter offers an excellent review of criticism.

Third-person. The narrator relates the story of others and normally is not a character in the story. (See omniscient.)

Third-person focused. The narrator has access to the mind of but one character, usually the principal one.

Third-person limited. The narrator lacks access to the minds of any of the characters. Like the omniscient, but oppositely, this rule may be qualified.

Joined. The narrator and a character share thoughts indistinguishably.

Alternating. The point of view shifts from one character to another or from one "person" to another.

Mixed. Like alternating, but in small compass.

Nonperson. Point of view absent in the sense that it is unlocatable.

Other varieties could be mentioned, but these are representative, with the last deriving chiefly from nonwestern narrative.

Three inferences of increasing importance may be drawn from those representative ideas about points of view. One is that writers are not always consistent. James himself, and even in his late novels, will use an authorial or narratorial "I" in passages where one of the characters is supposed to supply the point of view. Second, there are varieties of temporary narratorial retreat. Dialogue presented without the usual Austenian speech tags—"said she," "cried he"—is one example. Use of letters or documents is another. Of course the absented narrator must be presumed and will certainly be back soon. The third matter is the point made by Gérard Genette. Logically speaking, all narrative is first-person narrative. There can no more be third-person narration than second-person. Initially, openly, or in the end the telling must be referable to a teller whose self-reference can only be "I."[38] As he well observes, we have allowed ourselves "a regrettable confusion between . . . the question *who is the character whose point of view orients the narrative perspective?* and the very different question *who is the narrator?*—or more simply, the question is *who sees?* and *who speaks?*" (p. 186). Preferring to think of focalization rather than of points of view, Genette distinguishes three kinds: nonfocalized, as in "classical narrative"; internal focalization, which he distinguishes in three subvarieties; and external focalization (pp. 189–90). So as not to multiply terms, I shall continue with "point of view," asking leave to think it a question of narratorship, of *who knows and tells.* After all, even if there can be no narrator *of* drama, there can be narrators *in* a play.

It is not only a narrator who must use "I" for self-reference, but the

[38] Genette, 1981:161–211. This whole fourth chapter on "Mood" deserves study. Further references will be incorporated in the main discussion.

author as well. (The same thing obviously holds for characters, readers—
anybody.) For that and other reasons we need to inquire into the bases
and the necessities for distinguishing between narratorship and authorship. The issues are very difficult.

Aristotle said that Homer at times had his characters perform the imitation (which the philosopher liked and termed mimesis) and at times
performed the imitation himself (which Aristotle's teacher, Plato, termed
diegesis). The second possibility would probably be voted down in a
western critical plebiscite today. The closest idea that might prove acceptable is Wayne C. Booth's concept of the implied author (Booth,
1983:421–35).

Even when an author is not in evidence, the assumption that the author
exists is necessary. It is inescapable in a kind of modern Japanese prose
narrative for which no exact counterpart exists elsewhere. On the basis
of a German term, now forgotten, *Ich-Roman*, Japanese coined their own
term or terms: *shishōsetsu* or *watakushishōsetsu*. For the moment let us presume that *shōsetsu* can be adequately translated, which it cannot be, as
"novel." Both Japanese terms then mean, much like the German one, "I-
novel." Readers assume that the main character is the author, and that
diaries, letters to and from others, recalled conversations, and much else
that is actual go into the making of this kind of narrative. Yet it is also
assumed that this narrative differs from that of autobiography. In both
there is an identification of the narrator with the author, with whatever
caveats about reliability. The distinction between author and narrator in
these two kinds—and between these two kinds—is extremely difficult to
formulate.[39]

It is our habit in these matters to assume a degree of tidiness that does
not always exist. Authorship is a concept that varies considerably, at least
if by the author we mean the human agency responsible for particular
words on particular pages. Authorship involves a single person, or more
likely a team, normally of one author and one editor, although more
complex examples are not far to seek.[40]

---

[39] The features and distinctions of the *shishōsetsu* are much debated. For a wide-ranging
account surveying the Japanese scholarship and positing autobiography as a major distinction, see Hijiya-Kirschnereit, 1981, the first major western study. For a language and west-
ern-criticism based account, see E. Fowler, 1988. Reed, 1985 and 1988, seem to me to show
the shortcomings of linguistic models offered and to pare matters to their essentials.

[40] Take Eldershaw, 1984. "M. Barnard Eldershaw" is a pseudonym for Marjorie Barnard
and Flora Eldershaw. In addition to whatever normal editing they had, their first edition—
Melbourne: Georgian, 1947—was censored. Nearly forty years later the cut passages, including the present last two words of the title, were restored. On p. xv of the Virago modern classic edition one reads, "We have followed the original typescript version." The restored passages are identified. But it is not said who "we" may be, nor whether "the original

Narratorship is an easier concept than authorship, at least until one tries to define where one leaves off and the other begins. There are bound to be different interpretations or explanations. In *Great Expectations*, the mature Pip relates his fortunes from boyhood nearly to present age. Some might wish to posit an implied narrator or/and an implied author between Dickens and the narrating mature Pip. The same issue exists for *Huckleberry Finn*. In my view, it is simpler to assume that Dickens and Twain stand, so to speak, directly behind Pip and Huck, or in other words that the positing of an implied author or implied narrator is not necessary for either novel; that the author stands immediately behind the character-narrator.

It is not fashionable to make much of the author, at least not in certain circles in certain cultures. Since the existence of that agency is so patent, however, we are obliged to define some of the conditions involved. For one thing, the author must be considered as the historical person at a given task: Twain writing *Huckleberry Finn* rather than another of his stories. (It may be assumed I know that "Mark Twain" is a *nom de plume* for Samuel Langhorne Clemens, knowledge that does not provide, for me, a requiem for the author but plain evidence of the necessary terms under which an author may effect self-presentation, whether in narrative or lyric. A chief difference is that, because of the complexity of self-presentation in narrative, *noms de plume* are more frequent for narrative than for lyric writers.) The tasks of writing *Tom Sawyer, Huckleberry Finn*, and *A Connecticut Yankee* bring out different concerns, different features of the personality of, different versions of the style of, Mark Twain.

This may be called authorial self-stylizing, at least if we allow that concept to include artistic conventions of a given time or culture. Not only is an author historical; so is the writing of a book. As we all know, the history of writing one book (sonnet, or letter) differs from the history of writing another, and there is gratuitous evidence of authorial stylizing in the case of many a "classic nineteenth-century realistic novel" written under names like Mark Twain, Stendhal, and George Eliot. Perhaps to say "stylized author" is redundant, since there is no other kind of author.

Narrators and narratorship are also stylized. Conventions of a culture and historical conditions are necessarily involved. Many centuries were required in China and Europe before women could be thought of as narrators, whereas in Japan that was not the case. And if stylizing involves such matters as half the race, it also involves the niceties of beginning and

---

typescript" has "original" editing on it or whether, which is most unlikely, no changes were made in proof.

ending, of conveying a culture's values, and much else. Narratorship may also be surrogate and dispersed.

The Tale of Genji provides a good if disputed example of this. The most eminent scholars of the work agree that the story has a number of lesser narrators, ladies who served at court and heard various things which they pass on. One explanation of this is multiple point of view. An analogy may be drawn between the narration of *The Tale of Genji* and the scrolls drawn sometime later to illustrate it. The scrolls usually include an abridgment of a chapter, followed by one of its poems and then the picture. The picture relates more directly to the poem than to the prose, although the two are connected. The pictures have the convention of a removed roof, so that the inside of a house is visible. In lieu of perspective, the characters depicted usually gaze in directions that seem inconsistent with their being together. The narratorship is said to be like that: not singular but plural, dispersed.[41] Let us deal with the analogy first. If we are to follow the parallel with the scroll, then we may indeed take those various figures looking at different directions to represent a multiple narratorship. But we also unroll the scroll, reading and looking from right to left. That scrolling reading is an implied general narratorship—or authorship. Apart from the analogy, there is so much detail about what Genji and other characters think and what lovers do and say alone that, in addition to the multiple subsidiary narrators, a general (implied) narratorship or, if that fails to describe the situation, (implied) authorship must be presumed.

We need repeatedly to remind ourselves that narrative need not be literary. In particular, it is useful to get out of fixation with the novel. Here is Milton telling about part of his earlier life, exploiting the topos of "The Artist as a Young Man" well before Joyce.

> I must say therefore that after I had from my first yeeres by the ceaseless diligence and care of my father, whome God recompence, bin exercis'd to the tongues, and some sciences [kinds of knowledge], as my age would suffer, by sundry masters and teachers both at home and at the schools, it was found that whether ought was impos'd by them that had the overlooking, or betak'n to of my own choise in English, or other tongue, prosing or versing, but chiefly this latter, the style by certain vital signes it had, was likely to live. (Wolfe, 1953:808–809)

To insist again on what should be plain, a narrator is necessary for narration. In the example just given, moreover, a distinction between the

---

[41] This interpretation was presented by Professor Mitani Kuniaki in a lecture at Princeton University, Spring 1987.

narrator and John Milton is an unneeded contrivance, an unparsimonious supposition. The narrator-author is stylized, more openly self-concerned than his counterpart in *Areopagitica*, more controlled than the at times hysterical counterpart in *Ikonoklastes*.

Here now is another version of narrative (*Paradise Lost* 1, 13–19) with someone invoking the Muse:

> to my adventurous Song,
> That with no middle flight intends to soar
> Above th'*Aonian* Mount, while it pursues
> Things unattempted yet in Prose or Rhime.
> And chiefly Thou O Spirit, that dost prefer
> Before all Temples th'upright heart and pure,
> Instruct me . . .   (Patterson, 1931:2, pt. 1, 8–9)

The pride reminds us of the earlier passage in prose. The issue is whether it is more useful to identify the first person of the poem with Milton as stylized author or with a distinct agency, a narrator.

The answer depends on interpretation not only of what "author" and "narrator" mean but also upon interpretation of the entire poem. As I understand the poem, there is no single way of identifying the first-person. By Book 9, or more precisely by the fall of Adam, Milton seems to me to divide in considerable measure from his narrator, but that same division could be described as one found in the poet himself, between Milton the believer and Milton the one who knows that he would have fallen with Eve, too.

Alternatively, I should have no quarrel with someone who held that besides the main narrator of *Paradise Lost*, and in addition to the poet, there is a fictional construct, the Poet. On the other hand, at the beginning of Book 9, the stylized author and the narrator seem almost the same. I see no need for there to be a single, set relation between author and narrator.

At times or in a given complex work, numerous distinctions may be useful. One can say of Book 9 of *Paradise Lost* that at different points we have surrogate narrators (Eve, Adam, Satan), the first-person narrator, the self-presented author (or the Poet of the poem), a self-presenting author, at times perhaps an implied author, and at times Milton. I know of no critic who has thought Milton's narrator(s) to be female or Murasaki Shikibu's to be male. One can also say that the more factual or religious a narrative is, the less need there is to distinguish between author and narrator in radical terms (in the absence of countervailing evidence), whereas the more extreme a fiction or ironic a situation, the more the distinction becomes useful (in the absence of countervailing evidence).

If there is varying utility in distinguishing between Milton and his narrator in *Paradise Lost*, there are some writings in which a given distinction like that between narrator and author is more of a nuisance than an aid—Milton's prose narrative, for example. The same is true for near eastern Islamic cultures and east Asian cultures, with their strong lyric presumptions. This is not to say that it is assumed that the poet is *always* identifiable with the narrator. Apart from historical writing, the first originally literate and literary prose narrative extant in Japanese in its original form is Ki no Tsurayuki's *Tosa Diary* (*Tosa Nikki*; ca. 935). Although it is based on his return to the capital after a tour of duty as governor of Tosa, the diary is related as if by one of the women in his party. The fiction has been apparent from the outset.

Over seven centuries later Matsuo Bashō wrote one of his "diaries of the road," as he called them. He records a visit to what is probably, after Mount Fuji, the most famous beauty spot in Japan, Matsushima, a group of islands off the eastern shore near Sendai. Here is most of the ending:

> In the shade of the pines there were also one or two priests who had renounced the world, leading the lives of hermits in their grass-thatched huts, above which rose the thin smoke of fires built of pine cones or fallen needles. Of course I do not know them, but their life is appealing. As I approached them, the moon rose, sparkling upon the sea, creating a loveliness different from that in daylight. We went back to the inlet and looked for lodging. Our room was in the upper of two storeys, and we opened our window, enjoying our traveler's sleep in the freshest of breezes, borne upon us with the strangest feeling of delicacy. Sora wrote a poem. . . . I decided to be silent as a poet in such a place. (Miner, 1969:174)

I do not see what is gained by refusal to identify Bashō with his narrator here, or rather to say directly that Bashō relates. We can verify all but one thing here as fact from reading Sora's nonliterary diary. It is unusual for Bashō not to compose a *hokku* on a place he visits, especially if it is famous, or if it appeals to him. One is tempted to take his decision "to be silent as a poet in such a place" as a kind of Zennist nonpoem. In fact, Bashō is playing loose with facts on that one detail. He did compose a *hokku* at Matsushima, but it did not satisfy him, make him feel worthy of the place or himself. He was right. Even with this distortion of fact, it makes sense to identify Bashō with the narrator, as it does not Tsurayuki with the female narrator of *The Tosa Diary*. Because we have useful distinctions, it does not follow that we need always make them, or even always make them the same way for the seemingly same "I."

Two reasons have prompted this discussion, however brief, of narrative points of view. One has been to emphasize my sense of its importance and its multiplicity, in fact its untidiness, even impurity as a literary phenomenon in lengthy examples. It is important as a way of describing the cognitive process from authorial creation to presented expression. Because it is multiple, talk of "point of view" in the singular suggests a single cognitive scheme that is simply not honored in long narratives.

The other purpose has been to lay the grounds in what is reasonably familiar for a subject of equal importance to narrative but that has gone undiscussed, as far as I am aware.[42] As has been emphasized, the concept of narrative point of view metaphorically concerns the minds real or fictional who are knowing and relating in a narrative. My next concern with narrative is the counterpart of that knowing and relating: what is known, what is related. Given that the phrase "point of view" is so familiar and has counterparts in other languages, and given also the lack of need for unnecessary multiplication of categories of terms, I shall call the counterpart of narrative points of view the narrative points of attention, or simply point(s) of attention. It has some merit—or limitation—in suggesting an aural metaphor for what the reader "hears" related.

The omission of concern with the topic is strange within western literature and insupportable in other literatures. "Tell me, Muse, of the man of many ways," *The Odyssey* begins (in one translation), beseeching a little farther on, "From some point here, goddess, daughter of Zeus, speak, and begin our story" (Homer, 1975;11. 1, 10). In pre-Platonic literary ideas, the conception of the Muses is paramount (Harriott, 1960), and with that goes a concern with what is being told, or about to be told, that certainly marks literature for recitation.

The loss of concern with the matter must be attributed to the Academy's concern with mimesis. Aristotle's concern lay with imitating, with mimesis and diegesis, and the *what* of the imitation was the world of which the imitation was a simulacrum enriched with metaphor and based on distinctions between goodness and badness. That concern, however redefined, has remained a mimetic legacy. It presumes a world, an imitator (or Romantic imagination), and an imitation (currently, representation, *representation, Darstellung*) that is counterpart of that world. These truths that are self-evident lack the complexity of Homer:

---

[42] My own previous discussions of points of attention appeared in places too inaccessible to be worth citing.

Tell me, Muse, of the man of many ways, who was driven
far journeys, after he had sacked Troy's sacred citadel.
Many were they whose cities he saw, whose minds he learned of

   . . .

(Homer, 1975:11. 1–4)

No sooner has Odysseus become our object of attention than it turns out that he has his objects of attention, many people and their minds. No sooner do we accustom ourselves to him as the object of attention with, in turn his objects of attention, than the gods become the point of attention, with *their* points of attention (1. 19), and it is not long before we make, with Pallas Athene as transition, a shift to Telemachus as point of attention (1. 113 and through Book 4, with various divagations).

It seems highly desirable to alienate (render foreign, unusual) mimetic assumptions about the imitator, the world imitated, and the imitation of the world. There also will be no harm in doing so cheerfully. In 1785 a Japanese publisher named Tsuta Jūzaburō brought out a book called *Edo Umare Uwaki no Kabayaki*. The title is playfully complex. "Edo Umare" means "Born in Edo"; "Uwaki no Kabayaki" means "A Broiled Eel of a Dashing Lady-Killer." The best translation of the title is *Grilled Playboy, Edo Style.*[43]

The book consists of pictures drawn by Kitao Masanobu for a story by Santō Kyōden. On the first page the inept hero, Enjirō, is drawn stretched out reading scripts of plays. The written text appears across the top of the picture (and as a joke down the left-hand margin in a single dribble), except for the last two clauses given in the translation below. Those are the thoughts or words of Enjirō and so are written just above his head. The ensuing translation obeys the original more faithfully than it does the laws of usual translationese and perhaps of the English language to boot. It renders the entire written narration depicted; its first word means "In this picture" or "Below in this picture."

Here Enjirō, the only son of a shop worth a million and called Fickle Feeling, is grown to about eighteen or nineteen, and—"The disease of poverty causes no suffering here; / It is well if no other ill befalls"— taking pleasure in the life of a playboy, looking at books of plays of the puppet theater, thinking with envy of such exemplars as Idahachi of the Tamakiya or amorous Inosuke, having the yearning of an entire life to be a playboy and acquire the name of a ladykiller, thinking in due

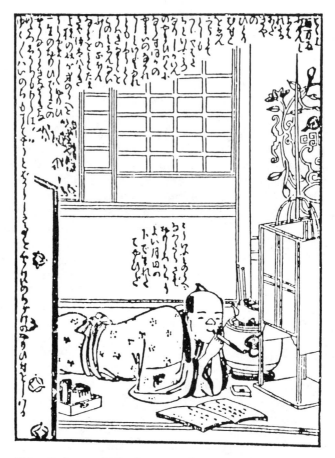

"Here Enjirō . . ." The first page of Santō Kyōden's *Edo Umare Uwaki no Kabayaki* (1785). From *Kibyōshi Sharebon Shū*, ed. Mizuno Minoru (Tokyo: Iwanami Shoten, 1958), p. 136.

course to throw away life in this, imagining such notions of a fool, decides to devote life to that end—

—it would be terrific to become that way—

that's being born with a great karma!

(Miner, 1983:87, revised)

The fact that the point of attention is crucial here can be demonstrated in many ways. First of all, there is the picture. There are also the words, "Here Enjirō . . .," so emphatic on what we should attend to, so little emphatic of narratorial presence. It is significant that when the narrator does wish to make himself known, it is desirable or necessary to intrude with a strong gesture, the dismissive comment, "imagining such notions of a fool."

Like Odysseus, Enjirō has his objects of attention: the play scripts, famous playboys of the time, and himself. As with any story, attention to point of view alone is empty except for narratorial thought and comment. The story cannot exist without its points of attention, and since people are the prime objects of attention, they as subjects have their own, other objects of attention, who may have . . .

This example may cause a certain giddiness in heads well trained mimetically. If so, the spin does not stop when we learn who the author and artist were. Santō Kyōden and Kitao Masanobu are names for the same person, also known as Kyōya Denzō, named after (or before) a shop, the Kyōya. Masanobu sometimes illustrated stories by others, and other artists sometimes illustrated Kyōden's. To obtain information about the writer, Santō Kyōden, one looks him up in a literary reference book. For Kita Masanobu, the same human being but a different artist, an artistic reference book is necessary. In either one, the investigator will discover that the real name of those artists and that shopkeeper was Iwase Sei, who is not listed in either the literary or pictorial reference books.[44] This is not Aristotle's cut-and-dried Homer imitating in two ways. It is various *personae artis* working together to produce the object of attention: "Here Enjirō . . ."

This delightful little comedy, prepared by those so closely connected but distinctly named artists, Masanobu and Kyōden, instructs us in how to attend. So instructed, we may consider some examples. But let us first use drama to make an allied point. It is necessary to consider the readers' points of view and the characters' points of view as distinct not only in themselves but from the author's narratorial point of view as well.

Because drama has no narration, there is no narrator and therefore no narrative point of view. *But our readerly point of attention remains.* And audience point of attention possesses the same cognitive status for drama as for readers or hearers of narrative (and lyric). As we take Hamlet as our point of attention, we find him taking in a soliloquy both himself and

44 In the most widely used Japanese dictionary, *Kōjien*, 3rd ed. (Tokyo: Iwanami Shoten, 1983), there are entries for our author, Santō Kyōden and for Kitao Masanobu, but none for Iwase Samuru, as that dictionary pronounces the character for the real man's given name (in the entry on Kyōden). Most literary dictionaries give, as I have done, "Sei." How Japanese: we know with certainty two made-up artistic names and a business name and are not sure of the "real name." Consider Murasaki Shikibu. The "Murasaki" is a nickname derived from the heroine of the first two sections of the work, and the "Shikibu" indicates that a male relative had a post in the Bureau of Rites. Her real surname was Fujiwara, and her real given name is not known.

Fortinbras. And in rapid dialogue, we find characters taking each other as points of attention, with our own switching with equal rapidity back and forth.

The general example from drama makes this a moment appropriate to fulfill the promise in the second chapter to deal with that strange ending of *Matsukaze*, in which it grows difficult for the audience (or reader) to tell who is speaking, whom the audience is to take as both the narrator and the point of attention. (This *nō* is unusual in other ways, being apparently unique among Zeami's work in having a *shitezure*, a "shite companion," Matsukaze's sister, Harusame.)

It will be recalled that, by convention, the chorus in *nō* gives the thoughts or words of the principal character, the *shite*. At the end of *Matsukaze*, however, we find that the chorus does not do that, but offers instead a play on the names of the two sisters. As the night has passed, there was a spring shower (i.e., Harusame) and now there remains only wind in the pines (Matsukaze). The normal function of the *nō* chorus has been abandoned in order to give us this figurative version of the two sisters.

Instead of our attending to the sisters as they attend (via the chorus) to their objects with their minds, we attend directly to the sisters as our objects of attention when they have been deprived of theirs. As a result, their past dreams become our present vision. There is *no dominating point of view* but only points of attention. What had seemed impossible to explain becomes amply clear once the conception of characters' and readers' points of attention is introduced.

Leaving the stage and its possibilities, its limits, we observe that narrative has its own possibilities, its limits. There may be points of attention for us in the theater, but in narrative there can be none without a narrator and points of view. It is equally true, however, that there can be no narrative without points of attention. And, as we have just been seeing—as we could also see in lyric on other grounds—under the conditions of western drama we have (dramatic) points of attention without a (dramatic or narrative) point of view. The only seeming exception occurs when drama encapsulates narrative, as in Othello's account of his wooing of Desdemona. Then he becomes the narrator. But since he is a character, and since there is no general narrator, his narration ends up being a long speech in the theater rather than any challenge to the conditions of the dramatic.

Western narrative sometimes takes on a semblance of features of Japanese or other affective-expressive literatures. Austen has a passage in *Persuasion* (vol. 2, ch. 2 or ch. 19) that resembles what we have just seen in Kyōden. The heroine, Anne Elliott, meets her once-rejected suitor, Frederick Wentworth. He has come to Bath in hope of persuading her with a second offer that she is eager to accept when made. Her vain father and elder sister do not help, and she is being pursued by her plausible but villainous cousin, William Elliott. On a day when she has an appointment with him, she happily encounters Wentworth by chance. Rain leads him to offer her his umbrella. To their mutual chagrin, Elliott comes by to claim her company. She leaves in his company with a smile to Wentworth. Whereupon we read:

> As soon as they were out of sight, the ladies of Captain Wentworth's party began talking of them.
>
> "Mr. Elliott does not dislike his cousin, I fancy?"
>
> "Oh! no, that is clear enough. One can guess what will happen there. He is always with them; half lives in the family, I believe. What a very good-looking man!"
>
> "Yes, and Miss Atkinson, who dined with him once at the Wallises, says he is the most agreeable man she was ever in company with."
>
> "She is pretty, I think; Anne Elliott; very pretty, when one comes to look at her. It is not the fashion to say so, but I confess I admire her more than her sister."
>
> "Oh! so do I."
>
> "And so do I. No comparison. But the men are all wild after Miss Elliott. Anne is too delicate for them."
>
> (Austen, 1926:5, 177–78)

The contrast between the narrator's introductory sequence and the dialogue is an extreme one. The narration is standard novel fare. The dialogue affords what the New Critics used to term a choral function, and it is this kind of run of conversation that has given Austen the name of a dramatic novelist. It is striking that both the narrator and "the ladies" refer to or name other characters: the same ones in fact. But the women who speak are not named, and there are no narratorial speech tags. By casting them into anonymity (all we can tell is that there are at least three of them), Austen confers correspondingly greater attention on Anne and her cousin.

The alert reader has another object of attention that the women do not: Wentworth. We know, as they do not, of his love for Anne (as we know of hers for him, as he does not), and we know that their words are a torture to him. This high degree of importance of the point of attention is typical of affective-expressive narrative like Japanese, as is also therefore the seemingly effortless switch from person to person attended to and voice to voice of the attenders. It may be coincidental, although I believe it altogether material, that this lack of specification of the names of speaking characters in *Persuasion* is unique in Austen's novels.

The women's comments seem to displace the narrator. In that sense, this passage is a foremother of the stream of consciousness practiced by Joyce and Woolf or, more generally, by a range of conventions developed by authors of the modern "lyrical novel."[45] *True* displacement of the narrator is of course impossible to narrative. But the effort to make the narrator less conspicuous is feasible, as is multiplication of the narratorial function by surrogates or shifts in point of view. We recognize in not a few recent western novels this tendency to damage narratorship by denying the narrator certain powers or making narratorship unreliable. Here is an antimimetic effort, a major element datable in English from Joyce, with whatever premonitions. The extreme version of this antimimesis has been denial, not of narratorial, but of authorial agency by critics (who nonetheless maintain their own self-entitling ordinance).

Those developments in western literary practice and critical argument have made it easier to teach nonwestern narrative. There remains, however, a great gap between antimimetic narrative—which necessarily feeds off what it opposes, mimetic presumptions—and the narrative in affective-expressive traditions. To show as much will require further examples.

The Diary of Izumi Shikibu (*Izumi Shikibu Nikki*) employs a variety of narrative techniques that make it seem like an odd Edwardian story laced with brief poems. That is true—in translation—and only as long as we use normal English sentences and, in particular, references such as names along with a liberal dose of pronouns. One of the most interesting examples of affective-expressive narrative and of the importance of points of attention in the *Diary* will tax a reader's patience. But they triumph who endure, or at least the fifty-seven clauses involved will surely demonstrate that what Austen sustains so rarely and briefly is far more readily handled in Japanese. The passage involves the prince who is the hero and features the Lady (Izumi Shikibu) who is the heroine and, most people think, the author.

They have been having a sporadic love affair in which the Lady wishes for certainty and security in his love. In the lengthy passage to be quoted, he is visiting her and unexpectedly proposes that she move into his palace. His official consort or principal wife lives there, and given the Lady's

---

[45] Freedman, 1963. This book has enjoyed great favor among students of nonwestern "novels." Its favor is owed partly to the author's insight into handlings of time and intensity that lend a lyric cast to certain novels, partly to the corresponding lyric elements in nonwestern narrative, and partly to seeming resemblances between antimimetic and affective-expressive art.

relatively low social status and the complex marital gradations of the time, for her to live with a prince of the blood would make her a concubine. As long as he commutes to her in her own house, her status is higher because ambiguous and, in a way, normal. Perhaps that is why the Lady somewhat unexpectedly hesitates.

Within the lengthy syntactic flow, the narrator's and reader's narrative points of attention—first the Prince, then the Lady, and finally, briefly the Prince—dominate point of view. While he is the reader's point of attention, she is his. It will be observed that he is allotted a smallish amount of thought and a long speech, that when the Lady is our object of attention, she is given more thought than speech, and that she herself, rather than the Prince, is her chief point of attention. These shifts are very smooth. One reason is that the distinction between thought and speech is grammatically less in Japanese. Another, stronger reason is that throughout the passage neither the Lady nor the Prince is specified by name, and not a single personal noun—counterparts of our pronouns—is used. (Honorifics in choice of verbs and other means serve to indicate who speaks or thinks.) With all the other liberties I take with my native tongue in the following, I bow to our pronominal tyranny.

To make discussion (and perhaps plain sense) possible, I shall designate whose words follow. "N" designates the beginning of narratorial words. "PT" and "PW" designate that until the next key these are the Prince's Thoughts and the Prince's Words. Similarly, "LT" and "LW" signal the Lady's Thoughts and Words. (For a normal version of the same passage, see Miner, 1969:126–28.)

> PT Only she looks so helpless in the world that it brings a pang of anguish to look on her, N and with great feeling he says, PW "It seems so tiresome an existence here, so although I have not wholly thought this through, do come live with me, for whatever reports
> 5 people have spread about you, I manage to visit you all too infrequently, and although I have not yet been seen doing so, people say the most painful things about my visits, and there have been times when I have called and have been so far unable to see you that I have felt miserable to the point of not being human—in fact
> 10 now and then there has seemed no point to continuing our relation, but perhaps because I am an old-fashioned sort who feels he must be faithful, I have felt keenly and have not given you up, even if it is so difficult to keep visiting you this way, so really, let us establish ourselves so that I am the moon coursing your sky, since
> 15 if life is as tedious here as you say, you ought to come with me, for even if my consort and others are there, it should not be that

troublesome, because from the outset it has been difficult to slip out at night, having as I do a position that requires appearance in the world, whereas if just the two of us might be together (it is not

20 all that interesting to perform sacred rites alone) I cannot help thinking what comfort there would be in our talking together, one mind and one heart," N and so forth, LT yet it is not at all clear she could take up so unaccustomed a life, and it also occurs to her that there has been talk of her serving his Abdicated Majesty, of which

25 nothing has come, and nothing else for that matter to help "to the other side of the hills" when there is such misery in a life feeling like a long dark night that never ends, and although there are many worthless men who only toy with a woman and there has been all that terrible gossip, having no one else to rely on—so why not do

30 so, then, after all? because even though the consort is there, they do live separately, and the old wet nurse seems to perform all manner of services, so that even if to go there means one's doings would become widely known, who wishes to live altogether hidden away? and what keeps one from going? since it would get

35 rid for good of that musty tale of other men visiting here, LW "What shall I say?— you know how my time is spent in such depressed uncertainty and how, having nothing other than your occasional visits—I suppose the situation is just as you describe it, and yet would you not be distressed by what others said? as I cer-

40 tainly would be if people took my moving as proof that the gossip about me is true," N to which his answer, PW "As for gossip, it is I who should bear its brunt, and since no one could think your position one to be pitied, let me have a place built for you hidden from prying eyes," N and with some other assurances, he departs

45 while it is still fully dark.

"The passage . . . is over thirty lines long in a revised edition of the *Nikki* and forms a single grammatical sentence reminiscent of James Joyce's long sentences in *Ulysses*."[46] The *Diary* does not, however, constitute stream of consciousness but rather what the prose of the time is capable of doing at length and clearly. It is not antimimetic, since there was no mimesis to oppose. It is rather affective-expressive, unmimetic narrative in which the points of attention (with subpoints of attention) may be of greater qualitative importance to the reader and a character

---

[46] Konishi, 1986A:304. He includes as well five earlier clauses in the "sentence." I am not sure that "sentence" is the proper designation, although the last verb does have a finality to it that earlier ones do not (Japanese verbs conclude clauses and sentences). On the other hand, "period" suggests western oratory too much. Hence, "passage."

than points of view. (Although that fact is made possible only by the point of view.) In fact it is not easy to identify the narrator. She is one who has access to the Prince's thoughts (11. 1–3), something that also occurs elsewhere in the work. That and the Lady's speaking (elsewhere) of herself as a third person would make it unnatural to think of her as the narrator of a western novel.

This is, however, some manner of diary, or rather of *nikki*.[47] Our choice in the matter is to accept the Lady of the diary as a narrator (though privy to the Prince's thoughts and given to speak of herself as a third person) or to say that Izumi Shikibu, the author, narrates. Japanese would make the latter choice, although either of them leaves us in the exquisite position of choosing a self-stylized version of the same person. The point is that the identity of the narrator and of points of view simply matters less here, because the affective nature of the points of attention leads us to devote ourselves to them as the important feature.

There is in fact little narration, little evidence of a general narrator: "and with great feeling he says" (2); "and so forth" (22); "to which his answer" (41); and final clause (44–45). What matters is what is attended to. That includes the Prince's Thoughts briefly (1–2) and his Words at length (2–22, 41–44) and the Lady's Thoughts at great length (22–35) and her Words more briefly (36–41). Moreover, the subsidiary object of attention of the Prince's Thoughts and Words, as also of the Lady's Thoughts is the Lady herself. Again: the emphasis on what is attended to is all the stronger in the original for the lack of use of even a single personal noun, equivalents of the pronouns that dot the English rendering.

This is not "Mimesis: The Representation of Reality in Western Literature," as Erich Auerbach's title so cogently puts it. It is rather an example of another poetics: the affective expression of reality in east Asian literature.

The passage from *The Diary of Izumi Shikibu* is not an eccentric one in classical Japanese literature. In fact, the importance of points of attention really requires consideration of *The Tale of Genji*. In a late chapter, "The Drake Fly" ("Kagerō"; ch. 52), there is a type-scene of male visual intrusion (*kaimami*) on a woman or women, something that highly placed la-

---

[47] A *nikki* is defined by Konishi, 1986A:256: "A prose composition, written in the present tense, that is concerned with the life of a historical person." Again: "Narration in the present tense is the governing principle of the nikki, although it is not an absolute convention" (257). (Given his point, the translation has been put in the English present tense, although in Miner, 1969 the past tense was used.) Since he says that Japanese verbs do not have tense, Konishi means that temporal phrases and designations (like our adverbs) situate the narrative relation in the present, whereas for *monogatari* like *The Tale of Genji* the narrative is situated in a past present.

dies sought utterly to avoid. The voyeur is the hero of the last ten chapters, Kaoru, Genji's putative son. He is good-willed and attractive, at once religious and amorous—in a fashion encouraging thought and discouraging resolute action—as also serious on the one hand and muddled in mind and motive on the other.

Whether we think of the presence of the author and a general narrator, the agency evident in the following quotation is rather a subsidiary narrator, whom we place as a court lady of some standing, since although she uses honorific verbs for Kaoru and the First Princess, she does not do so for the Princess's ladies. The code for the minds we gain access to (at once their points of view and ours of attention) is as follows, in order of appearance.

$$N = \text{Narrator}$$
$$K = \text{Kaoru} \qquad KS = \text{Kosaishō} \qquad P = \text{Princess}$$
$$L = \text{Lady of Lower Rank}$$

. . . ^{N} in the evening, when very few ladies were still waiting on the First Princess, Kaoru changed into informal court dress, having certain religious points to discuss with some of the officiating priests, but the priests had departed, and he went off toward the
5 water pavilion; with so few people attending the princess, Lady Kosaishō and others had set up temporary blinds to screen her; ^{K} "Could Kosaishō be here?—someone's robe is swishing," ^{N} he thought, and looking though a narrow gap in the blinds of the veranda: someone resembling no ordinary lady, for what with the
10 brightness of the scene and the unobstructed view provided by the gap in the hastily erected blinds, one could see, and splendid it was, far within where three ladies and a girl were working away at a block of ice set on some sort of tray; all four having removed their formal outer robes were so relaxed that they hardly seemed
15 in the royal presence, and yet the First Princess was there, changed into a filmy white robe, holding ice wrapped in paper in her hand, her face showing some amusement over the exertions of their chipping the ice, $^{N+K}$ and indescribably lovely; since the day had been almost unbearably hot, her abundant, wonderful hair had
20 been streamed to one side, and ^{K} "As her full face is now looking in my direction," there was no possibility of a comparison to her loveliness; "The rest of them are of good families, but I have never seen anyone to compare with her beauty," ^{N} he thought, for her servingladies were as clay by comparison, and since looking about
25 might settle one's thoughts—there in a yellow singlet and faint purple train, fanning herself with that profound self-possession of

hers, there *was* Lady Kosaishō saying, ᴷˢ "You have exerted your-
selves no end, and it is so hot; why not leave things as they
are?—ᴺ⁺ᴷ this with a lovely smile and attractive demeanor; her
30   voice revealed that she was indeed the one who had attracted him
so; ᴺ meanwhile, ᴺ⁺ᴷ having bestirred themselves, the others at
last each had ice in her hand, applying it with unusual freedom to
their heads and chests—some not looking so prepossessing—with
Kosaishō wrapping ice in paper for the Princess and herself, and
35   the Princess protesting with her very fair hands held out, ᴾ "No
thank you—the wet is already a trouble to me"; ᴷ hers was a very
soft voice, but hearing it brought him a thrill of joy to recall,
"When we were both still children, and I had no notion of these
things, I still thought her a lovely child; thereafter I have had no
40   direct news of her, and what favor of the gods and the Buddha can
have granted me this?—or is it a moment designed to agitate
me?"—ᴺ⁺ᴷ even as he stood there, gazing with such unsettled
thoughts, a lower-ranking lady whose room lay to the north hur-
ried back toward the blinds ajar, ᴸ "It would be dreadful if someone
45   were to look in here," ᴺ she thought, coming on in a fret and, on
seeing someone in male dress, ᴸ "Who can it be?" ᴺ she wondered
and, not minding how she exposed herself, she advanced straight
toward him, and then suddenly went in—ᴷ "No one must know I
am here, since it would smack too much of amorousness," ᴺ he
50   thought, concealing himself. . . .[48]

There are some passages here that I may have indicated improperly.
Lines 8–18 on the Princess's apartment seem to involve Kaoru's point of
view; but that is hard to sort with the degree of honorifics used. Much
the same thing can be said both ways of lines 25–31 on Lady Kosaishō.
On the other hand, perhaps 31–35 are to be imagined as from the Narrator alone. The clause in 40–41 is especially interesting (if not especially
important), since in one interpretation it is the thought of the Buddha and
the gods and should run, "It is a moment designed for agitation."
In any event, we observe the overlapping and fragmenting of various
points of view. There is a great deal of disruption, of displacement, of
switching from mind to mind. This volatility has its explanation in the
importance of the points of attention. The type-scene of male visual intrusion guarantees that, what with its highly erotic charge. Kaoru observes a group of women in dishabille, and not just any women but a
princess and her nobly born attendants. In addition to the scant clothing,

[48] Tamagami, 1968:286–89. For Seidensticker's translation of this passage into real English, see Murasaki Shikibu, 1976:2, 1030–31.

something any reader would instantly recognize as erotic, there is the central fact that the women are seen at all.

It seems incredible, but at that time lovers might not even know what each other looked like. Three months go by before the Prince in *The Diary of Izumi Shikibu* gets a clear look at the Lady, and she finds being seen embarrassing, although they have been making love that while (Miner, 1969:115–16). Similar things happen in *The Tale of Genji*, and both reflect contemporary mores.

In short, a kind of shudder must have gone through Murasaki Shikibu's contemporary or near contemporary female readers, and perhaps some erotic thrill through the male. But the author was a woman writing for female readers, including her royal mistress as well as certain male readers who lent support. The nature of the attention the author bestowed on her readers and they on this scene makes for fascinating conjecture. The issue can be given urgency by attention to another matter. Murasaki Shikibu uses the two most erotic images in classical literature: women's hair and moisture. The point of attention does matter for Kaoru and for us: that is what erotic—and other kinds of—attention depends on. Of course Kaoru is our immediate chief point of attention, and we must evaluate his understanding of what he sees. It is altogether characteristic of him that neither he nor we are able to disentangle the aesthetic, rational appreciation he feels from quickened eroticism.[49]

The essential character of Kaoru's mind, as also of the last ten chapters of *The Tale of Genji*, is muddle—of thought, intention, aim, fear, idealism, and perversity. One way of treating "the inconstancy of our actions," to borrow a phrase from Montaigne, is to do as the Bordelaise master did—and as Sei Shōnagon did before him in her *Pillow Book* (*Makura no Sōshi*). That is, to make the distinction between author and narrator negligible and then to absorb the world to that combined self. Because her kind of narrative, *monogatari*, concerned other, fictional characters, Murasaki Shikibu could not follow Sei Shōnagon's way. (In any event, they did not get on with each other.) Another way to achieve the same end is to make difficult if not negligible the distinction between the narrator and the character's thought. It is no accident that the work in many ways most like the Kaoru chapters is Richardson's *Clarissa*, which of course employs an epistolary method wherein the narrator is virtually impossible to discern except globally. All this is a way of emphasizing the centrality of points of attention in *The Tale of Genji*—and in narrative generally.

Our main point of attention is of course Kaoru. But the episode would

---

[49] For an excellent study of such matters in the *Genji*, and especially for what they imply for female experience in the last ten chapters, see Field, 1987:ch. 4. See also the pointed application of feminist criticism by Shirane, 1987:113–16, 147–48.

be as nothing if that point of attention did not incorporate his own points of attention, commonly while he is unaware that the person who is his point of attention is someone with her own points of attention, and not necessarily him. Often what he attends to is that favorite, solipsistic object, self. In some ways the finest example of that comes near the end of the passage, when the flustered serving-woman comes to close the gap in the blinds. We "see" Kaoru seeing her, her see him, and him see her seeing him while he worries about the figure he cuts. Narration determined solely by point of view simply could not achieve this degree of multiple, reflective subjectivity. In this passage, as in many others like it, the audible narrator repeatedly seems to fade out and in, whereas the author is everywhere, invisible.

Traditional criticism of *The Tale of Genji* distinguished five varieties of narrative. One is *ji* or *ji no bun*, ordinary narratorial relation, so-called third-person narration. There is some of that in the passage. Another kind is *sakusha no kotoba*, the author's words—authorial comment or intrusion, which western critics might prefer to term the narrator's comment or intrusion. There is no example of that in the passage, but it is symptomatic of a lyric-based poetics that the author should be presumed capable of speaking out in her own narrative. A third kind, *sōshiji*, is harder to define. It sometimes is taken to mean comment by the author or narrator, and sometimes a conflation of the two. A fairly literal rendering means "the book's narration" or "narration by the book." To the extent that that is what the term designates, the current western equivalent might be something like "the voice of the text." (Not in the sense "text" is used in this essay but in a sense I cannot, need not, define.) It is distinguished from the author's words pure and simple and from normal relation. It is also of course distinguished from the fourth variety, *kotoba*, words spoken by the characters.

The last category is one we have seen throughout the passage. It is *shinnaigo*, relation within the mind. This includes free indirect discourse (*erlebte Rede, style indirect libre*) but it is a larger category, sometimes overlapping with speech by a character. The simplest example is a character's reciting aloud, as the custom was, a poem or passage of verse that has presently come to mind. But as has been remarked, it is often difficult to decide whether something is outer or inner speech, words or thought— all being indicated by the same quotative particle. The ten last chapters are rich with this variety of narration, which is the best possible in the language for making the points of attention crucial.

It will be evident by now that the affective-expressive poetics based on lyric and kinds of history—the absence of mimetic preoccupations—led to different concepts of, and functions for, narration in Japan. That fact is clearly germane to the importance of points of attention. It is not that points of view do not matter. They do matter and seriously, as the differences between *nikki* (diary) and *monogatari* narrative show. But in affective-expressive systems they commonly do not matter as strikingly as points of attention. Put positively, the points of attention in affective-expressive narration are apt to have the centrality that points of view usually have in mimetic narration. This is a conclusion that can only be arrived at by intercultural comparative study.

In that kind of study it appears to be a sound principle that what is essential to one poetics will have a counterpart in another, as some Chinese and Japanese historiography fulfills the major functions of epic. If something matters so very much in one culture, there must be in another some echo of it, at however lower a volume or altered sound. Jane Austen has shown that, in her work, points of attention can, if rarely, be made to dominate points of view. It remains to show that the points of attention can be seen to matter in the work of a western master of point of view.

The inevitable name is of course Henry James. His late novels are famous for subtle and shifting points of view. Their effects require what even I would judge too lengthy quotation, however, and we must look elsewhere. Fortunately, there is an earlier work also famous for its handling of points of view, *What Maisie Knew*. In this novel, Maisie's parents divorce and remarry. Their new spouses form their own liaisons. The reason for being of the novel is that James enables us to understand this lurid situation only as the girl does. The novel is not told in her first person but by a narrator who is evident enough, as we shall see. What we mainly feel is a narratorship that is so-called third-person omniscient, except that omniscience takes out some kind of self-denying ordinance of telling only—in truth, only *seeming* to tell—through Maisie's mind. This means of course that she is the narrator's chief point of attention, which is to say that her subsidiary point of view is dominant and that her points of attention shift from one of the four parents or stepparents to another, and to herself. She in turn becomes the points of their attention as the awareness grows on them that she is coming to know what is going on.

That awareness leads them to seek, in troubled fashion, to discover just what she does or does not know. This is clearly, deliciously shown at the novel's end (in ch. 31), whose last three words give the novel its title, which is perfect for my ends. The "What" emphasizes Maisie's points of attention. "Maisie" declares that she is the author's point of attention and possessor of the main subsidiary point of view. And "Knew" makes clear that these metaphors of "points" involve subjects and objects of cognition, with one knower's object becoming the subject who knows another as object and so also the reciprocal.

In chapter 26 of *What Maisie Knew*, there is a passage quintessentially

Jamesian in its irony and, as to points of view, microcosmic of the whole novel. Mrs. Wix has asked Maisie, "Haven't you really and truly *any* moral sense?"[50] After an interval, Mrs. Wix resumes, "Have you absolutely none at all?" Sophisticated evil challenges innocence with lack of a moral sense. Our passage immediately follows Mrs. Wix's second question.

Because my proposition about the crucial importance of points of attention is novel, because my quotations are lengthy, and because coding will annoy some readers, I have restricted myself until this stage with coding *points of view*. Now that the method is at least clear it is time to emphasize the complexity by coding for points of attention as well. In the paragraph to be quoted there are the following persons whose minds may be the focus for a point of attention or of view. We shall see that the four are not sufficient, that an R = Reader is also involved.

N = Narrator	M = Maisie	
W = Mrs. Wix	B = Mrs. Beale	

N-W-M designates the narrator with Mrs. Wix as point of attention and her with Maisie as point of attention. N/M-W designates the narrator and Maisie sharing knowledge of Mrs. Wix. And N/M-M designates the narrator and Maisie sharing knowledge of Maisie. The other codings should be obvious.

> N-W-M She had no need now, as to the question itself at least, to be specific; that on the other hand was the eventual result of their quiet conjoined apprehension of the thing that—well, yes, since they must face it—Maisie absolutely and appallingly had so little
> 5 of. N-M-W This marked more particularly the moment of the child's perceiving that her friend had risen to a level which might—till superseded at all events—pass almost for sublime. Nothing more remarkable had taken place in the first heat of her own departure, no act of perception less to be overtraced by our rough method,
> 10 than her vision, the rest of that Boulogne day, of the manner in which she figured. N-M/R I so despair of [counting] her noiseless mental footsteps here that I must crudely give you my word for its being from this time forward a picture literally present to her. N-W-M Mrs. Wix saw her as a little person knowing so extraordi-
> 15 narily much that, for the account to be taken of it, what she didn't know would be ridiculous if it hadn't been embarrassing. N-W Mrs. Wix was in truth more than ever qualified to meet embarrassment;

[50] James, 1966:193. I have changed single to double quotation marks, have corrected the text at one point, and have added periods after instances of "Mrs." The sentence next quoted is from p. 194, and the passage thereafter is from pp. 194–95.

[N-M/R] I am not sure that Maisie had not even a dim discernment of the queer law of her own life that made her educate to that sort of
20   proficiency those elders with whom she was concerned. [N-M to N-M-B] She promoted, as it were, their development; nothing could have been more marked, for instance, than her success in promoting Mrs. Beale's. [N-M-W] She judged that if her whole history, for Mrs. Wix, had been the successive stages of her knowledge, so the very
25   climax of the concatenation would, in the same view, be the stage at which the knowledge should overflow. [N/M-M] As she was condemned to know more and more, how could it logically stop before she should know Most? It came to her in fact as they sat there on the sands that she was distinctly on the road to know Every-
30   thing. She had not had governesses for nothing: what in the world had she ever done but learn and learn and learn? She looked at the pink sky with a placid foreboding that she soon should have learnt all. [N-M/W] They lingered in the flushed air till at last it turned to grey and [N-M] she seemed fairly to receive new information from
35   every brush of the breeze. [N-M/W] By the time they moved homeward [N-W] it was as if this inevitability had become for Mrs. Wix a long tense cord, twitched by a nervous hand, on which the valued pearls of intelligence were to be neatly strung.

With this extraordinary paragraph, Maisie moves from having "absolutely none [moral knowledge] at all" to knowing "that she soon should have learnt All." The "none" and the "All" differ in the sense that Mrs. Wix's accusation in the guise of a question refers to "*any* moral sense," whereas Maisie's "All" will be total possession of the sordid carryings-on by "those elders with whom she was concerned." When Mrs. Wix asks her repeated question as to whether Maisie has any moral sense, she has come to the understanding that the girl knows very well about her elders. Mrs. Wix cannot understand why Maisie does not show revulsion. The paradox, if it is one, is that Maisie's innocence is preserved as her knowledge of adult evil steadily increases. (Although there is also Jamesian irony in Maisie's thinking that she really will obtain omniscience.)

The details of handling involve an obtruder, the self-styled "I," who takes his oath for a fact: "I must crudely give you my word" (12–13). He does so because he despairs of his ability to chart the progress of Maisie's knowledge. Narratorial activity and, yes, authorship are evident in other ways, particularly in the studied obliqueness that informs the writing and is essential to the donnée of the novel. There is the first sentence quoted: "She had no need now . . ." and so on—four commas, a semicolon, and two dashes.

The style is ceremoniously opaque. The reader faces a little crisis of decision with that first sentence: who is the object of attention here, Mrs. Wix or Maisie? It turns out to be Mrs. Wix although, with the second sentence, we shift to Maisie, who has Mrs. Wix as her point of attention. Beginning with line 9, "Nothing more remarkable . . . ," Maisie becomes the point of attention again, with herself gradually becoming her own point of attention.

Then we are shifted back to Mrs. Wix at a new stage of knowledge of the girl beside her on the strand: "what she still didn't know would be ridiculous," or laughable, although given the nature of evil involved, it "would be ridiculous if it hadn't been embarrassing." This is an exquisite moment. Mrs. Wix shifts to herself and the other "elders" as points of attention, with Maisie looking at them and knowing what they have been seeking to hide from the world. The narrator may well say drily (16–17), "Mrs. Wix was in truth more than ever qualified to meet embarrassment." After a semicolon we shift back to Maisie via a portentous double negative (18–20): "I am not sure that Maisie had not even a dim discernment. . . ."

Most of the rest of the paragraph is devoted to the rise in what Maisie knew, or would know from more to most to everything to all. At the end, however, we get the kind of easy, or at least quick, shift in point of attention that we see in the first third of the paragraph. The narrator is concerned with both Maisie and Mrs. Wix at the beginning of the last sentence but one, "They lingered. . . ." In the second clause, however, the concern is solely with Maisie, "she. . . ." (l. 34). The last sentence begins similarly, "By the time they . . . ," but again there is a switch in point of attention, now to Mrs. Wix, reminding us of the opening of the paragraph, but also serving with the reminder to show how far the narrator, Maisie, Mrs. Wix, and we readers have enlarged the dimensions of what all know that Maisie knows.

There are some questions to raise in all this. Who is that first-person obtruder? We have more than one choice: narrator, stylized author, author. If we choose the second, we are really choosing the third, because no author can write without self-stylizing. If we choose the first, a narrator, then we must posit that *What Maisie Knew* has at least two narrators, one who identifies himself as "I" on a few occasions, and another who goes unself-identified. The issue relates to that first appearance of the "I" narrator in l. 12: "I must crudely give you my word." Who is the "you?" The possibilities are: nobody, the stylized reader, and the reader. Once again, the second really means the third, the reader, who is necessarily stylized by what is known in following the narration (as well as by general culture, personality, etc.). The choice comes down to one between believing that a version of the author is addressing a version of the reader, or another that there are multiple narrators and that one of them at least can pretend to address a nonexistent audience. The former choice is typical of readers who have affective-expressive assumptions and the latter of readers who have mimetic presumptions.

Another issue involves the multiplicity of points of attention, which is to say their constant shifting. In a novel as highly psychological as *What Maisie Knew*, the characters keep taking each other as points of attention. Another way of putting the matter is to say that whatever is the case with the identity of the "I," or of the narrator, there are constantly shifting subsidiary points of view. For that matter, the "I" narrator or author takes himself as point of attention. The plurality deserves stress.

So does what might, with little exaggeration, be termed the mess. Points of view and points of attention are not fixed things. James may be subtle, but he has natural language at his disposal. His efforts to bend it with double negatives and other studied manipulations show no setting of such and such degrees of passage. Consistency is no more required in James than in other narrative authors. If we seek parsimony, simplicity in describing what James and we know of *What Maisie Knew*, we are well advised to take the affective-expressive position of an author's addressing an audience. And that is precisely what James seems to be striving to do: address, form, shape, stylize his readers by his strong bending of language.

The novel is a celebrated example of James's skill in handling point of view and, as we have seen, the narrator is an important presence at our elbow. Yet it will also be clear that to omit concern with points of attention is to miss the major triumph of the novel. Clearly, we cannot do without points of view in *What Maisie Knew*, for the obvious reason that there can be no point of attention without point of view, just as points of view cannot exist without points of attention. Also, in a highly psychological, subjective novel like this one, points of attention are really more important for study than are the points of view. Or rather, it is the combination of various points of attention and subsidiary points of view in which interest resides.

At this point it should be emphasized that the multiplicities or inconsistencies of major points of view are wholly common. Narrative is not lyric in presence and consistency. It does not matter if all fails to fit, since it is the continuance to fulfillment that counts for narrative. Another example (this time without codings!) will show that James is not in the least eccentric in his inconsistencies of narratorial point of view.

The Adventures of Huckleberry Finn is a commonly adduced example of so-called first-person narration. When people talk about the point of view used by Twain, they have passages like the opening sentences in mind. How perfect the accent seems.

> You don't know about me without you have a read a book by the name of "The Adventures of Tom Sawyer," but that ain't no matter. That book was made by Mr. Mark Twain, and he told the truth, mainly. There was things which he stretched, but mainly he told the truth. (Twain, 1985:1)

Yet more crucially than the example from James, this one provides the crux of an addressee: the very first word, "You." Again that entity is either a version of the reader or is nobody. One word is chosen carefully. *Tom Sawyer* was "*made* by Mr. Mark Twain." In fact, the earlier book is not told in Tom's first person but by Twain. The fiction of *Huckleberry Finn* is that it is "made" and told by Huck.

And so, in a sense, it is. But there is much in the novel that cannot reasonably be assigned to Huck as agency. One general matter may be mentioned. Huck is the cultural product of an Irish drunkard father and an education from a bumbling but benign Miss Watson. Nothing in either half of his nurture really makes credible his liberal attitudes toward Jim. So no doubt we assign the result to causation by character, but once we think of the matter it does not leave the mind, and in fact other things occur to confirm the inconsistent Twain/Huck point of view. An example will help clarify the point. In chapter 22, Colonel Sherburn faces the mob come to lynch him for killing a particularly silly local *miles gloriosus*. Here are some of Sherburn's scornful words:

> "The idea of *you* lynching anybody! It's amusing. The idea of you thinking you had pluck enough to lynch a *man*! Because you're brave enough to tar and feather poor friendless cast-out women that come along here, did that make you think you had grit enough to lay hands on a *man*? Why, a *man's* safe in the hands of ten thousand of your kind— as long as it's daytime and you're not behind him." (Twain, 1985:190)

Twain has Huck report this speech, or so common wisdom about point of view would posit. Actually, it is inconceivable as a product of Huck's mind. But there is no reason for Twain, any more than for James or whatever other author, to conceive of narrative agency in the simple, puristic way that is so common. One can say of Sherburn's words that Huck's point of view is simply suspended, or that the author is narrating them. The novel loses none of its magic, none of its character as narrative.

My own interest in points of attention derived from what seems special about the narrative emphasis in affective-expressive literary traditions, where they may seem to matter so much more than points of view that the handling of points of view may seem or be inconsistent. Actually, we see that James himself is not consistent in his handling of points of view. Much has been written as if the sky would fall if a decision on point of view, once made, were ever violated. Others have lately gloated over the perfidies of narration for shifting, being inconsistent.

It is useful to have evidence from other cultures to show us what we ought to have seen in our own. In fact it would be possible to employ the concepts developed to describe *The Tale of Genji* to describe *What Maisie Knew*. The concept of "relation in the mind" (*shinnaigo*) seems particularly appropriate. Yet Henry James is not Murasaki Shikibu, any more than modern English is classical Japanese. Writing in the mimetic tradition, he properly grounds his narrative on his narrator, a version of Aristotle's Homer engaged in imitation. The gulf between narrator and character, imitator and imitation, author and representation is decisively western. There are (in James, for example) none of those moments when a given sequence of words could be attributed to the narrator or to Kaoru, to Kaoru or divinities. As a result, we find James using double negatives and other devices to get from one topic to another. In a sense, it is not only mimesis but also rhetoric that prevails. We enter the chief object of attention, the mind of Maisie, by dint of James' immense skill. It is a smoothly functioning, complex machine, whereas Murasaki Shikibu offers us a sparkling stream in natural flow and visible to great depth.

A little summary may show where our exercise has taken us. It is appropriate that the concept of point of view should have arisen in a culture still surprisingly mimetic in main assumptions. It is widely assumed, even by those who would deny it, that the maker and the made, the representation and the world, fictionality and factuality are consistent elements of sturdy integrity. It seems to follow that "point of view" is a point singular. And the shifts in "point of view" by James and the *representation* of "stream of consciousness" by Joyce and Woolf seemed to be great departures from past simplicity.

As we have been seeing, however, what was recently so novel in our greatest modernist novelists (Proust, Flaubert, Mann—Woolf and Faulkner may be added) was effected centuries before by ladies at the Japanese court. (The fact would be all the clearer if we were reading *The Diary of Izumi Shikibu* and *The Tale of Genji* in Japanese rather than in English with its need to say who, its tyranny of pronouns.) The affective-expressive poetics derived from lyric with history naturally gave greater prize to narrative points of attention, and the plurality is evident, as also plain in authors' ability to shift with great rapidity, both to other points of attention or to engender shifts in point of view. It is not too many years since the differences of modern Japanese writers like Tanizaki Junichirō

and Kawabata Yasunari from familiar western novelists made some readers of those authors in English translation think their work bizarre, unfin-
ished. As has been observed, the rise of antimimetic narrative has changed
that, and the present danger is of a contrary kind. In spite of Murasaki
Shikibu's finding kinship between *monogatari*, history, and the sutras, it is
assumed by some that her affective-expressive beliefs led her to the kind
of nominalist, antirealist position congenial to so many recent critics.

Another set of things revealed by our exercise is that "point of view" is
not only plural but inconsistent, as the Japanese writers, as James and
Austen, in her way, have shown. Only consider the narrator (or the stylized author—or author) putting his hand on his heart to vouch for this or
that about Maisie. He seems to materialize from nowhere in a novel supposedly told from Maisie's "point of view." We see from the contradictions the validity of Genette's insight, that all narration is basically first-
person, and that the truly dominant point of view is that of the narrator
(back to the implied or stylized author). Maisie's is the main subordinate
point of view, and even that is interrupted by the author and by a switch,
not complete but real for all that, to Mrs. Wix's point of view. Your
Dickens or George Eliot would reveal the same, as of course would
Sterne—and Milton.

Points of attention offer the complement to points of view, and as the
selection from *The Diary of Izumi Shikibu* showed, the narrator's process
could "enter" the mind of the Prince as well as the Lady, showing him
taking her as point of attention and then her taking him, the world, and
herself as points of attention, within a narrative in which they both are,
properly speaking, the points of attention of the general narrator, a (self-)
creation of none other than Izumi Shikibu, who is also (self-) created as
the Lady in the narrative. It seems dizzying in description, and truly I
have never read literature told in language usage normal for its age that
resembled in difficulty the style of *The Tale of Genji*. Once commanded,
however, this rapidity of shift and exchange of points of view and points
of attention reveals a world of enormous subtlety and beauty.

Let me demystify it as far as possible with the reminder of what we
comprehend so easily in an opera. There is no narrator, of course, but the
various characters are our shifting points of attention, as they are for each
other within their points of view. And opera is also a group (*za*) art, like
renga, with two or even dozens sharing a point of view and one or more
points of attention as six named characters and a chorus close the last act.

As the examples given have shown, the narrative continuum is based
on frequent adjustments, constituting narrative units, of points of view
and points of attention. The handling of points of view is relatively far
more consistent, offering an inertia of sameness, of continuing as is.

Points of attention are relatively far more volatile, offering an inertia of change, of difference in the continuing. Shifts in subordinate point of view are also very frequent and beget change.

Although as we have seen there can be no general point of view in drama, the audience takes the characters on stage as points of attention, as the characters do each other. In lyric the speaker's equivalent of point of view is almost always fixed, and even the points of attention are simpler. The cynic observed that Wordsworth had one eye on the daffodils and the other on his canal stocks. That implies what is usually the case, the lyrical daffodil eye keeps the daffodils intently in view—during the daffodil moment. At another moment it may focus on a violet by a mossy stone or Tintern Abbey (or canal stocks). When they do occur in narrative, shifts in general point of view are more momentous than shifts in points of attention, although the latter shifts are the usual source of narrative energy.

Those shifts may be better described as junctures and disjunctures between a given point of view and a given point of attention. Simple continuance plainly requires sustaining the newly junctured, as alteration involves disjuncturing, which of course produces a new juncture. As we have had reason to observe before, in narrative, the factor of people far exceeds in importance places and times. We now possess an additional reason. A given character in a narrative who becomes an object of our attention is capable of having yet another person, thing, fault, or sensation as object of attention to that character's point of view. *The Tale of Genji* and *What Maisie Knew* show how complex and yet how easily managed these matters are in the finest narrative.

Junctures of point of view with points of attention constitute the *force* of narrative continuum. The first juncture brings beginning, and the last disjuncture closure. There is a modern tendency to esteem change, and my emphasis upon the ignored points of attention may seem to express the same preference. In one sense inertial change is crucial in the grand juncture of beginning and in lesser rebeginnings, as the complementary force of disjuncture brings lesser endings and at last the end. To be intelligible, however, such change must occur within a more comprehensive inertial sameness: if what changes does not pertain to the same set of things, there is either another story or the alteration makes no sense. It is also true, as Beckett's narratives show, that repetitive sameness—recurrence without (sufficient) change—may produce the comic meaning of meaninglessness.

As predicted, it has required greater effort, and length, to deal with continuum rather than with fulfillment as a principle of narrative. We are now ready to return to an earlier test case: the issue whether Japanese linked poetry is narrative. We may wish to call linked poetry lyric, in order to honor its intense presence. But by now I think we shall wish to count it narrative, recognizing that its code provides us with fulfillment and narrative continuance of the same elements, as its shifts provide disjunctures to a marked degree. Authorship keeps shifting. Point of view may or may not, given that it is established by the poets' group (*za*). Since point of attention does shift with each new stanza, point of view is logically more important to inertial continuance, as in all narrative. But points of attention, the volatile and disjunctive force, matter more in linked poetry, as befits an affective-expressive rather than a mimetic poetics.

To illustrate these matters we may close, in good narrative fashion, with the last stanzas from a *haikai* (properly *haikai renga*) linked sequence, that species with a decorum lower than *renga*. Here are the last units, then, from a *haikai* duo by Matsuo Bashō and Enomoto Kikaku (Miner-Odagiri, 1981:61–63). Bashō has just composed the thirty-first stanza.

	Aware ika ni	How it moves the heart
	Miyagino no bota	that the wind on Miyagi Moor
	fukishioru ran	withers the bug clover
32	Michinoku no ezo	Michinoku where barbarians
	shiranu ishiusu	know nothing of stone mortars
	Kikaku	

	Michinoku no ezo	Michinoku where barbarians
	shiranu ishiusu	know nothing of stone mortars
33	mononofu no	that ancient hero
	yoroi no marune	just took sleep in his full armor
	makura kasu	borrowing his pillow
	Bashō	

	Mononofu no	that ancient hero
	yoroi no marune	just took sleep in his full armor
	makura kasu	borrowing his pillow
34	yakoe no koma no	the horses neigh at dawn like cocks
	yuki o tsugetsutsu	announcing freshly fallen snow
	Kikaku	

	Yakoe no koma no	Horses may neigh at dawn like cocks
	yuki o tsugetsutsu	announcing freshly fallen snow
35	shi akindo	poetry is what I sell
	hana o musaboru	flowers not my debts concern me
	sakate kana	so I drink all the time

Kikaku

	Shi akindo	Poetry is what we sell
	hana o musaboru	flowers not our debts concern us
	sakate kana	so we drink all the time
36	SHUNKO hi kurete	As sun sets on the SPRINGTIME LAKE
	KYŌ NI NOSURU GIN.	AND PLEASURE HAS BROUGHT HOME OUR
	Bashō	POEM. [51]

In my judgment, this is narrative with a very high proportion of lyricism, a decision that others might reach more easily if they sat to translate a hundred-or ten-thousand-stanza sequence. [52] Some people might wish to hedge their bets saying that linked poetry occupies the narrow margin between narrative and lyric. The sage would no doubt say that it depends on which features one chooses to think crucial. My judgment is plain, and therefore, like the narrator of a Chinese story, I shall say that if you wonder about relativism in comparative poetics, you will find certain ideas in the next chapter.

[51] The capital letters in the last stanza designate Japanese presented as if it is Chinese. The last two stanzas violate what in *renga* proper is an inviolable rule against repetition: stanzas 35 and 36 repeat, with slight alteration, stanzas 1 and 2. This kind of thing appears from time to time, if rarely, in *haikai*, and as far as I know only at the beginning and end of a sequence.

[52] Paul Hernadi is unusually hospitable to a wide range of generic concepts. Although in his last chapter he argues "The Case for Polycentric Classifications" and urges us "Beyond Genre," he in effect welcomes a variety of approaches (Hernadi, 1972:152–56, 183–85 for the parts mentioned). Much the same may be said of Fowler, 1982. The pity is that their evidence is not intercultural, for reasons given in the Introduction and in Chapter 1. At the end of the latter there appears a table representing my own distinctions.

CHAPTER 5

❏
_____

Relativism

the *tertium comparationis* is not immediately given.

— Douwe W. Fokkema

COMPARATIVE POETICS AGAIN

Issues involving relativism will enable us to consider a few matters not
specifically, explicitly addressed and to raise a few others. This chapter
may well return at its beginning to the opening of this entire essay. In the
first chapter it was remarked that poetics is literally inconceivable without
the assumption of the autonomy of literature. That autonomy is presumed not only cognitively but also institutionally, socially. A corollary
of this assumption is that other kinds of thought and social practice are
also autonomous, if anything general is to be posited about them, indeed
if they are thought to exist: music and mathematics, philosophy and economics, and so on.

If each of these "subjects" is autonomous, their possibilities of relation
must be questioned. "Autonomous" must be more closely defined.
Clearly, the autonomy is not complete or mathematicians would not take
to music as they do, and there would be no possibility of discovering in
music mathematical proportions and relations. It is therefore necessary to
posit that the autonomy is qualified by the transferability of musical,
mathematical, or literary knowledge. One question therefore arises: are
all kinds of knowledge relative to each other in the same terms?

The answer was also given in less explicit form in the first chapter. The
relation of autonomous kinds of knowledge is not simply relative, because the relations are variant. That is, the nature and degree of transferability—or utility—of one kind differs from that of another. As was observed, mathematics and logic are (at least in their less arcane reaches)
autonomous and of great use to other kinds, whereas they absorb or use
relatively little of other kinds of knowledge. Literature, on the other hand
is of lesser utility, although it would go hard on linguists, historians, and
others if they were forbidden use of literature to their nonliterary ends.
In fact, the very absorptive power of literature makes it possible, as it

were, once again to refine from it historical and other knowledge (Miner, 1979A). We can go a step farther to recognize that the autonomies of knowledges are also defined by—to some extent confined to—families. Literature belongs to the family of the aesthetic, along with painting, music, dance, sculpture, architecture, and crafts. In general, it is less autonomous from, and a closer intellectual sibling of, music than of the other arts, as the combination of poetry and music fully reveals. Moreover, as the world's dominant poetics—the affective-expressive—shows, literature has a degree of autonomy from the other members of its aesthetic family in that its verbal medium allies it with its cousins, those nonaesthetic but verbally emphatic family members.

The autonomy is not complete, then, for literature or other kinds of knowledge. And its relation varies from other kind to other kind. To put matters differently, the relativism of autonomous bodies of knowledge is also qualified. We do not face the specter of indescribable relations (because of no relations or incoherent ones) between literature and other kinds of knowledge. That conclusion is sustained both logically and empirically. But experience also inevitably implies history, a subject that reintroduces relativism in another guise.

Just as any historical account rests on examined or unexamined principles—theories—so does study of theories (for us, poetics) depend for its evidence on history. It rests, that is, both on primal history, history as event, and on accounts of those events and of ideas about those events. History as account is founded on three rival presumptions (Miner, 1988, 1989). One may be termed intellectual and, in some versions, idealist. It presumes that the wellspring of history is the thought of individuals, of a group of class, of a nation or an age: Geistesgeschichte, l'esprit du temps, mentalités.

A second is determinist. In principle that should include the first, with mind determining material matters. In practice, however, it is usually taken to mean that agencies such as the material means of production or historical circumstances more widely conceived determine thought (including literature). The third—relativism—governs all historical thought to some degree, including the previous two kinds. What is actual or distinctive about given events is relative to the culture and the age in which they occurred. This presumption clearly relates to comparative poetics.

Only a few critics have shown awareness of the matter, including possible problems that it poses. James J. Y. Liu is one of the few. He entered a distinction between "historicism" and "relativism." His specific application is the issue of interpretation. The relevance of the issue extends much further, however, even if historians seem untroubled by the relativism they assume as a matter of course. The problem is one of defining relativism so that, as with the autonomy of literature, there are perceivable limits, relations to other autonomies, and family resemblances.

Liu held historicism to refer "to the attitude that, in order to understand a text produced in another age, we must assume the mentality of a reader of that age." Historical relativism refers instead "to the attitude that every age is bound to interpret in its own terms a text produced in another age and that no interpretation, including that of the author's own age or even of the author himself, has privileged status" (Liu, 1988:116). Since he goes on to explain the Chinese view that an author's words tell of the mind behind them and then to Gadamer, it is clear that he supports (with limitations) what he terms historicism rather than historical relativism.

It is not, logically, a matter of choice. And the definition of historical relativism deprives it of some of its potentiality. He seems to have "ages" of a single culture in mind. Perhaps that is inherent for him in the idea of *historical* relativism. The matter does not end there, however, since *a priori* the gaps of cultural relativism seem greater than the gaps between stages of an individual culture. And when we add the two—as in comparisons of Tudor and postcolonial Swahili, or Han and postmodernist Italian literatures—the gap grows immensely. We cannot simply choose "historicism," at least not where comparative poetics is concerned.

I shall not pretend to attempt to explain anything beyond practice of comparative poetics. As the first chapter makes clear, "comparatists" all but universally ignore comparison. My own small contribution is that of practice that appears to work. Not to repeat the first chapter, but to rephrase part of the argument, relativism can be overcome (the gap bridged) by linguistic and historical understanding of divergent literatures. The further conditions involve adequate definition of problems in poetics and, in particular, of those issues where there is formal identity no matter what the culture: the emergence of a systematic poetics has been the example. It is revealing, for instance, that both the varieties of affective-expressive poetics and the mimetic poetics traditionally held to the prior assumption of philosophical realism.

With those criteria in mind, we can make wry sense of the Indian position on mimesis. Indian poetics end up being affective-expressive by a most complex route, and it is otherwise interesting for being the sole such tradition to entertain seriously thoughts of imitation in the mimetic sense. Indian critics of drama held that imitation had to be rejected on at least two grounds. One is that it misplaces what is real, which is not the fiction that drama employs but its effect. It is also "psychologically untenable" (Gerow, 1977:265). This is precisely the response that readers of the first and second chapters here would expect from a poetics where affect (in *rasa*) is so central, and precisely in the area that such a reader would expect the issue to arise, drama. In short, cultural relativism and historical relativism can be acknowledged and dealt with providing we have feasible means and bases for comparison. That is not to dispose of all the issues, but it is enough to give heart.

THE RELATIVISM OF THE GENRES

It is taken as a basic premise of this study that a generative poetics is historically relative to a particular cultural complex. In particular, a systematic poetics emerges when literature is conceived of as an autonomous kind of knowledge, and when a gifted mind or minds define literature out of the then most esteemed kind of practice. These kinds have been termed foundation genres. They include drama, the foundation genre of western poetics and no other. They include lyric, the chief foundation for other poetics. To some extent they also include narrative, because in east Asia certain kinds of history were included with lyric, and because in Japan we have a definition of narrative literature so soon after the poetic system was founded.

Another example—one that must now be seen in its proper complexity—is that of Horace, who has been depicted hitherto as the completer of western poetics by his affective account of the reader and the poet. Was his poetics really a supplement to Aristotle, or was it an originative poetics? If the latter, then the claims of mimesis are yet smaller than has been suggested throughout this study. As is well known, Aristotle's *Poetics* was soon lost in antiquity, and Horace's *imitatio* does not designate the mimetic process of representation as in Aristotle but rather imitation of the Greeks, as Horace did so spectacularly in adapting Greek lyric forms to Latin. About one third of the *Ars Poetica* is devoted to drama, however, a fact difficult to explain, given the low reputation of the theater in Rome. There are different possible explanations. One is that the striking attention to drama testifies to a familiarity with Aristotle. Another is that one or more of the Pisos (to whom the epistle is addressed) was known by Horace to be interested in composing plays for the only way acceptable to dignified Romans—for reading aloud, declamation.

Clearly neither explanation has evidence sufficient for proof. The second seems more likely in sociological terms, but the Pisos are too little known for anything approaching certainty on the issue involved. The first seems a very awkward kind of acknowledgment of Aristotle. It seems that neither consideration proves much of anything and that with those avenues of evidence foreclosed it simply is not clear what drama means to Horace, whether he assumes mimesis and writes a supplement to it or whether he does not know mimesis and so writes a second western foundational poetics.

The best decision seems the probable one that Horace knew Aristotle through Alexandrian mediaries, that he probably knew him through summaries or characterizations rather than through first-hand knowledge (Brink, 1963–82). Presuming that, Horace's attention to drama is so much of his epistle-treatise is not gainsaid by either of the two possible significances attributed to it. I myself think that the crucial evidence is of another kind: little in Horace's views is downright contradictory of Aristotle, and the use of art as analogue (*ut pictura poesis*) at the beginning is in Aristotle's spirit, not simply as a variety of example but as an assumption of what may and what may not be relied on to carry conviction of truth.

In other words, I see no reason to reject the common assumption that Aristotle began and Horace added. At the same time, however, the issue is by no means closed to question, and not to repeat what has been said about the Middle Ages, in the Renaissance the Horatian *ends* of poetry were often of greater concern than the Aristotelian *means*.

The example of Horace raises, then, the basically historical question whether he was the author of an originative or supplementary poetics. The weight depending on that issue will vary with our interests. But the example is of special import in showing that it does *not* bear on the fundamental relativism of a poetics: its relativism to the genre that provides the norm. The evidence for this is historical, intercultural, and logical or theoretical. Without the evidence, which has been both alluded to (Miner, 1979B) and repeatedly attested to here, the concept of the genres continues to have empirical or practical support.

That is, the concept of genre fulfills three theoretical needs for discussion. These needs are, first, for a concept of a single poem, whose consideration is the basis for all further literary thought. Attention to the single poem ranges of course from a first reading to detailed explication employing a range of concepts and knowledge including the historical as well as the theoretical. At the other extreme, literary theory requires a conception of literature—the assumed total of poems but in fact a group of individual exemplars known, a canon. These extremes do not suffice, however, for all needs, and a third conception is clearly necessary: that of groupings or kinds of similar poems, something larger than the individual example but far smaller than the presumed total, literature (Miner, 1986A). At this point study becomes relative to those kinds distinguished at the end of Chapter 1, those including genres. Since these three objects of consideration (the poem, literature, kinds) relate to the evidence necessary, further justification of relativism to them is unnecessary.

In seeking to emphasize to undergraduates the cognitive validity—and nature—of the term "genres," I have sometimes used pictures from magazines as evidence. The upshot is of much greater theoretical interest than might be thought, although the details are tame enough. Students quickly identify a still scene from nature or a lovers' embrace as lyric ("presence" and "intensification," "matters of moment"). They will identify a defined area with people actively interinvolved as drama ("estrangement" and "engagement," "make-up"). And they will identify what seems to go on as narrative ("continuum" and "fulfillment," "movement"). Because these are conceptual, cognitive matters, it is easily possible to get students to change their identifications. When asked to imagine what happened after the scenes they identified as lyric and dramatic, they will reidentify them as narrative. When asked to imagine the things that go on or the lovers' embrace as occurring on a stage, they will of course transform both into drama.

Revealing enough, it is next to impossible to get what the students have identified as narrative or drama changed into lyric. One may say that there is a theoretical sense in which drama and narrative are more capacious, able to contain lyric, to transform it to their ends. Lyric is weaker in transformative power, being (whatever the case with individual examples) more intensely itself. That is why, as we have seen, lyric alone is nonselfinterruptible. As the irreducibly simple, affective genre, it is a natural one for the generation of systematic poetics. And since, at the other extreme, drama is the only necessarily fictional genre, it is appropriate that drama should be the genre on which one, if only one, of the world's poetics was founded. It is also important that drama can transform lyric and narrative fact into fiction.

The distinctions between the genres are, in a weak sense, entire. We are able to recognize them, even in their usual mixed forms. Yet as I have tried to emphasize, the distinctive features identified in each of the genres are shared by the others, relatively. Estrangement and engagement will be found in lyric and narrative as well as in drama. By the same token, the presence and intensification of lyric can also be found in drama and narrative; the moving continuance and fulfillment of narrative can be found in the other two genres. That is simple enough, apparent enough to require no elucidation.

Another kind of relativism is involved, however—one that makes the explanation difficult.[1] It is far from easy to identify the critical degree of narrative or lyric that enables us to recognize them in a drama. A strongly moving moment in a well-acted play need not move us because of *lyric*

---

[1] Close readers will observe some shift in what "relativism" is taken to mean from time to time in this chapter. Since the same class of problem is involved, I have decided to simplify by using just one name.

intensity but because the drama has grown intense. On the other hand, Shakespeare depicts his Romans as generous to their dead opponents and, after the antagonism, that gesture brings a much valued dramatic resolution—in a scene sometimes inescapably narrative.

The "critical degree" spoken of involves our decisions in response to the poet's decisions (whatever the degree of our consonance or dissonance, fit or misfit with the poet). When we, or one of us, decides that what we have been knowing in one set of terms (e.g., dramatic) has altered sufficiently beyond what drama shares with the other two genres, we decide that the alteration has reached the critical degree. The issue then becomes that of what difference suffices to seem decisive. It may be just the conviction that, to the natural propensity of drama to include features of narrative and drama, what has been added is sufficient to give a lyric cast to what nonetheless remains dominantly dramatic.

> Count no man happy till he is dead.
> (Various Greek plays)

> Lord, what these weders are cold!
> (*Second Shepherd's Play*)

> Tomorrow and tomorrow and tomorrow . . .
> (*Macbeth*)

> Beneath the fruit the aspic [asp] lies.
> (*All for Love*)

The same holds true for lyric intensification of narrative that remains dominantly narrative.

> Mens immota manet lacrimae volvuntur inanes.
> (The mind remains unshaken while tears fall in vain.)
> (*Aeneid*)

> Yamazato no hikari.
> (She was the radiance of the mountain village.)
> (*The Tale of Genji*)

> Those thoughts that wander through eternity.
> (*Paradise Lost*)

> Bliss was it in that dawn to be alive.
> (*The Prelude*)

In such fashions may drama or narrative appropriate lyricism without yielding to it. Significantly enough, the lyricism is often unobserved in context. We may have to seize on an individual line, almost to examine it for its *rasa* in the manner of Indian critics, to recognize the lyric potential.

The next stage involves the relativism of the genres to each other. Enough examples of narrative and dramatic features in lyrics were given in the second chapter. It remains to raise the theoretical and practical question how dramatic features may enter into lyric or narrative. The founding convention of drama—that it is presented by players on the boards—cannot be accounted for by the other genres, because if the convention were adopted, they would instantly become drama. We may pass by marginal examples such as a song at a concert, a story read over the radio, and analogous procedures. We are interested in the harder task of explaining the presence of a dramatic element in lyrics and narratives read, and meant to be read, in a "print culture."

The clue to dealing with this problem will be found in the fact that drama is noninterruptive of lyrics whereas it is interruptive of narrative and of itself. In narrative the issue is whether the narrator's role is temporarily superseded. A run of dialogue without speech tags frequently marks the writing of novelists as different otherwise as Austen and Ivy Compton-Burnett. The result is a nonsupersessive dramatic element. We presume a narrator at our elbow abiding her time to declare herself in charge when she pleases. It is quite another thing when we have a situation such as Byron presents in the third canto of *Don Juan* (stanzas 82ff.). Byron there brings into his narrative a Greek "poet," who "sings some sort of hymn" (86). His hymn is highly lyrical, but the mode of presentation is, by Byron's irony, so distanced and occasioned as to present an interruptive scene in which the hypocritical Greek poet temporarily has a kind of stage of his own. That is, there is not only an interruption but a marking of it. It is marked by going on for sixteen stanzas of "The isles of Greece, the isles of Greece," and so on; it is marked by separate numbering of the stanzas between the eighty-sixth and eighty-seventh of the narrative; above all, it is marked by a different meter and stanza form. The narrator's irony both largely creates and largely contains the dramatic character of the interruption. The lyric affectivism of the interlude also promises that it cannot long continue, that the narrator will reassert himself, and the narrative continuum will resume.

Donne and Herbert's dramatic lyrics (discussed in the third chapter) show that drama may enter lyric with ease but not interrupt it. The poet may include dramatic features but cannot use them to intermit the lyric as Byron intermits his narrative. Of course there are popular songs for performance on stage, cantatas like Dryden's St. Cecilia Day odes, and so on to opera. But we must raise the question in terms of nonperformed lyrics: with ordinary, literary lyricism. The very strength of its presence, its intensity of moment, subjects a dramatic feature to just that role, a feature within the lyric dominance.

This relativism of the genres is not, then, mutual or equal. Drama can accommodate—by allowing interruption—lyric and narrative in their actual versions of moment and movement, whereas drama cannot be fully incorporated, *in its stage make-up*, into the other two genres. Some explanation is therefore required for the ease with which a relative degree of the dramatic may enter into lyric and narrative.

The solution to this seemingly intractable problem will be found in the necessary fictionality of drama alone among the three genres. In narrative of a factual kind, in historical narrative for example, speeches by characters provide a subordinate dramatic character. It is significant that the fictionality of historians' speeches has been recognized—and allowed as a convention—for centuries.

The situation does not greatly differ with lyric, although it is somewhat more complex. In Donne's dramatic lyric, "The Indifferent," the outrageous declamations of the first two stanzas emphasize the fictionality of the poem, the distinction between the declaiming speaker and the amused poet. By the same token, Asian lyrics are either factual or, when fictional, taken to have an independent speaker (e.g., a male poet writing love poetry as if he were a woman). Of course fictionality does not ensure drama in narrative or lyrics: they may be fictional on other grounds to begin with. All that is argued is that when drama is taken into lyric or narrative, its characteristic force of make-up typically introduces a fictionality into factual literature or heightens the degree of fictionality in what is already fictional.

FACT AND FICTION ONCE MORE

This logic also implies a relativism of fiction to fact. We have seen that in his *Poetics* (ch. 9) Aristotle writes of characters ("names") that they may be either actual (historical) or fictional, and that the former should be preferred, because that which has been is more evidently possible. If that is true even of western literature, and of drama in particular, it is yet more abundantly true of literatures with affective-expressive poetics. To take the issue at its hardest, we can ask for the grounds on which the factual exists in fiction. As examples, we may take the stanzas after the first stanza of *Three Poets at Minase* and *Bleak House*.

The *renga* code determines that the opening stanza of *Three Poets* is factual. (See pp. 169–73.) The poets sit to compose a sequence of linked poetry in very early spring: a little snow is left, but haze, a Japanese poetic emblem of spring, veils to some extent the bases of the hills and the evening along the Minase River scene. The rest of the stanzas are fictional, and the main point is that we do not really notice a difference. "We" here means both people acquainted with the *renga* code and those who are not. It might seem that that is because in his first stanza Sōgi alludes to a famous poem by Gotoba, whose reign was distinctive for the poets he supported, and whose poem was written about the very scene, season, and time of day when the three poets sat. Some of the language of Sōgi's opening stanza is in fact taken from Gotoba's poem, and it could be argued that the allusive nature of the opening stanza deprives it of a factual status, reducing it to a fictionality like that of other stanzas. Or, it could be argued that Gotoba's poem, although composed on a set topic, is also factual.

The issue can be posed in other terms. Why should that hazy, evocative first stanza be taken to be more factual than the addition by Sōchō (77) to a stanza by Shōhaku?

	Uenu kusaba no	Shrubs uncultivated by the owner
	shigeki shiba no to	stand thick by the wattled door
77	katawara ni	in that vicinity
	kakiho no arata	the rampant field by the hedgerow
	kaeshi sute	covers the discarded hoe
		(Miner, 1979C:215)

These stanzas are fictional and yet may seem more factual than the opening stanza. An important reason why a fictional passage may seem factual is that realism in literature is expressed in certain styles, by certain conventions. As "poststructuralist" criticism has well taught us, the appearance of fact here is delusory, and what we have is a conventional decorum of the humble, a lowered fiction rather than a genuine fact (although the fiction is founded on the presumption of fact that wattled doors, hedgerows, and farming tools exist in the world). This is shown by the stanza added by Sōgi to Sōchō's.

	Katawara ni	In that vicinity
	kakiho no arata	the overgrown field by the hedgerow
	kaeshi sute	covers the neglected hoe
78	yuku hito kasumu	the traveler returns drifting in haze
	ame no kuregata	brought by twilight in light rain[2]
		(Ibid.)

[2] As has been explained, linked poetry involves semantic connection only of one stanza to its predecessor, as also therefore to its successor, like links of a chain. Sōgi's use of haze here entails absolutely no recollection of the same phenomenon in his opening stanza. It is, however, a favorite scenic feature with him, especially when he wishes to raise the impressiveness of a sequence. This "design" stanza is written to set off Sōchō's excellent "ground" stanza (77).

Here the decorum, the style, alters and the fictionality is more evident. That is true, but not the whole truth. We do presume the world to possess travelers, haze, and gentle rain—along with deserted buildings, tall weeds, unwanted bushes, and tools thrown away. If there were not such things known to us as fact, the poet would lack power to make a fiction including those elements, and we would lack power to make sense of the fiction. The same holds for *Bleak House*. The world does hold smog ("fog"), brickmakers and lawyers, scriveners dominated by their wives and aristocrats in decline, rain and smallpox. We may call all these fictional in Dickens' novel, but each fictional item depends for its existence on the possibility provided by fact. Large-scale literary fictionality, as in literary Dadaism, becomes less and less intelligible as it becomes more and more fictional. To say it again, an entirely fictional work would be unintelligible.

To restate this matter: both in those fictional *renga* stanzas and in *Bleak House* fact is dependently relative to fiction in the sense that we gain access to factuality only through what is granted to be fictional. Yet the opposite is more fundamentally true: presumed fiction is impossible without presumed fact. "Fact" derives from the perfect participle, "factum," of "facere," to make. That is the Latin counterpart of Greek "poiein," also meaning to make, the root of "poet" and "poetry." "Fiction" from "fictio" derives from "fingere," to form or devise. Chinese would think that it makes perfect sense that "fact" and "poetry" can be traced to a single confluence, and that they should differ from fiction.

Without the presumption of fact, there can be no grounds for fiction, whether in a realistic novel, a novel of the minimal, or writing where meaning is deferred or even denied. Samuel Beckett is a great artist of the minimal, and in *Malone Dies* we have the absurdist impossibility of a small window through which Malone sees sunrise on one occasion and sunset at another. Aporia. It certainly is a physical impossibility, yet an impossibility itself impossible without a presumption of the factuality of windows, of sunrises and sunsets, of east and west. The presumed play of fiction requires a presumption of fact.

These conditions hold as well in what I shall call literature of deferred meaning: both the kind with the other, better or larger meaning of allegory and the kind with the worse, lesser meaning of irony. Without actual woods in existence, Spenser would lack means to create an allegorical forest of error, and without babies and the human need to eat, Swift would have no means to propose slaughtering infants for food. The concepts of the factual and the fictional are relative to each other, but fact is logically prior to fiction. The situation holds for all literatures, although in practice the degree of factuality and of fictionality varies.

There are other kinds of relativities that may hold for a single literature

or illuminate differences between literatures. Drama offers examples. We
have seen that to much of the Middle Ages drama meant the Ciceronian
dialogue (Behrens, 1940). It is yet more interesting to consider the Se-
mitic literatures, in which drama properly conceived did not exist. A little
thought recalls variants, as in a passage about the behavior of David on a
certain occasion (2 Samuel 6:12–15).

> So David went and brought up the ark of God from the house of Obed-
> edom into the city with gladness.
> And it was so, that when they that bare the ark of the Lord had gone
> six paces, he sacrificed oxen and fatlings.
> And David danced before the Lord with all his might; and David was
> girded with [only] a linen ephod.
> So David and all the house of Israel brought up the ark of the Lord
> with shouting, and with the sound of the trumpet.

This episode did not lead to the development of drama in biblical times.
(Properly speaking it is a narrative of a ludic event.) It is, however, the
kind of performance related to religion that led to drama in Greece, as
Aristotle related (*Poetics*, ch. 4), and to the development of medieval English drama from enacting the "Quem quaeritis" trope first in and then
outside churches. In Arabic literature the situation differs, although there
is a quasi-counterpart to drama. Arabic practice of reciting panegyrics on
set occasions illustrates the principle: a counterpart of drama in estrangement from the ordinary and in performance in a designated area. The
necessary estrangement is also present in the incident of David's scantily
clad dance before the Ark of the Lord, assuming—as we cannot assume—
that the episode was acted by a player representing David. If we have not
realized already that this is narrative, however, we discover it in the verse
(16) following the last quoted: "And as the ark of the Lord came into the
city of David, Michal Saul's daughter looked through a window, and saw
king David leaping and dancing before the Lord; and she despised him in
her heart."[3]

Epic provides another example. In the terms employed here, epic is not
a genre but an example of one genre, narrative. There is a western tendency to conceive of epic in narrow terms. To the Greeks and Romans,
it had to be composed in dactylic hexameters, which would rule out the

---

[3] In his brief account of this episode, Alter makes no mention of the dramatic possibilities
or nature of the episode, although he does talk about David's "festive procession" and
Michal as "an unhappy spectator" (Alter, 1981:123). For something of a Christian version,
very different in tone, see the account of the dancing by Herodias to get the head of John
the Baptist: Matthew 14:6–10, Mark 6:21–28. The version in Matthew has more dramatic
potential—with place and motive suggested—than that in Mark.

vernacular languages. To those who define epic in terms of the clean narrative line of classical and neoclassical epic, the episodic nature of the *Beowulf* and the *Nibelungenlied* might rule them out, along with Ariosto, Tasso, and Spenser—and Ovid. No doubt each of the narrow definitions serves some use, or they would not exist.

Surely, however, there is more to be gained than lost in considering Joyce's *Ulysses* a comic epic in prose—and in a sense greater than Fielding's claim to be writing a serio-comic epic in prose (a double contradiction to his contemporaries). If we allow Joyce along with Bunyan and Fielding to write heroically (if also comically), then a forteriori we must grant an even higher claim to east Asian history in prose, whether factual or fictional or mixed, on the secure grounds that it serves the epic functions of foundation, destiny, and the awesome. I sometimes think that clarity would be gained, if it ever is to be gained in this matter, by beginning with the world's oldest narrative, the Sanskrit and moving on from there.

Sanskrit literature provides the nearest thing we have to a worldwide or neutral phenomenon. At least matters central to both east and west emerged from its culture, and its poetics is remarkably inclusive. Sanskrit literature contains all three genres and, given its antiquity as well, it shows that we do not have to play the game of "Why don't *they* (who are not *we*) have it, too?" One could waste time as well by asking, Where is the western *fu* or the western *monogatari*? Actually, it might be argued that epideictic oratory and prose poems serve functions of the *fu* and that western romances serve functions of *monogatari*.

The effort to find counterparts must employ some criteria, whether formal, ideological, or functional. And there are certain things about which we should not deceive ourselves. Relative likeness is not identity, whether David dancing and whooping it up as a counterpart of drama or the western romance as a counterpart of *monogatari*. On the other hand, were literatures identical, there would be nothing to compare.

The most serious deception of all is to think that relativism allows us to privilege western phenomena over others. There is all too little danger that Sanskrit poems or *nō* will be taken as forms that require us to depreciate western equivalents. Quite the opposite. There is instead a hegemonic presumption that western practice provides the norm for which we must dig and dig to find some counterpart in another literature, something that will be certain to differ enough as to prove the point that it is inferior. People who know their own literature thoroughly are either more humble, or ought to be, as the example of what epic may be shows. Perhaps the most offensive failure of comparison involves the "novel" (Walker, 1987). Given the fact that, in its various versions, fictional-factual prose narrative is the premier example of modern and contemporary literature, there is a tendency that can only be termed vicious to judge modern—and even premodern—literary prose narrative written outside the west by culture-specific novelistic features construed normatively. This is not relativism, nor is it comparative literature. It is Eurocentrism based on ignorance and fear. We have enough real problems without needing to invent delusive ones.

RELATIVISM IN LITERARY HISTORY

"Historical relativism" designates the widespread modern assumption that events vary relative to the place and time, the culture and stage, of their occurrence. The view is seldom if ever held in isolation from other views. If one holds to an assumption that human nature is essentially the same at all times and places, one then may also hold to a cyclical point of view: like situations will lead to like results. On such a view, history teaches lessons or enables one to predict the future. One of the most widespread such conceptions is that dominant civilizations or peoples or institutions have their rises, their flourishings, and their declines. To the Sinocentric view, that is in brief the outline of the history of dynasty after dynasty receiving and losing the mandate of heaven. Other views include a belief in progress, whether on the assumption that truth accumulates and error decreases, whether some analogy to Darwinism is made, or whether imminent eschatology is believed. And there are those who hold the contrary, because entropy is assumed to be a general law or because the race seems at last to have taken some decisively disastrous path. In fact, more than one of these and other ideas is usually held by each of us, regardless of contradiction.

Literary history is conceived of in somewhat similar although by no means identical terms. It is impossible to argue convincingly that the greatest literature is produced by the most just society, although it is possible to maintain that a society markedly unjust by then contemporaneous standards is unlikely to produce literature of lasting claim. Two other features of literary history do resemble history of other kinds, however. One is the ambiguousness of the word "history," designating as it does both presumed actual or primal *event* and ensuing oral or written *account*.[4] The latter is seldom an unmediated account of the former; in fact what is labeled "history" is almost invariably writing based on previous writings along with adoption of, or reactions to, ideologies past and present. In

---

[4] See Miner, 1988, or in greater detail, Miner, 1989. Certain considerations are omitted here as not relevant to the main topic of relativism.

addition, it is necessary to remind ourselves that inertial sameness is a stronger force than innovative change. Our being enamored by the concept of change may lead us to prefer to think of "revolutions in French literature." In order for the phrase to make any sense, the inertial force of "French" must be greater than any sense of "revolution." "Revolutions in French literature" is far more relative to French literature than to revolutionary alterations.

The principle has specific generic relevance to literary history. That is, literary history (our concern is particularly with "history" in the second, recorded sense) after the explicit or implicit foundation of a poetics remains dominated by the foundational poetics. Subsequent alterations, great and small, are relative to the foundational poetics in the sense that they are understandable only as versions and alterations of the poetics of a given literary system. As we have seen, traditional western preoccupations have been relatable to mimesis, even when the alteration takes the extreme form of antimimesis. Recognition of this relativism to the basic assumption does not, however, preclude various relativisms to other, lesser assumptions and to considerable variety within the history of a given literature. Of course the inertial identity of that literature makes the variety seem much scantier when judged by someone assuming as historical norms the main features of the history of another literature.

That somewhat generalized account can be illustrated by examining more and less familiar stretches of literary histories. A literary history of early seventeenth-century literature can be told with some brevity by drawing on the literary elements posited at the end of the first chapter. That is, early seventeenth-century English literature is dominated by three kinds of writing: drama, lyric poetry, and unplotted narrative prose. Drama is distinguishable into tragic, comic, and tragicomic varieties more or less identified respectively with verse, prose, and mixed rhythms. There is in addition another kind of drama, the masque, whose purposes find expression in the rites of panegyric. Apart from the narrative variety of satire, poetry is dominantly lyric, and the lyric is dominantly private or social in mode, with striking dramatic subgeneric traits. After Herbert, however, the subgenre becomes increasingly narrative, and then the modal balance of private-social yields to the new one of the social-public. In the middle of the century, both factual and fictional verse narrative with plot comes to be written, whereas the theaters are closed. Unplotted verse and prose narrative continue to be written. During the last four decades, verse becomes yet more dominantly narrative, whether plotted or unplotted, as well as more public in mode, and satire flourishes alongside panegyric. Drama reemerges in tragic, comic, and tragicomic versions, but satiric elements outweigh panegyric, which moves to verse for characteristic expression. Unplotted verse and prose narrative come to be written, but the gifted seers at the time would have singled out for attention the fictional, plotted, prose narratives commonly termed romances.

During the first half of the eighteenth century several significant shifts take place. Lyric is of relatively little importance as a separate practice, and the drama loses creative force except in stage production. Verse narrative becomes dominantly unplotted, and its public mode becomes increasingly qualified by dissident private elements. As the periodical essay shows, varieties of unplotted prose narrative strikingly coexist with plotted counterparts. Yet the greatest shift is that exemplified by the emergent novel. Not only is this a new kind of *fictional* narrative, but more importantly it shifts the attitude of narrative from the high heroic to the humbler. Characters "lower"—less impressive—than the heroic and even less than the author and ourselves become the object of literary attention. With the lower attitude for the characters goes a corresponding lower attitude for the setting, "the world" of the characters. In fact, such perceived lowness was construed normatively, and not until the twentieth century was the novel taken in full seriousness as a literary kind worth of study, teaching, and theoretical examination. The history of this kind was sometimes considered, but "the rise of the novel" became an urgent subject only well after the middle of the century.

The account could be continued or be retold in greater detail. It is enough to observe that historical explanation is hardly feasible without attention to genres and the other literary elements or distinctions used. There are, however, other features of that literary history that require telling, and most importantly there is the relativism to genres conceived in normative terms. From even earlier to even later than the temporal extent described, there is a shift in prestige and therefore of prominence among the genres. Drama remained strong in terms of mimetic conceptions of literature, but in practice narrative and lyric are preferred. The reason is evident: drama was a suspected kind associated with theaters, plague, prostitution, profanity, and lies. Its players had no admiration from the respectable, and there was an outcry when even the learned Benjamin Jonson published plays as parts of his *Works*. Drama had a higher reputation later in the century. (Pepys referred to Dryden as a "play poet," and Dryden to individual plays as "A Poem" in subtitles.) But the esteemed genre was narrative, or rather narrative of the heroic kind, epic.

We observe a discrepancy between conceptions and estimations based on a theory of literature relative to drama and application of that theory to actual poems written in the other two genres. If that was true of the early seventeenth century, by the late there was a conflict between assumptions held from the foundation genre, drama, and assumptions held from the genre and rhythm most esteemed in practice, heroic narrative verse. The mimetic and the conflicting narrative norms held through the eighteenth century, becoming more complex with the popular if not critical esteem of the novel and with the return of lyric practice.

Conflicts of these kinds have given way to more extreme versions. The Romantics (England remains the focus) introduced an essentially lyric poetics suitably emphatic of affect and expression focused on the poet rather than the reader (who was not entirely ignored). Subsequently, in a development culminating toward the end of the twentieth century, expression (language) excluded both the poet's and the reader's affectivism and gradually became the center of critical assumptions for many. Lyric criticism became almost skeletal with the exclusion of poet and reader and affect. One widespread result was the "hermeneutics of suspicion" of the poet, replacing a "hermeneutics of trust"; and another was the elevation of "the text." Whatever that "text" may be, it has often been assigned features attributable to human agency. It is said to do, to demand, to read (itself), and to perform numerous other actions previously attributed with more likelihood to poets and readers. The main point, however, is that a skewed lyric relativism has been used to oppose a nonetheless continuously dominant mimeticism, even in antimimesis.

To appreciate the specialness of that run of English literary history, it will be useful to alienate it by attention (in less detail) to features of Japanese literary history. As we have observed, its literary system was explicitly founded on lyric, with certain kinds of history. That is to say, the poetics was relative to kinds of writing yielding an affective-expressive poetics along with an affinity for narrative and a strong streak of philosophical realism somehow co-existent with Buddhism. Within a century of the founding, *The Tale of Genji* appeared. The greatest work in the literature, this long narrative also has a number of comments on literature and other arts, exhibiting as it were submission to the lyric-based affective-expressive poetics and yet emphatic of consonance with history. This double emphasis was confirmed about a century later by critics praising *The Tale of Genji* for its value to lyric poets and to history. The dual relativism to lyric and narrative was signaled by the elevation of linked poetry (*renga*) to status as a premier literature. Not long thereafter, Zeami managed to expand the bounds of literature yet further by having *nō* and its comic interludes (*kyōgen*) accepted as premier literature. The feat was achieved by affirmation of the affective-expressive assumptions inherited from lyric, and its effect was to make that poetics yet more comprehensive. In all this, language of certain kinds contributing to an attitude of elevation was assumed to be necessary. In general, any appreciable lowering of that attitude was taken to foreclose the possibility of a subsequent new kind of writing being considered literary.

In other words, as in China and Korea (although with numerous differences), normative definitions of literature prevailed in Japan. What counted as true literature was relative to the basic poetics but also to norms of language and of attitude. Many dismissals of new kinds on those normative grounds now seem insupportable. The linked poetry (*haikai renga*) of Bashō and Buson, the puppet (*jōruri, bunraku*) and actors' (*kabuki*) theater of a Chikamatsu seem greatly more important today than vast numbers of court poems that were regarded as the epitome of literary art. In addition, during the second half of the twentieth century there was a steadily increasing discovery of the literary value of varieties of popular prose narrative that may be typified by, but not limited to, the ingenious Ihara Saikaku (1642–93). Like English literary history as recounted, Japanese is relative to shifting emphases on genres, attitude, rhythm, and others of the literary constituents mentioned in the first chapter.

Such relativism to literary constituents is inevitable by definition, although actual results vary radically, as we have just observed. In addition, there are with each literary history problems of crises of commission and omission. None of us can long remain indifferent to the problems within the systematic poetics developing in a given literary history. Yet those problems need not concern us further: it has been enough to establish that literary histories involve relativism to construals of the range of literary constituents. There is, however, another set of problems of relativism that arise when, as comparatists, we seriously essay to compare the theoretical and historical actualities of differing literary systems.

PROBLEMS OF RELATIVISM

The very relativism necessary to comparative study poses difficult problems, especially when taken in extreme form. The intellectualist view of history appeals to our sense that history is made by people who think and have purpose. But when heightened to idealism or concepts of the unique soul of a people, it is a dangerous concept. Similarly, we think that whatever happens is the effect of causes, whether remote, proximate, or immediate. But rigorous determinism is repugnant. Surely the same logic applies to relativism, and the same problem of avoiding what may be termed rigorous relativism is one that faces the comparatist.

The problem can be identified in terms of a preference for a given genre. At one time or another in the west, drama, narrative, and lyric have each been preferred. As we have been seeing from the beginning of this study, only one literary system, the western, is founded on drama, whereas the rest were founded on lyric (or in the Indian case came to definition in terms of an affective-expressive poetics like that founded on lyric). It seems equally irrational to think that this daunting evidence signifies either that a vote has been taken and western literature should be dismissed with its critical baggage, or that there is one right system, the western, with the rest heretical. We must live with the fact that, historically, there is always a hierarchy of genres. Of course there is no guarantee that the choice of one age will be that of the next.

If preferences for genres differ so much within a single culture, what hope do we have for comparative poetics, a kind of comparative study necessarily *inter*cultural? Naturally we make choices, because we have to get on. And most of us try to make them on relativistic grounds. The problem has been stated with elegant concision and dry irony: "the *tertium comparationis* is not immediately given" (Fokkema, 1984:250). That will be examined shortly. Behind its cogency we find a very strong critique of cultural relativism in a series of propositions. First, rigorous cultural relativism implies ethical relativism, a restriction of judgment on things outside one's own culture, something as dubious as tolerance for all in one's own culture.[5] There is no easy way out:

> the complications of cultural relativism . . . are . . . far from being solved. Whether we speak of cultural relativism in its moderate or extreme form, the concept betrays its European origin and as such is bound to be a contradiction in terms: cultural relativism, which consists of an attitude of tolerance towards other patterns of culture, introduces that attitude into the investigation of cultures which may lack such tolerance. The contradiction is not restricted to the level of ethical judgment, but occurs also at the epistemological level. Scientific research aims to achieve results that are universally valid, and this runs counter to the principle of cultural relativism. (Ibid., 240)

As if recognizing the dangers of Eurocentrism in this, Fokkema goes on to propose a number of pragmatic recommendations: for example, "what I propose is merely that in our text analysis we respect as far as possible the linguistic, stylistic or rhetorical distinctions offered by the text, instead of immediately imposing allegedly universal parameters on it" (248). One can only agree with such conclusions. But it seems to me that the problem has a bit more staying power, and that recognizing its features enables us to know something about the limits and possibilities of comparative poetics.

[5] Fokkema, 1984:239. Nothing in my selection of ideas from his study should lead to the assumption that Fokkema is unsympathetic to intercultural comparative study.

Often the method used to deal with the problem transforms comparison into another intellectual exercise. For example, not only may Jonson and Shakespeare be compared, but they have been. And not only they but Bo Juyi and Du Fu, Goethe and Schiller, . . . Two methods of introducing further criteria cannot be claimed to offer a *tertium comparationis*, however common those methods may be. One is to add one or more additional writers: Marlowe, let us say, Li Bo, or Lessing. This addition of course introduces a third set of variables rather than any *tertium comparationis*. But the addition of other writers of the age can have genuine explanatory power. Of that there is no doubt, any more than that the explanation has been historical rather than comparative. Similarly, one may bring to bear a Freudian or Marxist overview. The set of assumptions will certainly provide a context for a pair of writers. But once more the result is not comparative. It is ideological, or theoretical in guise.

Both history and theory are important, and either or both may be relative without being comparative. In fact we ought to use historical information where we can, beginning with it when possible. It would make little evident sense to compare Shakespeare's tragedies to Jonson's masques. On the other hand, where there is historical evidence to show that a play by Shakespeare was performed at a court to glorify members of the audience, then there are real grounds for comparison. Somewhat differently, it should be evident that each of us reads and writes with certain theoretical, ideological preoccupations. There is a clear advantage in having our ideological and theoretical presumptions clear to others and certainly to ourselves. Concern with social classes or groups makes sense for *Twelfth Night* and *The Alchemist* and can provide a portal to comparison, even if the social standard lacks comparative power. There are even approaches—feminist study springs at once to mind—that combine historical and theoretical concerns. Of such it may be said that a multidimensional approach has no special claim to being comparative. It may not even be unified, even if the constituents are both or all considered to be feminist, Marxist, or whatever.

In literary study, the *tertium comparationis* is not only not immediately given. It is not given at all. The best solution to this problem of controlling relativism known to me is that offered in the first chapter: identification of formally identical features in the things being compared. Even then, success is not ensured, because one may have assumed a degree of identity—of comparability—that in fact does not exist. Nonetheless, it *is* the best way known to me. Much as I think historical and theoretical rigor are necessary, I cannot in honesty omit to report that what usually happens with historically based "comparison" is the discovery of trivial likeness and difference, and that what happens with theoretically based "comparison" is the very nonsurprising identical conclusion each time.

My sole alternative is to return to what has proved useful not only to me but what seems to have worked in the comparisons made by others. In doing so now, I hope to describe three approaches. The three are undertaken so as to exorcise, if that is possible, the specter of relativism.

The first approach may be termed inferential. This has been the method employed in the previous chapters. It starts (using my example) with the historical facts that Aristotle's poetics is based on drama as the esteemed genre and that other generative poetics are based on lyric (with or without kinds of history). The task then becomes one of drawing inferences about the significance of a choice of that nature. The basis of relativism is shifted to a given systematic poetics as series of inferences relative to the genre used for founding. Once we discover the results of giving a genre pride of place, we are able to enter on our usual comparative business. Attention to relativism of genre to system within a single poetics and thereafter to comparison does not do away with relativism on the level of comparison among differing systems. But it tames the relativism for a comparatist by rendering it familiar. Since that has been the chief course followed here, there is no need to rehearse what has been said.

A second approach may be called judicial, the deliberate suspension and examination of personal assumptions. It involves identifying one's principles, taking them as prejudices, seeing where they have taken one, and exploring alternatives. As is well known, Gadamer has been most influential in showing that the identification and uses of our prejudices (*Vorurteile*) are basic to interpretation.[6] Given that our prejudices are likely to seem axioms to us, such judgment is made with difficulty. But if it can be done in interpretation, it can be done in poetics, as a now familiar and specific issue will serve to show. Chinese in particular have identified—in the absence of proof to the contrary—the speaker of a lyric with the biographical poet. On the judicial line being proposed, we should choose to suspend, to controvert our western hostility to the Chinese view. The choice is a difficult one for a westerner (as I shall soon admit), but less difficult in some contexts than others. Inquiry of our writers, especially lyric poets, will show that they assume they "put" themselves into their writing. By identifying our prejudice and reflecting on it, we understand,

[6] Gadamer, 1982:234–74. These pages are a portion of the crucial Second Part of the book, "The extension of the question of truth to understanding in the human sciences." The pages mentioned must be seen in the context of that title as well as of what precedes and follows. He begins the Second Part with the shift from Enlightenment to Romantic hermeneutics. Then, in the pages cited, he treats the issues of the hermeneutic circle and of prejudices as part of the necessary historical basis of understanding. That done, he is free to return to Aristotle's example and even to the maieutic dialogues by Plato.

moreover, the basis for our easy synecdoche in saying "Mallarmé" or "Borges" when we mean their literary writings.

This encounter of mine with the Chinese principle is offered because the Chinese view has been a particularly difficult one for me to accept. My critical training engrained in me the principle of the "genetic fallacy." My prejudice remains, although the passage of time has enabled me to suspend it to the point of acknowledging two things. One is that in Chinese lyrics the distinction between what I have termed the self-stylized poet and the speaker is often a useless one. The second is that counterparts may, after all, exist in a Wordsworth or a Dickinson, and that in fact we assume the possibility in reading a Mallarmé, a Pound, or a Neruda. We may also reflect that the displacement of the poet from the poem need not be taken to be a modern western discovery. The assumption is wholly natural to a mimetic tradition founded on drama, and yet it must be granted that we do not read Sappho or Alcaeus in the same way that we would experience a play by Sophocles in the theater. Using our prejudices requires knowing them. In other words, this judicial approach is an extension of the inferential one first suggested.

The third approach is pragmatic, not the dismissal of relativism but a recognition of it, so extending the judicial approach. It is pragmatic in that the grounds for choice in a relativist dilemma are those of manifest utility rather than quick certainty. Moreover the utility of a given choice can only be adequately understood in the context of the utilities of other choices. Although this approach is the most difficult to describe theoretically, it is in some ways the easiest to practice. So far is that so, that two ethical versions of the pragmatic can be set forth.

There are various kinds of affectivist poetics. Horace posited both moral and pleasurable varieties, the "pleasurable" being taken to include a wide range of what moves us in other than strictly moral terms. Is one to be chosen over the other? The debate can be considered in intracultural terms—*within* a western, Indian, Islamic, or east Asian culture—since there have been long debates over the matter. But the intercultural evidence is obviously more important. In the main, Chinese preferred the moral version. In the main, Japanese preferred the wide range of non-moralistic affectivism. If a choice is to be made—and we all choose, whether idly or consideringly—the pragmatic decision based on the principle of justice or inclusiveness must be made in favor of Horace over the Chinese and Japanese versions. His version has the pragmatic advantage of including much of what is in theirs, as theirs do not his to the same degree. Having tentatively decided that, we ought to ask ourselves what we might gain by choosing the Chinese or Japanese version. Here the ethical principle is mercy, recognition of the special. Each of them, or both together, has the attraction of giving its alternative in a fuller, purer version that Horace allows for. For some purposes one or the other may be chosen to illuminate a theoretical or practical issue. But in the end the pragmatic, just choice remains with Horace.

The second example is similar. It involves the issue of whether literature is necessarily fictional or whether it may be factual, not simply in necessary premises for fiction but in the cognitive nature of the whole. It is my all but uniform experience that westerners think the question is simple if not naive. One answerer will remind us (historically) that modern ideas of literature as a fully separate belles-lettres is an idea dating only from the eighteenth century: *of course* factual writing is included. At another extreme, there are those who deny (theoretically) the usefulness of the distinction itself. All writing is of one textualist kind, one generalized *écriture*. Things return by that route to *la pensée sauvage*, all kinds of knowledge existing but in undifferentiated form. Yet another answerer argues that the writing of the critic is on a par of importance with the writing of the author being discussed. There may even be a "meta" version: some replies to some critics are superior to the critic replied to. But when the issue is truly joined, these western answerers posit fictionality and representation as bases of literature taken in its familiar versions of drama, lyric, and narrative.

Once again, the pragmatic decision according to justice favors the more capacious conception: literature as something either dominantly factual or fictional, or indeed intermittently identifiable as now one and then the other. Since the choice is easy, we must ask what would be gained by choosing according to mercy fictionality alone as the basis for literature. Since by definition it allows only a single basis for literature, it is a tidier conception. Since our studies are aimed to clarify by using basic principles to produce order, there are attractions in fictionality as the single criterion. But the just choice is superior for historical, theoretical, and logical reasons.

The historical evidence is plain. Factual writing has been and still is included in the category of literature, particularly in east Asia, where kinds of histories are included in the basic canon by which the poetics was defined. The theoretical issues are far more complex. Chikamatsu's idea of art as that which occupies the narrow margin between truth and falsehood has an advantage and a disadvantage in the present context. The advantage is that it enables us to posit a term larger than the fictional but inclusive of it. This was earlier termed the virtual. That is invaluable help. In the present context, however, it does not deal with the other term, fact, for which neither the virtual nor the true is necessarily synonymous. There are ways in which it is useful to think of literature being true, but those ways must be understood in a pluralistic fashion, and the argument is too complex to follow through here.[7] To mention the matter is, however, to imply the inadequacy of fiction as a concept coextensive with literature.

There are also two logical difficulties with considering that fiction defines literariness. For one thing, there are fictions that are not literary: "fictio" emerged as a concept in Roman law, and legal fictions abound to this day. For another thing, literature is a species not only of the genus of writing but also of the aesthetic. None of the other arts that, with literature, make up the category of the aesthetic can usefully be termed fictional. The advantage of using fiction as the criterion for literature seems to be that, like any standard for description or definition, fictionality can rule out as well as in. The problem is that it rules out more than we can afford to lose, and in ruling out the other arts of the aesthetic genus it rules out also some desirable literary things.

Ruling in and ruling out poses other possible difficulties. Of the many that might be mentioned, one pair seems especially illuminating: universalism and exceptionalism. They may even appear together, as when it is assumed that English (or Chinese) literature is exceptional in being the greatest and, at the same time, universalist in defining the terms on which literary norms are defined. (This is a special case of pleading justice and mercy together.) That is of course nothing other than cultural centrism. The benign version assuming both poles is that all developed literary traditions are part of a universally conceived conception of literature and that all literatures are exceptional in having distinct features. That is of course a premise of this study.

There are also versions of a single choice. As a huge continental people with a lengthy history, Chinese are given to assuming that Chinese literature defines universal literature. Certainly that was the attitude for centuries. The literature by the four classes of barbarians (depending on the quarter they lived around the Middle Kingdom) was of interest only when written in Chinese. As an insular people with borrowed religion and writing system, Japanese are given to assuming that their literature is exceptional, indescribable by foreign standards and fundamentally unknowable by foreign readers. What is here exemplified as Chinese has its counterparts (European), as does what is Japanese (Hebrew). Since both claims are founded on presumptions of exclusivity, of ruling out, the excluded reader is tempted to ignore the literature of the claimant. To ig-

---

[7] Of course the factual, the fictional, and the virtual are all versions of the important but neglected subject of literary truth statuses. It is just that this is not the place for the discussion.

nore, that is, as long as cultural politics allows it. Only the benign version of combination permits genuine comparative study.

These remarks on relativism do not resolve the dilemma, and there is a further feature of the issue that I do not remember seeing raised. If we take relativism seriously and alone, we are left without anything other than conditions true of a moment and a place. Historians (literary ones included) blithely assume that by presuming *history* as a category of study relativism (each phenomenon a product of its age and place) poses no problems. This is as illogical as the statement that language is indeterminate. It *is* true that some minds live more easily than do others with the relative, and that a few can enjoy the chaos of uncontrolled relativism. It is even truer that most people do not even pose the question, much less search for an answer.

In practice the problem is less serious than it is in theory, because the historian (or comparatist) silently assumes *other*, different grounds for what is being understood. (It is as if the historian presumes Liu's historicism as well as his historical relativism.) The historian assumes a structuralist premise, as it may be termed: the entities termed France, the middle classes in Europe, Europe in the toils of the First World War. It is assumed that "France," "the middle classes," and "Europe" are continuous entities, and that relativist assumptions about the discrete nature of each age, year, or minute are controlled as necessary by the entities mentioned. This approach solves the problem by ignoring its major. It follows that this highly illogical but familiar historicizing has grown comfortable by now: like the family dog, it will not bite us (we suppose), for all its teeth.

There is, on the other hand, no way to examine anything, at least of importance, in comparative (or other) study if all is relativized or denied. Like the historian just mentioned, we need to assume some stable entity, some reasonable conception, some logic of connections and distinctions. Given purposes require all too different kinds of security, and at times what one of us wishes to assume may be the point of contention for another person. That "one" and that "another" may be ourselves at different times. Properly speaking, the best we can do (beyond the things specified above) is to define our terms for others and attend with charity to what others need to posit in order to get on with their enterprises—something that, for one of us, is more easily said than done. Since we have grown used to doing so in historical writings, perhaps this worrying of the problem is excessive. But I think that with comparative poetics—with intercultural comparative study of other kinds as well—the stakes are so high, the possible gains and risks so great, that it is desirable to identify and worry about problems so familiar that we do not see them.

Like a family, an intellectual field of study can be defined both in terms of the entirety or in terms of the individual members. Comparative poetics is a member of the families of poetics and of comparative literature, and like other kinds of still-novel intercultural study, its history consists of only the last entries in the family Bible. There are those who are particularly desirous to identify an American or French, a Japanese or Chinese school of "comparative literature." It will surprise no reader who has journeyed this far in this study to be told that I find it more important to seek out two other things: the literatures of those countries and the desirable nature of comparative study.

René Wellek has often told us that the work of comparatists is to study *literature*. That widening of our horizon may itself be broadened. Not all theoretical and methodological problems about literature are immediately comparative, but comparative poetics certainly is, by definition. We need also to construe both literature and poetics pluralistically, with all the problems of relativism that doing so may entail. The more diverse the literatures drawn on for evidence, the better founded will be any poetics we derive—as also the more difficult will be any issues of relativism. And because diverse literatures have diverse histories, if we are to claim any lasting basis for our judgments, the histories must be considered not merely in terms of a single century or movement. For all the many hazards, however, only intercultural evidence is adequate for an account of comparative poetics. Many issues besides those raised here are proper to this field, and comparative poetics is a destined end of comparative literature, as Etiemble was quoted as saying near the beginning of this study.

The reason is inescapable. The great gain from intercultural comparative study is that it avoids taking the local for the universal, the momentary for the constant and, above all, the familiar for the inevitable.

MONOGRAPHS, articles in journals, and editions of single works are normally entered under the (original) author's name. The need for clarity and simplicity leads to exceptions. For example, Gottfried von Straussburg and his *Tristan* are not entered under Gottfried, which would be correct, nor under von Straussburg, which would be incorrect, but under the names of his editor and his translator, Closs and Hatto, with a cross reference from his name. Editions of multiple works are entered under the editor's name, with cross reference from the name of the original author.

Alsina, 1985. J. Alsina, ed. *Le personnage en question: Actes du Ve colloque du S. E. L.* Toulouse: Université de Toulouse-Le Mirail.

Alter, 1981. Robert Alter. *The Art of Biblical Narrative.* New York: Basic Books.

Anderson, 1986. William S. Anderson. "The Theory and Practice of Poëtic Arrangement from Vergil to Ovid." In Fraistat, 1986, pp. 44–65.

Aristotle. See Else; R. McKeon.

Auerbach, 1971. Erich Auerbach. *Mimesis: The Representation of Reality in Western Literature.* Princeton: Princeton University Press.

Austen, 1926. Jane Austen. *The Novels of Jane Austen.* 5 vols. Ed. R. W. Chapman. Vol. 3 (*Mansfield Park*). Vol. 5 (*Northanger Abbey* and *Persuasion*). Oxford: Clarendon Press. (*Persuasion* is in the second run of pagination.)

Bakhtin, 1984. Bakhtin, Mikhail Mikhailovich. *Rabelais and His World.* Bloomington: Indiana University Press.

[Matsuo] Bashō. See Miner, 1976; Miner-Odagiri, 1981.

Bayly, 1789. Anselm Bayly. *The Alliance of Musick, Poetry and Oratory . . . [in] the Epic and Dramatic Poems, as It Exists in the Iliad, Aeneid and Paradise Lost.* London: n. pub.

Beckett, 1956. Samuel Beckett. *Waiting for Godot.* London: Faber & Faber.

Behrens, 1940. Irene Behrens. *Die Lehre von der Einleitung der Dichtkunst.* Beihefte zur *Zeitschrift für Romanische Philologie* 92.

Blessington, 1979. Francis C. Blessington. *Paradise Lost and the classical epic.* Boston and London: Routledge and Kegan Paul.

Bloom, 1973. Harold Bloom. *The Anxiety of Influence.* New York: Oxford University Press.

———, 1975. *A Map of Misreading.* New York: Oxford University Press.

———, 1982. *Agon: Towards a Theory of Literary Revisionism.* New York: Oxford University Press.

Booth, 1983. Wayne C. Booth. *The Rhetoric of Fiction.* 2nd ed. Chicago: University of Chicago Press.

Bowring, 1982. Richard Bowring. *Murasaki Shikibu: Her Diary and Poetic Mem-*

oirs. Princeton: Princeton University Press. Including a translation of *The Diary of Murasaki Shikibu (Murasaki Shikibu Nikki)*.

Brink, 1963–82. Charles Oscar Brink. *Horace on Poetry*. 3 vols. Cambridge: Cambridge University Press. The *Ars Poetica* is in vol. 2, 1971.

Brower-Miner, 1961. Robert H. Brower and Earl Miner. *Japanese Court Poetry*. Stanford: Stanford University Press.

Cao, 1973–86. Cao Xueqin. *The Story of the Stone (Shitouji)*. The same story as *The Dream of the Red Chamber (Hungloumeng)*. 5 vols. Trans. David Hawkes and John Minford. Harmondsworth: Penguin. See Plaks, 1976.

Chatman, 1983. Seymour Chatman. *Story and Discourse: Narrative Structure in Fiction and Film*. Ithaca: Cornell University Press.

Christ, 1977. Winfried Christ. *Rhetorik und Roman. Untersuchungen zu Gottfrieds von Straussburg 'Tristan und Isold' (Deutsche Studien*, vol. 31). Meisenheim am Glan: Verlag Anton Hain.

Closs, 1944. August Closs, ed. *Tristan und Isolt. A Poem by Gottfried von Straussburg. German Medieval Series*, section A, vol. 3. Oxford: Basil Blackwell.

Cohen, 1987. Michael Cohen. *Engaging English Art*. Tuscaloosa: University of Alabama Press.

Damrosch, 1985. Leopold Damrosch, Jr. *God's Plot and Men's Stories: Studies in the Fictional Imagination from Milton to Fielding*. Chicago: University of Chicago Press.

Davenant, 1971. Sir William Davenant. *Sir William Davenant's Gondibert*. Ed. David F. Gladish. Oxford: Clarendon Press.

Dickinson, 1960. Emily Dickinson. *The Complete Poems*. Ed. Thomas H. Johnson. Boston: Little, Brown.

Doležel, 1988. Lubomír Doležel. "Mimesis and Possible Worlds." *Poetics Today* 9:475–96.

Donne, John. See A. J. Smith.

Dryden, John. See Watson, 1962; Miner, 1985A.

Duffet, 1675. Thomas Duffet. *The Mock-Tempest*. London: n.pub.

Eldershaw, 1984. M. Barnard Eldershaw (pseud. for Marjorie Barnard and Flora Eldershaw). *Tomorrow & Tomorrow & Tomorrow*. New York: Dial Press. Original censored version, Melbourne: Georgian House, 1947.

Ellrodt, 1960. Robert Ellrodt. *L'Inspiration personnelle et l'esprit du temps chez Les poètes métaphysiques anglais*. 3 vols. Paris: Libraire José Corti. Vols. 1 and 2 repr. 1973.

Else, 1967. Gerald F. Else. *Aristotle's Poetics: The Argument*. Cambridge, MA: Harvard University Press.

Etiemble, 1963. [René] Etiemble. *Comparaison n'est pas raison: La Crise de la littérature comparée*. Paris: Gallimard.

———, 1966. *The Crisis in Comparative Literature*. Trans. Herbert Weisinger and Georges Joyaux. East Lansing: Michigan State University Press.

Field, 1987. Norma Field. *The Splendor of Longing in The Tale of Genji*. Princeton: Princeton University Press.

Fokkema, 1984. Douwe W. Fokkema. "Cultural Relativism Reconsidered: Comparative Literature and Intercultural Relations." *Douze cas d'interaction culturelle dans l'Europe ancienne et l'Orient proche ou lointain*. Paris: UNESCO, pp. 239–55.

Fong, 1987. Grace S. Fong. *Wu Wenying and the Art of Southern Song Ci Poetry*. Princeton: Princeton University Press.

A. Fowler, 1982. Alastair Fowler. *Kinds of Literature: An Introduction to the Theory of Genres*. Cambridge, MA: Harvard University Press.

E. Fowler, 1988. Edward Fowler. *The Rhetoric of Confession: Shishōsetsu in Early 20th-Century Japanese Fiction*. Berkeley and Los Angeles: University of California Press.

Fraistat, 1986. Neil Fraistat, ed. *Poems in Their Place*. Chapel Hill: University of North Carolina Press.

Freedman, 1963. Ralph Freedman. *The Lyrical Novel: Studies in Hermann Hesse, André Gide, and Virginia Woolf*. Princeton: Princeton University Press.

Fu, 1983. Fu Shen. *Six Records of a Floating Life (Fu Shen Liuji)*. Harmondsworth: Penguin. The translators, Leonard Pratt and Chiang Su-hui, give the author's name as Shen Fu.

Gadamer, 1982. Hans-Georg Gadamer. *Truth and Method*. New York: Crossroad.

Gendarme de Bérotte, 1911. Georges Gendarme de Bérotte. *La Légende de Don Juan*. 2 vols. Paris: Hachette.

Genette, 1981. Gérard Genette. *Narrative Discourse*. Ithaca: Cornell University Press.

Gerow, 1977. Edwin Gerow. *Indian Poetics*. This is fascicle 3 of vol. 5 of *A History of Indian Literature*, ed. Jan Gonda. Wiesbaden: Otto Harrasowitz.

Getto, 1951. Giovanni Getto. *Interpretazione del Tasso*. Napoli: Edizioni Scientifche Italiane.

Goldman, 1975. Michael Goldman. *The Actor's Freedom: Toward a Theory of Drama*. New York: Viking Press.

Gottfried von Straussburg. See Closs, 1944; Hatto, 1967.

Greene, 1985. Roland Arthur Greene. "Origins and Innovations of the Western Lyric Sequence." Princeton University diss.

Habermas, 1978. Jürgen Habermas. *Poetik, Kunst, Religion*. Stuttgart: Reclam.

Hardy, 1977. Barbara Hardy. *The Advantage of Lyric: Essays on Feeling in Poetry*. Bloomington: Indiana University Press.

Harriott, 1960. Rosemary Harriott. *Literary Criticism Before Plato*. London: Methuen.

Hatto, 1967. A. T. Hatto, trans. Gottfried von Straussburg, *Tristan*. Harmondsworth: Penguin.

D. Hawkes, 1967. David Hawkes. *A Little Primer of Tu Fu*. Oxford: Clarendon Press.

T. Hawkes, 1977. Terence Hawkes. *Structuralism & Semiotics*. Berkeley and Los Angeles: University of California Press.

Herbert, George. See Hutchinson, 1953; Patrides, 1974.

Hernadi, 1972. Paul Hernadi. *Beyond Genre: New Directions in Literary Classification*. Ithaca: Cornell University Press.

Hijiya-Kirschnereit, 1981. Irmela Hijiya-Kirschnereit. *Selbstentblössungsrituale: Zur Theorie und Geschichte der autobiographischen Gattung "Shishōsetsu" in der modernen japanischen Literatur.* Wiesbaden: Franz Steiner.

Hochman, 1985. Baruch Hochman. *Character in Literature.* Ithaca: Cornell University Press.

Homer, 1975. *The Odyssey of Homer.* Trans. Richmond Lattimer. New York: Harper & Row.

Hošek-Parker, 1985. Chaviva Hošek and Patricia A. Parker. *Lyric Poetry: Beyond the New Criticism.* Ithaca: Cornell University Press.

Hrushovski, 1984. Benjamin Hrushovski. "Poetic Metaphor and Frames of Reference." *Poetics Today* 5:5–43.

Huizinga, 1949. Johan Huizinga. *Homo Ludens: A Study of the Play-Element in Culture.* London: Routledge & Kegan Paul.

Hutchinson, 1953. George Hutchinson, ed. *The Works of George Herbert.* Oxford: Clarendon Press.

Ingalls, 1972. Daniel H. H. Ingalls. *Sanskrit Poetry.* Cambridge, MA: Harvard University Press.

Izumi Shikibu, 1965. Izumi Shikibu. *Zenkō Izumi Shikibu Nikki.* Ed. Enchi Fumiko and Suzuki Kazuo. Tokyo: Shibundō. As she says in her introduction, Enchi's role was largely confined to it. See also Miner, 1976.

Jaeger, 1977. C. Stephen Jaeger. *Medieval Humanism in Gottfried von Strassburg's Tristan und Isolde (Germanische Bibliothek,* 3rd series). Heidelberg: Carl Winter.

James, 1966. Henry James. *What Maisie Knew.* Harmondsworth: Penguin.

Kayser, 1962. Wolfgang Kayser. *Das sprachliche Kunstwerk. Eine Einführung in die Literaturwissenschaft.* Bern: A. Francke.

Kermode, 1967. Frank Kermode. *The Sense of an Ending.* New York: Oxford University Press.

[Enomoto] Kikaku. See Miner-Odagiri, 1981.

Killy, 1972. Walther Killy. *Elemente der Lyrik.* Munich: Beck.

Ki no Tsurayuki. See Miner, 1976.

Kleist, Heinrich von. See Laaths, 1952.

Konishi, 1958. Konishi Jin'ichi. "Association and Progression: Principles of Integration in the Anthologies and Sequences of Japanese Court Poetry, A.D. 900–1350." *Harvard Journal of Asiatic Studies* 21:67–127.

———, 1971. *Sōgi.* Tokyo: Chikuma Shobō.

———, 1973. *Image and Ambiguity: The Impact of Zen Buddhism on Japanese Literature.* Tokyo: Tokyo University of Education.

———, 1974. *Zeami Shū.* Tokyo: Chikuma Shobō.

———, 1984. *A History of Japanese Literature.* Vol. 1. Princeton: Princeton University Press.

———, 1986A. *A History of Japanese Literature.* Vol. 2. Princeton: Princeton University Press.

———, 1986B. *Nihon Bungeishi.* Vol. 3. Tokyo: Kōdansha.

Laaths, 1952. Erwin Laaths, ed. *Heinrich von Kleist. Sämtliche Werke*. Munich: Droemersche Verlanganstalt.

Laird, 1988. Holly A. Laird. *Self and Sequence: The Poetry of D. H. Lawrence*. Charlottesville: University Press of Virginia.

Lanham, 1968. Richard A. Lanham. *A Handlist of Rhetorical Terms*. Berkeley and Los Angeles: University of California Press.

Lanser, 1981. Susan Sniader Lanser. *The Narrative Act: Point of View in Prose Fiction*. Princeton: Princeton University Press.

Lee, 1983. Peter H. Lee. *Critical Issues in East Asian Literature*. Seoul: International Cultural Society of Korea.

Legge, 1970. James Legge. *The Chinese Classics*. 5 vols. N.p: n. pub. This edition was first published in 1872. The *Shijin* and its prefaces are in vol. 4, the sole one of this ed. used here.

Levy, 1988. Dore J. Levy. *Chinese Narrative Poetry. The Late Han through the T'ang Dynasties*. Durham: Duke University Press.

Lewalski, 1985. Barbara Kiefer Lewaalski. *"Paradise Lost" and the Rhetoric of Literary Forms*. Princeton: Princeton University Press.

———, 1986. Ed. *Renaissance Genres: Essays on Theory, History, and Interpretation*. Cambridge, MA: Harvard University Press.

Liddell-Scott, 1951. Henry George Liddell and Robert Scott. *A Greek-English Lexicon*. New rev. ed. 1940 by Henry Stuart Jones et al. Oxford: Clarendon Press.

Liu, 1962. James J. Y. Liu. *The Art of Chinese Poetry*. Chicago: University of Chicago Press.

———, 1975. *Chinese Theories of Literature*. Chicago: University of Chicago Press.

———, 1977. "Towards a Synthesis of Chinese and Western Theories of Literature." *Journal of Chinese Philosophy* 4:1–24.

———, 1982. *The Interlingual Critic: Interpreting Chinese Poetry*. Bloomington: Indiana University Press.

———, 1988. *Language-Paradox-Poetics: A Chinese Perspective*. Princeton: Princeton University Press.

Martz, 1954. Louis L. Martz. *The Poetry of Meditation*. New Haven: Yale University Press.

M. McKeon, 1987. Michael McKeon. *The Origins of the English Novel, 1600–1740*. Baltimore: Johns Hopkins University Press.

R. McKeon, 1947. Richard McKeon, ed. *Introduction to Aristotle*. New York: The Modern Library (Random House). The Ingram Bywater translation of the *Poetics* is on pp. 624–67.

B. S. Miller, 1987. Barbara Stoler Miller. "Legends of Authorship and Implicit Poetics in Sanskrit Literature." A paper for the second Sino-American symposium on comparative literature, Princeton University.

J. H. Miller, 1976. J. Hillis Miller. "Ariadne's Thread: Repetition and the Narrative Line." *Critical Inquiry* 3:57–77.

J. S. Miller, 1988. J. Scott Miller. "The Hybrid Nature of Kyōden's *Sharebon*." *Monumenta Nipponica* 43:133–52.

Milton, John. See Patterson, 1931–38. See also Wolfe, 1953.

Miner, 1967. Earl Miner. *Dryden's Poetry*. Bloomington: Indiana University Press.

———, 1968. *An Introduction to Japanese Court Poetry*. Stanford: Stanford University Press.

———, 1969. *The Metaphysical Mode from Donne to Cowley*. Princeton: Princeton University Press.

———, 1976. *Japanese Poetic Diaries*. Berkeley and Los Angeles: University of California Press. 2nd, corrected ed.; orig. 1969. Includes Ki no Tsurayuki's *Tosa Diary* (*Tosa Nikki*), *The Diary of Izumi Shikibu* (*Izumi Shikibu Nikki*), and Matsuo Bashō's *Narrow Road Through the Provinces* (*Oku no Hosomichi*).

———, 1979A. "Some Remarks on the Question of Literary Values." *Southern Review* (Adelaide) 12:124–34.

———, 1979B. "On the Genesis and Development of Literary Systems." *Critical Inquiry* 5:339–53, 553–68.

———, 1979C. *Japanese Linked Poetry*. Princeton: Princeton University Press. This includes the *renga* sequences *Three Poets at Minase* by Sōgi, Shōhaku, and Sōchō and *Sōgi Alone*.

———, 1982. "Narrative Parts and Conceptions" and "Résumé of Events in 'Ukifune.' " In Pekarik, 1982, pp. 223–50, 251–57.

———, 1983. "The Grounds of Mimetic and Nonmimetic Art: The Western Sister Arts in a Japanese Mirror." In Wendorf, 1983, pp. 70–97.

———, 1985A. Ed. *Selected Poetry and Prose of John Dryden*. New York: Random House.

———, 1985B. Ed. *Principles of Classical Japanese Literature*. Princeton: Princeton University Press; "The Collective and the Individual: Literary Practice and Its Social Implications," pp. 17–62.

———, 1986A. "Some Issues of Literary 'Species, or Distinct Kind.' " In Lewalski, 1986, pp. 15–44.

———, 1986B. "Some Issues for Study of Integrated Collections." In Fraistat, 1986, pp. 18–43.

———, 1987. "Comparative Poetics: Some Theoretical and Methodological Topics for Comparative Literature." *Poetics Today* 8:123–40.

———, 1988. "Literatures, Histories, Literary Histories." (Kansai Daigaku) *Tōzai Gaukujutsu Kenkyū Kiyō*, no. 21, pp. 1–12.

———, 1989. "Literatures, Histories, Literary Histories." In Yang-Yue, 1989, pp. 1–40. A considerably augmented version of the preceding.

Miner-Guffey-Zimmerman, 1976. Earl Miner, George R. Guffey, and Franklin B. Zimmerman, eds. *The Works of John Dryden*. Vol. 15. Berkeley and Los Angeles: University of California Press. This includes *Amphitryon*.

Miner-Odagiri, 1981. Earl Miner and Hiroko Odagiri. *The Monkey's Straw Raincoat and Other Poetry of the Bashō School*. Princeton: Princeton University

Press. Includes the *haikai* sequence, *Poetry Is What I Sell (Shi Akindo no Maki)* by Bashō and Kikaku.

Miner-Odagiri-Morrell, 1985. Earl Miner, Hiroko Odagiri, and Robert E. Morrell. *The Princeton Companion to Classical Japanese Literature*. Princeton: Princeton University Press.

Molière, 1966. Jean-Baptiste Molière. *Amphitryon*. Ed. Michel Autrand. Paris: Bardas (Les petits classiques Bardas).

Murasaki Shikibu, 1976. Murasaki Shikibu. *The Tale of Genji (Genji Monogatari)*. 2 vols. Trans. Edward G. Seidensticker. New York: Alfred A. Knopf. See also Bowring, 1982; Tamagami, 1968.

Nakamura, 1962. Nakamura Hajime. *Shin Bukkyō Jiten (New Dictionary of Buddhism)*. Tokyo: Seishin Shobō.

Passage-Mantinband, 1974. Charles E. Passage and James H. Mantinband. *Amphitryon . . . Together with a Comprehensive Account of the Evolution of the Legend and Its Subsequent History on the Stage*. University of North Carolina Studies in Comparative Literature, no. 57. Chapel Hill: University of North Carolina Press. This includes verse translations of the versions by Platus, Molière, and Kleist.

Patrides, 1974. C. A. Patrides, ed. *The English Poems of George Herbert*. London: Dent.

Patterson, 1931–38. Frank Allen Patterson, ed. *The Works of John Milton*. Vol. 2, pt. 1 (*Paradise Lost*, 1–8. Vol. 3, pt. 1 (*Reason of Church-Government*).

Pekarik, 1982. Andrew Pekarik, ed. *Ukifune: Love in The Tale of Genji*. New York: Columbia University Press.

Pfister, 1977. Manfred Pfister. *Das Drama: Theorie und Analyse*. Munich: Wilhelm Fink Verlag.

Plaks, 1976. Andrew H. Plaks. *Archetype and Allegory in The Dream of the Red Chamber*. Princeton: Princeton University Press. See Cao, 1973–86. *The Dream of the Red Chamber* (i.e., *Hungloumeng*) and *The Story of the Stone* are alternate titles.

———, 1987. "Where the Lines Meet: Parallelism in Chinese and Western Literature." A paper for the second Sino-American symposium on comparative literature, Princeton University.

Plautus, 1960. Titus Maccius Plautus. *Amphitruo*. Ed. W. B. Sedgwick. Manchester: Manchester University Press.

Preminger, 1974. Alex Preminger et al., eds. *The Princeton Encyclopedia of Poetry and Poetics*. Enlarged ed. Princeton: Princeton University Press.

Puttenham, 1968. George Puttenham. *The Arte of English Poesie*. Menston: Scolar Press.

Quintilian, 1953. Marcus Fabius Quintilianus. *Institutio Oratoria*. 4 vols. Trans. H. E. Butler. Cambridge, MA: Harvard University Press (Loeb Classical Library, (orig. 1921–22).

Rank, 1975. Otto Rank. *The Don Juan Legend*. Princeton: Princeton University Press.

Reed, 1985. Barbara Mito Reed. "Language, Narrative Structure, and the Shō-setsu." Princeton University diss.

———, 1988. "Chikamatsu Shūko: An Inquiry into Narrative Modes in Modern Japanese Fiction." *Journal of Japanese Studies* 14:59–76.

Reiss, 1982. Timothy J. Reiss. *The Discourse of Modernism*. Ithaca: Cornell University Press.

Rickett, 1978. Adele Austin Rickett, ed. *Chinese Approaches to Literature from Confucius to Liang Ch'i-ch'ao*. Princeton: Princeton University Press.

Ricoeur, 1984. Paul Ricoeur. *The Rule of Metaphor*. Trans. Robert Czerny et al. Toronto: University of Toronto Press.

———, 1984–85. *Time and Narrative*. 3 vols. Trans. Kathleen McLaughlin and David Pellauer. Chicago: University of Chicago Press.

Rimer-Yamazaki, 1984. J. Thomas Rimer and Yamazaki Masakazu. *On the Art of the Nō Drama: The Major Treatises of Zeami*. Princeton: Princeton University Press.

Roche, 1989. Thomas P. Roche. *Petrarch and the English Sonnet Sequence*. New York: AMS Press, 1989.

Saintsbury, 1967. George Saintsbury. *A History of [English] Prose Rhythm*. Bloomington: Indiana University Press (orig. 1912).

Scholes-Kellogg, 1966. Robert Scholes and Robert Kellogg. *The Nature of Narrative*. New York: Oxford University Press.

Shakespeare, 1972. William Shakespeare. *The Complete Signet Classic Shakespeare*. Ed. Sylvan Barnet. New York: Harcourt Brace Jovanovich.

Shen Fu. See Fu, 1983.

Shirane, 1987. Haruo Shirane. *The Bridge of Dreams: A Poetics of "The Tale of Genji."* Stanford: Stanford University Press.

Shōhaku. See Miner, 1979C.

Sloman, 1985. Judith Sloman. *Dryden: The Poetics of Translation*. Toronto: University of Toronto Press.

A. J. Smith, 1975. A. J. Smith, ed. *John Donne: The Complete English Poems*. Harmondsworth: Penguin.

B. H. Smith, 1968. Barbara Herrnstein Smith. *Poetic Closure: A Study of How Poems End*. Chicago: University of Chicago Press.

G. G. Smith, 1904. G. G. Smith, ed. *Elizabethan Critical Essays*. 2 vols. Oxford: Clarendon Press.

Sōchō. See Miner, 1979C.

Sōgi. See Miner, 1979C.

Staiger, 1939. Emil Staiger. *Die Zeit als Einbildungskraft des Dichters*. Zurich and Leipzig: Max Niehans Verlag.

Starr, 1965. George Starr. *Defoe and Puritan Spiritual Autobiography*. Princeton: Princeton University Press.

Stinchecum, 1980. Amanda Mayer Stinchecum. "Who Tells the Tale? 'Ukifune': A Study in Narrative Voice." *Monumenta Nipponica* 35:375–403.

Sun, 1983. Cecile Chu-chin Sun. "Comparing Chinese and English Lyrics: The Correlative Mode of Presentation." *Tamkang Review* 14:487–507.

————, 1985. "Ch'ing and Ching: Correlation Between Inner Feeling and Outer Reality in Chinese and English Poetry." *Proceedings of the Xth Congress of The International Comparative Literature Association.* New York: Garland Press. Vol. 2:409–414.

Szondi, 1965. Peter Szondi. *Theorie des modernen Dramas (1880–1950).* Frankfurt am Main: Suhrkamp Verlag.

Takeshita, 1988. Takeshita Yutaka. "*Horikawa Hyakushu* no Chimei Uta no Ichi-yōsō." (Osaka Joshi Daigaku) *Joshidai Bungaku,* no. 39, pp. 35–47.

Tamagami, 1968. Tamagami Takuya. Murasaki Shikibu, *Genji Monogatari Hyō-shaku.* Vol. 12 (of 20). Tokyo: Kadokawa Shoten.

Three Kingdoms, 1959. *The Romance of the Three Kingdoms (Sanguo Zhiyenyi).* 2 vols. Trans. C. H. Brewitt-Taylor. Taipei: Dunhuang Shuju (orig. ca. 1925).

Twain, 1985. Mark Twain. *Adventures of Huckleberry Finn.* Ed. Walter Blair and Victor Fischer. Berkeley and Los Angeles: University of California Press.

Valdés, 1982. Mario J. Valdés. *Shadows in the Cave: A Phenomenological Approach to Literary Criticism Based on Hispanic Texts.* Toronto: University of Toronto Press.

————, 1987. *Phenomenological Hermeneutics and the Study of Literature.* Toronto: University of Toronto Press.

Walker, 1987. Janet A. Walker. " 'The Novel': One of the Modern Period's Most Guilty Terms." Paper presented at the American Comparative Literature Association meeting, Atlanta. Revised, awaiting publication: "On the Applicability of the Term 'Novel' to Modern Non-Western Lengthy Fictions." *Yearbook of Comparative Literature and General Literature* 38 (forthcoming 1990).

Walton, 1962. Izaak Walton. *The Lives.* Intro. George Saintsbury. London: Oxford University Press (Crown Classics; orig. 1927).

Watson, 1962. George Watson, ed. *John Dryden: Of Dramatic Poesy and Other Critical Essays.* 2 vols. London: Dent (Everyman).

Webster, 1956. T.B.L. Webster. *Greek Theatre Production.* London: Methuen.

Welsh, 1978. Andrew Welsh. *The Roots of Lyric: Primitive Poetry and Modern Poetics.* Princeton: Princeton University Press.

Wendorf, 1983. Richard Wendorf, ed. *Articulate Images: The Sister Arts from Hogarth to Tennyson.* Minneapolis: University of Minnesota Press.

Whitman, 1973. Walt Whitman. *Leaves of Grass.* Ed. Sculley Bradley and Harold W. Blodgett. New York: W. W. Norton.

Wilding, 1975. Michael Wilding. *The West Midland Underground.* St. Lucia: Queensland University Press.

Wolfe, 1953. Don M. Wolfe, ed. *Complete Prose Works of John Milton.* Vol. 1. New Haven: Yale University Press.

Yokomichi-Omote, 1973. Yokomichi Mario and Omote Akira. Vol. 1 (of 2). *Yōkyokushū.* Tokyo: Iwanami Shoten (orig. 1960). *Nihon Koten Bungaku Taikei* 40.

Yang-Yue, 1989. Yang Zhouhan and Yue Daiyun, eds. *Literatures, Histories, Literary Histories.* Shenyang: Liaoming University Press.

Yu, 1981. Pauline Yu. "Metaphor and Chinese Poetry." *Chinese Literature: Essays, Articles, Reviews* 3:205–24.

——, 1982. "Allegory, *Allegoresis*, and the *Classic of Poetry*." *Harvard Journal of Asiatic Studies* 43:377–412.

——, 1987. *The Reading of Imagery in the Chinese Poetic Tradition*. Princeton: Princeton University Press.

Zelditch, 1971. Morris Zelditch. "Intelligible Comparisons." In *Comparative Methods in Sociology*. Ed. Ivan Vallier, pp. 267–307. Berkeley and Los Angeles: University of California Press.

GIVEN the nature of this book, a large number of subjects is included, commonly with double entries. Except for anonymous works, titles indicate more than illustrative usage—quotation or discussion. Otherwise titles are represented here by authors' names, and dates are supplied for historical authors, defined as those who predeceased 1900. Dates are of the Common Era unless otherwise noted.

THIS BOOK HAS BEEN COMPOSED AND PRINTED BY
Princeton University Press
DESIGNED BY *Jan Lilly*
TYPOGRAPHY: *Linotron Bembo*
PAPER: *Glatfelter Supple Opaque Regular Finish*